DIRECTORY OF LITERARY MAGAZINES 1994–95

DIRECTORY OF LITERARY MAGAZINES 1994–95

Prepared in Cooperation with the
Council of Literary Magazines and Presses

Moyer Bell Limited : Wakefield, Rhode Island & London

Published by Moyer Bell
This Edition 1994

LIBRARY OF CONGRESS CATALOGING-IN-PUBLICATION DATA

Directory of literary magazines / prepared by the Council of Literary Magazines and Presses—1984—New York: The Council c1984.

v.; 22cm

Annual.
Continues: CLMP literary magazine directory
ISSN 0884-6006 = Directory of literary magazines

1. Literature—Periodicals—Bibliography. 2. American periodicals—Directories. 3. Little magazines—United States—Directories. I. Council of Literary Magazines and Presses (U.S.)

Z6513.C37 85-648720
PN2 AACR 2 MARC-S

ISBN 1-55921-112-1 Pb

Printed in the United States of America
Distributed in North America by Publishers Group West, P.O. Box 8843, Emeryville, CA 94662, 800-788-3123 (in California 510-658-3453), and in Europe by Gazelle Book Services Ltd., Falcon House, Queen Square, Lancaster LA1 1RN England.

> The little magazine is something I have always fostered, for without it, I myself would have been early silenced. To me it is one magazine, not several. . . . When it is in any way successful it is because it fills a need in someone's mind to keep going. When it dies, someone else takes it up in some other part of the country—quite by accident—out of a desire to get the writing down on paper.
>
> —William Carlos Williams*

The *Directory of Literary Magazines* is compiled as a guide to the changing world of literary magazines of which Williams speaks. The literary magazine is a particularly American tradition that has provided early publishing opportunities for many of our important writers—including T.S. Eliot, E.L. Doctorow, Elizabeth Bishop, Ernest Hemingway, Ralph Ellison, Robert Lowell, Katherine Anne Porter, Raymond Carver, Richard Wright, Ezra Pound, Maxine Hong Kingston and Amiri Baraka. Through the medium of literary magazines, writers see their art in print and are given a permanent place in our culture. At the same time, readers are given an opportunity to discover new voices and talents and to experience a wide range of serious literature which is excluded from or underrepresented in the commercial marketplace.

This year's *Directory* includes nearly 600 magazines from the United States, Canada and Europe. Entries are designed to include information asked for by **readers, writers, librarians, publishers**, and others.

Entries include:

- descriptions of each magazine in the editor's own words in order to clarify for prospective **writers** the magazine's editorial directions and interests. Writers are strongly urged to research magazines before submitting work by using these entries, and most importantly, by purchasing and supporting the magazines that interest them;

* *The Autobiography of William Carlos Williams*, © 1951 William Carlos Williams. Reprinted by permission of New Directions Publishing Corporation.

- listings of types of material published by each magazine, subscription rates, ISSN numbers for use by **librarians** in selecting additions to their collections, and distributors for use by **bookstores** interested in increasing their magazine sections;

- advertising information for **publishers'** use, including ad rates and sizes as a complement to the activities of CLMP's Ad Program which offers advertising space in specially designed packages of literary magazines to interested publishers. For more information on ad rates and CLMP's advertising services to publishers, please contact CLMP.

The Council of Literary Magazines and Presses (CLMP) is dedicated to serving and supporting alternative publishing in the United States. As a membership service and advocacy organization, it works on behalf of literary magazines and small presses to strengthen the field from within, promote its many and varied accomplishments to the public, and provide an ongoing forum for the discussion of issues relevant to the greater literary community.

CLMP provides an array of programs and services to its member magazines and presses. The organization has also taken a leading role in field development, activities which benefit the entire field of literature (writers, readers, publishers, librarians, booksellers, literary centers), of which its members are a vital part. This work involves creating and implementing mechanisms for emerging publishers to learn from established ones; for literary publishers to collaborate with literary presenters; for the media, funders and other groups to be better informed about literary publishing and its role in America's cultural life; for research and data collection about the field to be undertaken and the results made public; for ensuring that literature has a place at the table where the politics of cultural policy are debated and decided; and ultimately for facilitating the flow of literature from the hands of writers into the hands of readers in America.

If you would like to receive further information about CLMP or becoming a member, please write us at 154 Christopher Street, Suite 3C, New York, NY 10014-2839.

We hope you are well-served by this edition of the *Directory of Literary Magazines*. CLMP would like to thank the staff at Moyer Bell for their dedication to this project. CLMP would also like to thank the National Endowment for the Arts and the New York State Council on the Arts for their general support, and the Andrew W. Mellon Foundation and the Lila Wallace-Reader's Digest Fund for their generous program support.

KEY

NAME OF MAGAZINE
Editor(s)
Address
Telephone number

Material published
Magazine description
Recent contributors
Unsolicited Manuscripts Received/Published per Year
Reading Period
Payment to contributors
Reporting time
Copyright
First year of publication; frequency; circulation
Subscription rate; single copy price; discount for resale
Number of pages; size of magazine
Advertising rates and sizes
International Standard Serial Number
Distributors

Abbreviations

ea—each
ind—individual
inst—institutional
irreg—irregular
pp—pages
var—varies
v—volume
yr—year

All entries contain the fullest information available at date of *Directory* publication.

Index by State (see p. 262)

ABACUS

Peter Ganick
181 Edgemont Ave.
Elmwood, CT 06110
(203) 233-2023

Poetry.

A 12 to 20 page, newsletter format, single-author-per-issue periodical devoted to experimental and language poetry.

Clark Coolidge, Jackson Mac Low, Carla Harryman, Laura Moriarty, Joan Retallack, Leslie Scalapino.

Unsolicited Manuscripts Received/ Published per Year: 100/8.

Payment: 10 copies.

Reporting Time: variable.

Copyright held by author.

No ads

ISSN: 0886-4047

SPD, Small Press Traffic

ABIKO LITERARY QUARTERLY RAG

Laurel Sicks, Managing Editor & Publisher; Dr. Hamada, Director; Jesse Glass, Poetry Editor; D.C. Palter, Fiction Editor
8-1-8 Namiki
Abiko, Chiba 270-11 JAPAN
0471-84-7904

James Joyce Finnegans Wake papers, poetry, fiction.

ALQR is primarily a James Joyce Finnegans Wake study journal, with poetry and fiction. Presently we allot ⅓ of the magazine to each category.

Burton Raffel, Skip Fox, Leo Connellan, Cid Corman.

Unsolicited Manuscripts Received/ Published per Year: varies—most mss. from contests/123.

Reading Period: Sept.—Dec. 31.

Payment: 1 copy/poets, 2 copies/fiction; $1,500 prize money.

Reporting Time: 2 weeks.

1988; 2/year; 600

$40/4 issues; $10/ea

250 pp; B-5

Ad Rates: $200/page; $500/½ page/; $50/¼; $500/back cover

Japan Publications Trading Co. Ltd.

ABRAXAS

Ingrid Swanberg, Warren Woessner
2518 Gregory St.
Madison, WI 53711
(608) 238-0175

Poetry, criticism, essays, reviews, translations, photographs, graphics/artwork, "found" cultural artifacts. No unsolicited

manuscripts, except as announced.
Contemporary poetry: (non-academic). Emphasis on the lyric and experimental. Unusual graphics and "found" poems. Interested in poetry in translation and Native American poetry. Criticism and essays on the contemporary scene.
César Vallejo, Ivan Argüelles, Próspero Saíz, Andrei Codrescu, Andrea Moorhead.
Unsolicited Manuscripts Received/Published per Year: 3,000/20.
Payment: in copies.
Reporting Time: varies per project.
Copyright held by Abraxas Press, Inc.; reverts to author upon publication.
1968; irregular; 500
$16/4 issues; $4/ea; 40%
80 pp; 6 x 9
Ad Rates: $60/page (5 x 8); $35/½ page (5 x 3½)
ISSN: 0361-1663

ACM (Another Chicago Magazine)

Barry Silesky
3709 N. Kenmore
Chicago, IL 60613
(312) 248-7665

Poetry, fiction, reviews, essays, interviews.
Literary, contemporary, non-regional, socio-political outlook.
S.L. Wisenberg, Pablo Antonio Cuadra, Ariel Dorfman, Maxine Chernoff, Lore Segal, Sterling Plumpp.
Reading Period: year–round.
Unsolicited Manuscripts Received/Published per Year: 7,500/65.
Payment: $5–$25.
Reporting Time: 8 weeks.
Copyright held by magazine; reverts to author upon publication.
1977; 2/yr; 750
$15/ind, $15/inst; $8/ea; 40%
220 pp; 5½ x 8½
Ad Rates: $150/page (5 x 8); $75/½ page (5 x 3⅞)
ISSN: 0272-4359
Ingram

AEGEAN REVIEW

Dino Siotis
220 West 19th St., 2A
New York, NY 10011

Modern Greek literature in translation. Works inspired by Greece by American authors.
Fiction, essays, interviews, poetry, art and photography.
Jorge Luis Borges, Lawrence Durrell, Truman Capote, Yannis Ritsos, Alice Bloom.
Payment: $25–$50.
Reporting Time: 6 weeks.
1985; 2/yr; 4,000

$10/yr ind, $18/yr inst; $5/ea; 40%
80 pp; 7½ x 10
Ad Rates: $265/page
ISSN: 0891-7213
DeBoer

AERIAL

Rod Smith
P.O. Box 25642
Washington, D.C. 20007
(202) 244-6258, 965-5200

Poetry, fiction, criticism, essays, reviews, translations, photos, graphics.
AERIAL 6/7 is devoted to John Cage & others. **AERIAL** #8 will be a special issue on Barrett Watten.
Jessica Grim, Rachel Blau DuPlessis, Lyn Hejinian, Bob Perelman, Elizabeth Robinson
Unsolicited Manuscripts Received/Published per Year: 3,000/25–35.
Payment: copies.
Copyright held by magazine; we reserve the right to reprint accepted materials in anthology or other form. All other rights revert to author.
1985; irregular; 1,000
$20/2 issues; $35/3 issues inst; $7.50/ea; 6/7 $15; 40%
approx. 200 pp; 6 x 9; 6/7, 8½ x 10
Ad Rates: Contact CLMP for information.
Ubiquity, SPD

AFRICAN AMERICAN REVIEW

Joe Weixlmann
Department of English
Indiana State University
Terre Haute, IN 47809
(812) 237-2968

Poetry, fiction, criticism, reviews, interviews, photographs, graphics/
artwork, bibliographies.
Essays on African American literature, theater, film, art, music, dance, and culture; interviews; poems; fiction; book reviews; bibliographies; and graphics on black themes.
Amiri Baraka, Gwendolyn Brooks, Ishmael Reed, Houston A. Baker, Jr., Rita Dove, Henry Louis Gates, Jr.
Unsolicited Manuscripts Received/Published per Year: 250/50.
Payment: depends on grants.
Reporting Time: 3 months.
Copyright held by author.
1967; 4/yr; 3,098
$24/yr ind, $44/yr inst; $10/ea; 40%
176 pp; 7 x 10
$180/page (5 x 8½); $100/½ page (5 x 4¼)
ISSN: 1062-4783

THE AFRO-HISPANIC REVIEW

Marvin Lewis & Edward Mullen
Department of Romance Languages
U Missouri: 143 Arts & Science Building
Columbia, MO 65211
(314) 882-2030

Scholarly articles, translations of Afro-Hispanic texts.

A bilingual journal of Afro-Hispanic literature and culture, publishing literary criticism, book reviews, translations, creative writing, and relevant developments in the field. Jointly published by the Department of Romance Languages and the Black Studies Program of the University of Missouri-Columbia.

William W. Megenney, E. Valerie Smith, Jerry Williams, Guillermo Bowie, Miriam DeCosta-Willis.

Unsolicited Manuscripts Received/Published per Year: 44/15.
Payment: none.
Reporting Time: 3 months.
Copyright held by University of Missouri.
1982; 2/yr; 500
$15/yr inst; $5/ea; $1 off inst. rate
8½ x 11
No ads
ISSN: 0278-8969
Faxon, Ebsco

AGADA

Reuven Goldfarb
2020 Essex St.
Berkeley, CA 94703
(510) 848-0965

Poetry, fiction, midrash, memoir, essay, translation, and graphic.

AGADA has a specifically Jewish orientation and emphasis along with a universalist perspective and publishes work touching on traditional Jewish themes and contemporary concerns. It seeks to share the insights, memories, and vision of creative Jewish people with people everywhere.

Thomas Friedmann, Yael Mesinai, Robert Stern, Shulamith Surhamer, Roger White.

Unsolicited Manuscripts Received/Published per Year: 160/20.
Payment: in copies.
Reporting Time: 2–3 months.
Copyright reverts to author.
1981; 1yr; 1,000
$12/2 issues; $6.50/ea; 40%
64 pp; 7 x 10
ISSN: 0740-2392

AGNI

Boston University Creative Writing Program
Askold Melnyczuk, Editor
236 Bay State Rd
Boston, MA 02215

Poetry, fiction, artwork, essays.

AGNI publishes poetry and fiction, translations, commissioned essays and reviews. Our special interests are new and underappreciated writers.

Thom Gunn, Ai, Patricia Traxler, Donald Hall, Maria Floor, John Updike, Ha Jin, Martin Espada, Robert Pinsky, Seamus Heaney, Tom Sleigh, Derek Walcott.

Reading Period: Oct. 1—May 1.

Unsolicited Manuscripts Received/ Published per Year: 2,000/50.

Payment: $10/page up to $150.

Reporting Time: 2–4 months.

Copyright held by The Agni Review, Inc.; reverts to author upon publication.

1972; 2/yr; 1,500

$12/yr; $7/ea; 40%

250–320 pp; 5½ x 8½

Ad Rates: $200/page (4½ x 7); $125/½ page (4½ x 3½)

ISSN: 0191-3352

DeBoer

ALABAMA LITERARY REVIEW

Theron Montgomery and Jim Davis
253 Smith Hall
Troy State University
Troy, AL 36082
(205) 670-3307

Fiction, poetry, essays, photography, and short drama.

A state literary medium for local as well as national artists; supported by National Endowment for the Arts.

Eve Shelnutt, Paul Grant, Joe Colicchio, Elizabeth Dodd, F.R. Lewis, Paul Ruffin, A. Nanette Mansey.

Unsolicited Manuscripts Received/ Published per Year: 3,000/36.

Payment: In copies.

Reporting Time: 2 months (except August).

1987; 2/yr; 850+

$9/yr; $4.50/ea; 40%

100 pp; 9 x 6

Ad Rates: swap equal ad or $25/8 x 5 page

ISSN: 0890-1554

ALASKA QUARTERLY REVIEW

Ronald Spatz, Executive Editor
University of Alaska Anchorage
College of Arts & Sciences
3221 Providence Drive
Anchorage, AK 99508
(907) 786-4775

Fiction, poetry, creative nonfiction, philosophy.

A journal devoted to contemporary literature and philosophy of literature.

Stuart Dybek, Jerome Charyn, Tracy Kidder, Arthur Danto, Maura Stanton, Sam Hamill,

Bill Van Wert, Grace Paley, Amy Hempel, Rosellen Brown, Tobias Wolff, Jane Smiley.
Unsolicited Manuscripts Received/ Published per Year: 1,500 fiction, 400 poetry, 100 other/24 fiction, 20 poetry.
Reading Period: Sept.—May 10.
Payment: in copies; other payment depends on grants.
Reporting Time: 3–12 weeks.
Copyright held by University of Alaska Anchorage.
1981; 2/yr; 1,400
$8/yr ind, $10/yr inst; $5/ea; 50%
192 pp; 6 x 9
ISSN: 0737-268X
DeBoer, Fine Print

ALBATROSS

Richard Smyth, Richard Brobst
Box 7787
North Port, FL 34287-0787
Poetry, interviews, graphics/artwork.
Since we see the albatross as a metaphor for an environment that must survive, we are primarily interested in ecological/environmental/nature themes, written in a narrative style; however, this is not to say that we do not consider other themes and forms.
Walter Griffin, Daniel Comiskey, Stephen Meats, Duane Locke, Peter Meinke.
Unsolicited Manuscripts Received /Published per Year: 300-400/15-20.
Payment: in contributor's copies.
1986; 2/yr; 500
$5/yr ind/inst; $3/ea; 40%
32–44 pp; 5½ x 8
ISSN: 0887-4239

ALDEBARAN LITERARY MAGAZINE

Quantella Owens
Roger Williams University
1 Old Ferry Rd.
Bristol, RI 02809
(401) 253-1040
Fiction and poetry in all styles and genres.
We are an eclectic magazine that publishes both fiction and poetry in all forms, styles and topics. We accept submissions from amateurs and established writers.
Unsolicited Manuscripts Received/ Published per Year: varies per year/50-100.
Payment: 2 free copies of issue published in.
Reporting Time: 6–12 weeks normally.
Copyright reverts to authors upon publication.
1971; A or S-A; 250–300

$5/ea; $4/past issues
50–100 pp; 6 x 9 or 5½ x 8½.
Ad Rates: write to us for information.

AMBERGRIS

Mark Kissling
P.O. Box 29919
Cincinnati, OH 45229

Fiction, essays, graphics/artwork.

AMBERGRIS is dedicated to quality art and literature, and to fostering the emerging author and artist. **AMBERGRIS** gives special, but not exclusive consideration to works by Ohio writers and artists, and to works with Midwestern themes in general.

William Allen, Nicole Cooley, Mona Simpson.

Unsolicited Manuscripts Received/Published per Year: 800-1000/8-10.

Reading Period: Aug.—April.

Payment: $5/published page; $50 maximum. Plus two contributor copies.

Reporting Time: 3 months for 1st round; up to 1 year for final decisions.

Copyright held by magazine; reverts to author upon publication.

1987; 1/yr; 800

$4.95/ea; 40%

160 pp; 5½ x 8½

ISSN: 1044-2006

AMELIA

Frederick A. Raborg, Jr.
329 "E" St.
Bakersfield, CA 93304
(805) 323-4064

Fiction, poetry, plays, graphics/artwork, criticism, reviews, essays, photographs, translation.

AMELIA is a reader's magazine, intended to be enjoyed over a period of time, offering a unique blend of the traditional with the contemporary in virtually every printed art form by both "name" and unknown writers and artists of superior talents. Contributors from its pages have been included in Pushcart Prizes, The Artist Market and other prestigious reprint anthologies.

Pattiann Rogers, David Ray, Lawrence P. Spingarn, Larry Rubin, Stuart Friebert, Merrill Joan Gerber, Maxine Kumin.

Unsolicited Manuscripts Received/Published per Year: 12,000+/600+.

Payment: poetry/$2–$25; fiction/$10–$35; nonfiction/$10/1,000 words; artwork/$5–$50.

Reporting Time: 2 weeks–3 months.

Copyright held by magazine; reverts to author upon publication.

1984; 4/yr; 1,250

$25/yr ind, $25/yr inst; $7.95/ea; 40%

156 pp; 5½ x 8½

Ad Rates: $250/page (4½ x 7½); $140/½ page (4½ x 3¾); $80/¼ page (4½ x 1¾)

ISSN: 0743-2755

AMERICAN BOOK REVIEW

Ronald Sukenick, Rochelle Ratner, John Tytell, Editors; Don Laing, Managing Editor

English Department Publications Center

Campus Box 494

University of Colorado

Boulder, CO 80309-0494

(303) 492-8947

Criticism, essays, reviews.

AMERICAN BOOK REVIEW is offered as a guide to current books of literary interest published by the small, large, university, regional, third world, women's and other presses. It is edited and produced by writers for writers and the general public.

Hayden Carruth, Robert Creeley, Diane Wakoski, Marge Piercy, Joe McElroy, Kirkpatrick Sale, Ihab Hassan, Ishmael Reed.

Unsolicited Manuscripts Received/ Published per Year: 100/15–25.

Payment: $50 per review.

Reporting Time: 2 weeks to 2 months.

Copyright held by **ABR**; reverts to author upon publication.

1977; 6/yr; 12,000

$24/yr ind, $30/yr inst; $4/ea; 40%

32 pp; 10 x 14

Ad Rates: $425/page (10 x 14); $260/½ page (5 x 14); $150/¼ page (5 x 7); $100/½ col (2¼ x 6¾); $60/¼ col (2¼ x 3¾); discounts available.

Ingram, Interstate, Armadillo, LS, Ubiquity

AMERICAN DANE

Jennifer Denning-Kock

3717 Harney St.

Omaha, NE 68131-3844

(402) 341-5049

Fiction, historical, essays.

AMERICAN DANE Magazine is the official publication of the Danish Brotherhood in America—whose purpose is "to promote and perpetuate Danish culture and traditions and to provide fraternal benefits and family protection."

Unsolicited Manuscripts Received/ Published per Year: 30/12–24.

Payment: approx. $35.

Reporting Time: 2 weeks.

Copyright returns to contributor after publication.

1916; 12/yr; 6,000
$12/yr, $15/yr foreign; $1/ea
8¼ x 11
Ad Rates: query
ISSN: 0739-9170
Danish Brotherhood in America

THE AMERICAN POETRY REVIEW

Stephen Berg, David Bonanno, Arthur Vogelsang
1721 Walnut St.
Philadelphia, PA 19103
(215) 496-0439

Poetry, translation, criticism, reviews, interviews, essays.
Lucille Clifton, Sam Hamill, W.S. Merwin, Jane Miller, Carolyn Forche.
Unsolicited Manuscripts Received/Published per Year: 8,400/60.
Payment: $1.25/line for poetry; $75/page for prose.
Reporting Time: 10 weeks.
Copyright held by World Poetry, Inc.; reverts to author upon publication.
1972; 6/yr; 20,000
$13/yr ind, $13/yr inst; $2.75/ea; 50%
52 pp; 9¾ x 13¾
Ad Rates: $725/page (9¾ x 13¾); $440/½ page (9¾ x 6¾); $240/¼ page (4¾ x 6¾)
ISSN: 0360-3709
Eastern News

THE AMERICAN VOICE

Frederick Smock, Sallie Bingham
332 W. Broadway, Suite 1215
Louisville, KY 40202
(502) 562-0045

Fiction, poetry, essays, criticism, photographs.
THE AMERICAN VOICE publishes daring new writers and the more radical work of established writers. Feminist, multicultural pan-American.
Isabel Allende, Maya Angelou, Chaim Potok, Minnie Bruce Pratt, Suzanne Gardinier.
Unsolicited Manuscripts Received/Published per Year: 5,000/60.
Payment: varies.
Reporting Time: 2–3 weeks.
Copyright: first rights held by magazine; reverts to author upon publication.
1985; 3/yr; 2,000
$15/yr ind; $5/ea; 40%
130 pp
Ad Rates: swaps/$100 per page.
ISSN: 0884-4536
DeBoer, Ingram

THE AMERICAS REVIEW (formerly REVISTA CHICANO-RIQUENA)

Julian Olivares, Evangelina Vigil-Pinon
Arte Publico Press
University of Houston

Houston, TX 77204-3784
(713) 749-4833
Poetry, fiction, criticism, review, interviews, photographs, graphics/artwork.
THE AMERICAS REVIEW, A Review of Hispanic Literature and Art of the USA, is the oldest (20 years) and most prestigious U.S. Hispanic literary magazine. It publishes works by outstanding Hispanic writers and artists of the USA, as well as works by new and emerging writers and artists. Analysis, interviews, commentary and reviews of U.S. Hispanic works and writers.
Sandra Cisneros, Denise Chavez, Tato Laviera, Ed Vega, Gary Soto.
Unsolicited Manuscripts Received/Published per Year: 200/30-35.
Payment: varies.
Reporting Time: 3–4 months.
Copyright held by Arte Publico Press.
1972; 3/yr (2 + double issue); 3,000
$15/yr ind, $20/yr inst; $5/ea ($10/double issue); 40%
128 pp; 224 pp double issue; 5½ x 8½
Ad Rates: $200/page (5 x 8); $125/½ page (4 x 5); $75/¼ page (2½ x 4)
ISSN: 0360-7860
Ebsco, Ubiquity, Homing Pigeon, Armadillo

ANEMONE

Nanette Morin, Editor; Bill Griffin, Art Editor
Box 369
Chester, VT 05143
Poetry, reviews, interviews, translations, photographs, graphics/artwork, paintings.
ANEMONE is a quarterly literary arts journal publishing the expressive voice of the people. Our purpose is to help bring the spirit of man closer to his true self through art. We look for work that is different, always looking for the new voice. **ANEMONE** encourages "political" and "social" poetry.
Robert Chute, Arthur Winfield Knight, Teresa Volta, Sesshu Foster, John Oliver Simon.
Unsolicited Manuscripts Received/Published per Year: 1,600/240.
Payment: 1 year's subscription and 5 gifts.
Reporting Time: variable.
Copyright held by Anemone Press Inc.; permission given to publish with mention.
1984; 4/yr; 3,000
$10/yr ind, $10/yr inst; $2.50/ea; 40%
32 pp; 10 x 15

Ad Rates: $200/page (10 x 15); $100/½ page (10 x 7 or 5 x 15); $50/¼ page (5 x 7)
ISSN: 8756-7709

ANTAEUS

Daniel Halpern
100 West Broad St.
Hopewell, NJ 08525
(609) 466-4748

Poetry, fiction, essays, criticism, translation, interviews.

ANTAEUS features a broad spectrum of current, previously unpublished fiction and poetry by both new and established authors, as well as essays and documents. Frequently publishes special issues offering essays on particular subjects (nature, autobiography, art, etc.).

Czeslaw Milosz, Robert Hass, Jorie Graham, Gail Godwin, Paul Bowles.

Unsolicited Manuscripts Received/Published per Year: 5000/varies.
Payment: $10/page.
Reporting Time: 10 weeks.
Copyright held by magazine; reverts to the author upon publication.
1970; 2/yr; 7,500
$30/2 yr ind, $30/2 yr inst; $10/ea; 20%
288 pp; 6 x 9
Ad Rates: $500/page (5½ x 8); $300/½ page (2¾ x 8); $200/¼ page (2¾ x 4)
ISSN: 0003-5319
W.W. Norton, Ingram, DeBoer

ANTIETAM REVIEW

Ann B. Knox, Crystal Brown, & Susanne Kass
7 W. Franklin St.
Hagerstown, MD 21740
(301) 791-3132

Poetry, fiction, photographs.

The **ANTIETAM REVIEW** is a literary magazine for fiction writers, poets and photographers who are natives or residents of Delaware, Maryland, Pennsylvania, Virginia, West Virginia, and the District of Columbia; however, we look for strong literary and artistic quality rather than local interest. Guidelines available.

Wayne Karlin, Joyce Kornblatt, Amy Clampitt, Linda Pasten, Dick Scanlan, Myra Sklarew.

Unsolicited Manuscripts Received/Published per Year: 450–500 fiction, 1,500 poems/8-10 fiction, 16-20 poems.
Reading Period: Sept—Feb. 1.
Payment: $100 for fiction; $20 for poems.
Reporting Time: 6 weeks—4 months depending on pub. date.
Copyright held by Washington

County Arts Council; reverts to author upon publication.
1984; 1 or 2/yr; 1,600
$5.25/yr; $5.25/ea; 20%
60 pp; 8½ x 11
No ads

ANTIGONISH REVIEW
George Sanderson
Box 135
St. Francis Xavier University
Antigonish, Nova Scotia B2G 1C0
CANADA
(902) 867-3962
Poetry, fiction, reviews, articles.
Literary quarterly; new and established writers; short fiction; reviews and light critical articles.
Michael Hulse, Sr. Bernetta Quinn, Achy Obejas, Louis Dudek, Omar Pound.
Reading Period: year–round.
Unsolicited Manuscripts Received/Published per Year: 1,300-1,500/200.
Payment: copies.
Reporting Time: poetry, 2 months; fiction, 4 months.
Copyright retained by author.
1970; 4/yr; 900
$20/yr; $7/ea; 20%
150 pp; 6 x 9
ISSN: 0003-5661
Canadian Magazine Publishers Association

ANTIOCH REVIEW
Robert S. Fogarty
P.O. Box 148
Yellow Springs, OH 45387
Poetry, fiction, criticism, essays, reviews.
ANTIOCH REVIEW is an independent quarterly of critical and creative thought which prints articles of interest to both the liberal scholar and the educated layman. Authors of articles on the arts, politics, social and cultural problems as well as short fiction and poetry find a friendly reception regardless of formal reputation.
Emile Capouya, Raymond Carver, Perri Klass, Gordon Lish, Joyce Carol Oates.
Unsolicited Manuscripts Received/Published per Year: 3,200/25–30.
Reading Period: year–round, except poetry; (Sept.—May 14.)
Payment: $15/published page.
Reporting Time: 3–6 weeks.
Copyright held by **ANTIOCH REVIEW**.
1941; 4/yr; 4,500
$30/yr ind; $42/yr inst; $6/sample
160 pp; 6 x 9
Ad Rates: $250/page (4½ x 7⅞); $150/½ page; $100/¼ page
ISSN: 0003-5769
Eastern News

ANTIPODES

Marian Arkin, Robert Ross
190 Sixth Ave.
Brooklyn, NY 11217
(718) 482-5680 or (718) 789-5826

Fiction, reviews, criticism, essays, poetry, interviews, photographs, graphics/artwork.

Focus is on Australian literature.

Thomas Keneally, A.D. Hope, Judith Wright, Thea Astley, Olga Masters.

Unsolicited Manuscripts Received/Published per Year: 300/50.

Payment: in copies.

1987; 2/yr; 600

$20/yr ind, $35/yr inst; overseas $27/yr ind, $42/yr inst;

60–75 pp; 8½ x 11

Ad Rates: $300/page (7½ x 10); $175/½ page (7½ x 5 or 3½ x 10); $90/¼ page (7½ x 2½ or 3½ x 5)

APALACHEE QUARTERLY

Barbara Hamby, Bruce Boehrer, Paul McCall, Mary Jane Ryals, Monifa Love
P.O. Box 20106
Tallahassee, FL 32316

Poetry, fiction, reviews, translation, photographs, graphics/artwork.

We are interested in well-crafted, modern fiction and poetry. Stylistic innovation is encouraged except when it interferes with narrative intent.

Peter Meinke, G.S. Sharat Chandra, Janet Burroway, Michael Shaara, David Kirby.

Unsolicited Manuscripts Received/Published per Year: 1,000/70–100.

Reading Period: Sept.—May.

Payment: in copies and money when grants permit.

Reporting Time: 12 weeks.

Copyright reverts to author upon publication.

1971; 3/yr; 500

$15/yr; $5 ea

100–200 pp; 6 x 9

Ad Rates: $50/page

APPEARANCES

Robert Witz, Joe Lewis, Bill Mutter
165 West 26th St.
New York, NY 10001
(212) 675-3026

Poetry, fiction, interviews, photographs, graphics/artwork.

APPEARANCES. Literature, art, civilization. New talent. The works. Why wait.

Ron Kolm, j-poet, Nathaniel Burkins, Max Blagg, Jack Wark, Rodolpho Torres.

Unsolicited Manuscripts Received/Published per Year: 150/3 or 4 to 10.

Payment: occasional.
Copyright held by magazine; reverts to author upon publication.
1976; 2/yr; 900
$15/3 issues; $5/ea; 40%
76 pp; 8½ x 11
Ad Rates: $180/page (7½ x 10); $110/½ page (7 x 5½); $80/¼ page (3½ x 5)

ARACHNE
Susan L. Leach
162 Sturges St.
Jamestown, NY 14701
(716) 488-2601
Poetry, fiction.
ARACHNE is a small press dedicated to publishing well written poetry with a largely, but not exclusively, rural theme. We are interested in new poets and in poets who have been writing but have not been largely published. We publish 4 contributors' issues yearly.
Gary Fincke, Penny Kemp, Norbert Krapf, Walt Franklin, Wallace Whatley.
Unsolicited Manuscripts Received/Published per Year: 1,000/85.
Payment: in copies.
Reporting Time: 1 week—2 months.
1980; 4/yr; 250
$18/yr ind, $20/yr inst; $5/ea; 40%
28 pp; 5¼ x 8¼

ARARAT
Leo Hamalian
585 Saddle River Rd.
Saddle Brook, NJ 07662
(201) 797-7600
Fiction, poetry, expository prose.
Publishes material relevant to Armenian culture or history; quality fiction and poetry.
Laura Kalpakian, Edward Alexander, James Hatch, David Kherdian, Ronald Suny, David Ignatius, Diana Der Houanessian.
Unsolicited Manuscripts Received/Published per Year: 70/10-15.
Payment: $50-$100
Reporting Time: 6 weeks.
Copyright reverts to author.
1960; 4/yr; 1500
$24/yr; $7/ea
72 pp; 9 x 11
Ad Rates: call office
ISSN: 003-7583

ARDEN
Scott P. Burke
P.O. Box 326
Lafayette Hills, PA 19444
Fiction, poetry, essays, reviews.
THE ARDEN publishes a wide range of material by new and established writers.
Bruce Curley, Patsy A. Bickerstaff, Mark A. Rossi, Joseph Sollish.

Payment: 1 copy.
Reporting Time: 2 months or less.
Copyright held by magazine; reverts to author upon publication.
1992; 2/yr; 200
$10/yr; $6/ea
90–130 pp; 5 x 11
No ads
ISSN: 1069-0816

ARSHILE: A Magazine of the Arts

Mark Salerno
P.O. Box 3749
Los Angeles, CA 90078

Poetry, fiction, essay, art.
The bulk goes to (1) poetry; (2) fiction; (3) essays on art. Editorial policy: to show everything rather than focus on one part of the picture. Also: to mix established artists with up-and-coming.
Notley, Corbett, Coolidge, Bronk, Myles, Ashton.
Reading Period: December & June.
Payment: copies.
Reporting Time: 3 months.
Copyright reverts to author upon publication.
1993; 2/yr; 1,000
$18/yr; $10/ea
172 pp; 5½ x 11½
Ad Rates: $250/page (4 x 7½)
ISSN: 1066-8721
DeBoer, SPD, Fine Print, Armadillo

ARTFUL DODGE

Daniel Bourne
Department of English
The College of Wooster
Wooster, OH 44691
(216) 262-8353

Poetry, fiction, translation, graphics, reviews.
ARTFUL DODGE is open not just to American work combining the human and the aesthetic, but also to translation, especially from Eastern Europe and the Third World. We also have an ongoing section on American poets who translate, featuring the poet's own work and his or her adaptations of work going on in landscapes other than English.
Stuart Dybek, Naomi Shihab Nye, Jorge Luis Borges, Alberta Turner, Charles Simic, Jim Daniels, William Stafford, Zbigniew Herbert.
Unsolicited Manuscripts Received/Published per Year: 2,500/60
Reading Period: year–round.
Payment: in copies, plus $5 honorarium, as funding allows.
Reporting Time: 1–4 months.
Copyright reverts to author.
1979; 2/yr; 1,000

$10/yr; $5/ea
150-200 pp; 6 x 9
ISSN: 0196-691X
DeBoer

ASCENT
Audrey Curley
P.O. Box 967
Urbana, IL 61801
Fiction, poetry.
Eclectic.
L. J. Schneiderman, Michael Bugeja, George H. Rosen, Nance Van Winckel, Robbie Clipper Sethi.
Unsolicited Manuscripts Received/ Published per Year: 1,050/40.
Reading Period: year–round.
Payment: 3 copies.
Reporting Time: 1 week—2 months.
Copyright held by magazine; reverts to author upon publication.
1975; 3/yr; 750
$6/yr; $3/ea; 40%
64 pp; 6 x 9
ISSN: 0098-9363

ASIAN PACIFIC AMERICAN JOURNAL
Asian American Writers' Workshop; Curtis Chin, Managing Editor; Julie Koo, Soo Mee Kwon, Co-Editors
296 Elizabeth St., 2R
New York, NY 10012
(212) 228-6718
Poetry, fiction, essays.
The **APA JOURNAL** aims to publish the best of contemporary Asian American poetry and prose by new and emerging writers not yet established in the mainstream literary world. In this endeavor, we serve Asian American writers by providing them a space in which to publish and widely disseminate their work, and we serve Asian American readers by giving them access to the work of these talented artists.
Koon Woon, Justin Chin, Zamora Linmark, Susan Ito.
Payment: 2 complimentary issues upon publication, discounts on other copies.
Reporting Time: 2–3 months.
Copyright reverts to author upon publication.
1992; 2/yr; 1,500
$16/yr, $30/2yr; $40/yr inst; $12/ea; 40%
150 pp; 5⅜ x 8⅜
Ad Rates: $250/page (4¼ x 7¼); $120/½ page (4¼ x 3⅜); $60/¼ page (2 x 3½)
Inland, Fine Print, SPD, Armadillo

ASYLUM ANNUAL
Greg Boyd
P.O. Box 6203
Santa Maria, CA 93456
(805) 928-8774
Fiction, poetry, prose poems,

essays, criticism, reviews, translation, photographs, graphics/artwork.

Contemporary literature: some emphasis on short prose forms, experimental writing, dream works and surrealism.

Kenneth Bernard, Stephen Dixon, Robert Peters, Stephen-Paul Martin, Edouard Roditi, Carolyn Stoloff, Russell Edson, Charles Bukowski.

Unsolicited Manuscripts Received/Published per Year: 1,500/80

Payment: in copies.

Reporting Time: 2 weeks–6 months.

Copyright held by magazine; reverts to author upon publication.

1985; 1/yr; 2,500

$10/yr; $7.95/back issue

160 pp; 8½ x 11

Ad Rates: $80/page; $55/½ page

ISSN: 0896-1344

ATOM MIND (Mother Road Publications)

Gregory Smith
P.O. Box 22068
Albuquerque, NM 87154

Poetry, short fiction, essays, artwork, photographs.

ATOM MIND, originally published in 1968–70, is a throwback to Jack Kerouac and the Beats, Steinbeck, Faulkner and Hemingway, a reflection of the original voices in American literature.

Charles Plymell, Charles Bukowski, Adrian C. Louis.

Unsolicited Manuscripts Received/Published per Year: 1,000+/120

Reading Period: year–round.

Payment: copies, occasional small cash payments.

Reporting Time: 2–4 weeks.

Copyright held by Mother Road Publications, with all rights reverting to authors.

1993; 4/yr; 800+

$16/yr; $5/ea; 40%

94 pp; 8½ x 11

Ad Rates: $80/page; $50/½ page; $30/¼ page

ISSN: 0-9636829-6-2

AURA LITERARY/ARTS REVIEW

Mark Valenta
P.O. Box 76
University Center UAB
Birmingham, AL 35294–1150
(205) 934-3354

Poetry, fiction, interviews, essay

Contemporary poetry and prose. Experimental, traditional or genre. Looking for work that distinguishes itself from the crowd yet remains successful.

Interested in documentary photography.
Payment: 2 copies.
Reporting Time: 3 months.
Copyright reverts to author.
1974; 2/yr; 500
$6/yr; $3/ea
120 pp; 6 x 9
ISSN: 0889-7433

A/B: AUTO/BIOGRAPHY STUDIES

Rebecca Hogan
English Department
University of Wisconsin
Whitewater, WI 53190
and/or
Timothy Dow Adams
English Department
University of West Virginia
Morgantown, WV 26506

Criticism, reviews, bibliographical and newsletter information.
Purpose of magazine is to publish essays—literary and critical—about autobiography and biography. Emphasis of recent issues has been on special topics: women's autobiography, Mexican, therapeutic (forthcoming), European, etc. The journal serves also as a clearinghouse for information about convention panels, members' interests, etc.
Lynn Bloom, Janet Verner Gunn, Richard D. Woods, G. Thomas Couser, Silonie Smith.
Payment: none.
Copyright held by author.
1985; 4/yr; 200
$15/yr ind, $45/yr inst
70 pp; 7 x 8½
Ad Rates: $150/page (7 x 8½); $75/½ page (7 x 4¼); $40/¼ page (3½ x 4¼)

AVEC

Cydney Chadwick
P.O. Box 1059
Penngrove, CA 94951
(707) 762-2370; Fax (707) 769-0880

Contemporary poetry, prose, & translations.
Innovative, challenging work from established and emerging writers. **AVEC** is particularly interested in translations of recent French writing and the Russian avant–garde.
Norma Cole, Michael Davidson, Lydia Davis, Dominique Fourcade, Jackson Mac Low, Michael Palmer, Claude Royet-Journoud, Leslie Scalapino, Aleksei Parshchikov.
Unsolicited Manuscripts Received/Published per Year: 1,000+/15+.
Reporting Time: 8 weeks.

Copyright reverts to author upon publication.
1988; 2/yr
$12/yr; $7.50/ea; 40%
192 pp
Ad Rates: $200/page (7½ x 10); $100/½ page (7½ x 4¾) $75/¼ page (3¼ x 4¾)
ISSN: 0899-3750
Inland, BookPeople, SPD, Spectacular Diseases (UK)

AZOREAN EXPRESS

Art Coelho
P.O. Box 249
Timber, MT 59011

Southern Appalachian Mountains, Okie American West, Hobo, Rural, Working Class, American Indian.
There's a focus on themes where people work with their hands; there's a celebration of life like in the poems of Sandburg and the stories of London and Gerald Haslam.
Badger Stone, C.L. Rawlins, Ann Fox Chandonnet.
Unsolicited Manuscripts Received/ Published per Year: 500/35.
Payment: in copies.
Reporting Time: 1 week.
1985; 1/yr; 500
$6.75 (post paid); 30%
80 pp; 5 ½ x 8 ½

B

B CITY

Connie Deanovich
517 North Fourth St.
DeKalb, IL 60115
(815) 758-4633

Poetry: special issue, 8–sestina.
David Trinidad, Susan Wheeler, Ron Padgett, Anne Waldman, Bernadette Mayer, Maxine Chernoff, Clayton Eshleman.
Unsolicited Manuscripts Received/ Published per Year: 700/2%.
Reading Period: Dec.—Feb.
Payment: small honorarium when available.
$5/yr ind, $6/yr inst; $5/ea; 40%

THE BAFFLER

Thomas Frank
P.O. Box 378293
Chicago, IL 60637
(312) 538-3812

Essays, stories, poetry.
THE BAFFLER publishes essays, criticism, and literature that derive from its unique interpretation of 20th century culture. The American Mercury of the '90s.
Thomas Frank, Steve Albini, Janice Edius, Owen Hatteras.
Unsolicited Manuscripts Received/ Published per Year: 200/5.

Reading Period: year–round.
Reporting Time: 5 months.
Copyright retained by magazine.
1988; 2/yr; 3500
$8/yr, $5/ea; 40%
136 pp, 6 x 9
Ad Rates: $175/page (6 x 8½); $90/½ page (6 x 4)
ISSN: 1059-9789
Ubiquity, Speedinpex, Fine Print, Desert Moon, Small Changes, Dormouse

BAKUNIN

Jordan Jones
P.O. Box 1853
Simi Valley, CA 93062-1853

Poetry, fiction, essays, reviews, artwork, drama.

BAKUNIN, a magazine for the dead Russian anarchist in all of us, seeks well-crafted and challenging writing and artwork, especially of sexual and social critique.

Sandra McPherson, Benjamin Saltman, Dorianne Laux, Stephen Dixon.

Unsolicited Manuscripts Received/Published per Year: 1,000/60.
Payment: 2 copies.
Reporting Time: 2 weeks—12 weeks.
Copyright reverts to author on publication.
1990; 2/yr; 750
$8/yr, $10/yr inst. and foreign; $5/ea; 40%
100 pp, 5½ x 8½
Ad Rates: $100/page; $50/½ page
ISSN: 1052-3154
Ubiquity, Fine Print, Armadillo

BALL MAGAZINE

Douglas M. Kimball, Editor; Jen Jarrell, Poetry Editor; Collin Coggins, Music Editor
Box 775
Northampton, MA 01061-0775
(413) 634-5687

Reviews (music, art, lit, sci-fi), fiction, nonfiction.

BALL MAGAZINE publishes all work of quality received biannually. Our format and content evolve according to what is received.

Des Lewis, Byron Coley, Matt Ernst, Lenora Rogers.

Unsolicited Manuscripts Received/Published per Year: 500/50+.
Reading Period: year–round.
Payment: copies.
Reporting Time: 2 weeks—2 months.
Copyright: magazine holds first rights.
1993; 2/yr; 2,000
$8/yr, $4.95/ea; 40%
80 pp, 8½ x 11

Ad Rates: \$100/page; \$60/½ page; \$35/¼ page; \$20/⅛ page; \$12/classifieds
Fine Print

BAMBOO RIDGE: The Hawaii Writers' Quarterly

Eric Chock and Darrell Lum
P.O. Box 61781
Honolulu, HI 96839-1781
Poetry, fiction.
BAMBOO RIDGE has special interest in literature reflecting the multi-ethnic cultures and peoples of the Hawaiian Islands.
Juliet Kono, Wing Tek Lum, Garrett Hongo, Sylvia Watanabe, Rodney Morales, Cathy Song, Lois-Ann Yamanaka.
Unsolicited Manuscripts Received/Published per Year: 500-700/60-80
Payment: \$25/poem; \$50/short story; plus 2 copies and 1 year subscription.
Reporting Time: 3–6 months.
Copyright held by Bamboo Ridge Press; reverts to author upon publication.
1978; 4/yr; 1,000
\$16/yr; \$5/sample copy; 40%
120 pp; 6 x 9
Ad Rates: \$100/page (5¼ x 8¼)
ISSN: 0733-0308
SPD

THE BEACON

Varies from year to year
The Beacon, SWOCC
1988 Newmark
Coos Bay, OR 97420-2956
888-2525 ext. 335
Short stories, poetry, plays, essays, line drawings and black and white photograph.
Magazine varies each year.
Public and students, local submissions only.
Unsolicited Manuscripts Received/Published per year: varies/varies.
\$4/ea
Page number and size of magazine varies with editor.

BEAT SCENE

Kevin Ring
27 Court Leet
Binley Woods
Coventry, England CV32JQ
(020) 354-3604
Beat influenced interviews, reviews, features.
SOS America onwards. Heavy emphasis on Beat generation writers such as Jack Kerouac, William Burroughs, Charles Bukowski. Interviews, features, and information magazine. Full colour covers/glossy pages.
Charles Bukowski, Allen Ginsberg, William Burroughs, Gary Snyder.

Copyright with contributors
1988; 4/yr; 8,000
$28/yr; $8/ea; all payments must be in actual US dollars—no checks please.
50 pp.
Ad Rates: $150/page; $75/½ page; $40/¼ page
Caroline International, Beat Scene

BELLES LETTRES: A Review of Books by Women

Janet Mullaney
11151 Captain's Walk Ct.
North Potomac, MD 20878
(301) 294-0278 Fax (301) 294-0023

Reviews, criticism, essays, interviews, personal essays, photographs, graphics/artwork.

BELLES LETTRES reviews literature by women in all genres. Our purpose is to promote and celebrate writing by women and to inform and entertain. Interviews, rediscoveries, retrospectives, theme reviews, and publishing news are regularly featured. Queries from writers are welcome.

Jewelle Gomez, Cheryl Clarke, Lynne Sharon Schwartz, Carole Maso, Deirdre Bair, Faye Moskowitz.

Unsolicited Manuscripts Received/Published per Year: 300/10.

Payment: in subscriptions, copies & honorarium, depending on grant funding.

Copyright held by magazine; reverts to author upon publication.
1985; 4/yr; 5,000
$20/yr ind, $40/yr inst; $5/ea; 40%
64 pp; 8½ x 11
Ad Rates: $400/page (7½ x 10); $350/back page (7¼ x 8½ or 8½ 7¼); $300/⅔ page (4¾ x 10 or 7½ x 6½); $250/½ page (3½ x 10 or 7½ x 5); $125/¼ page (3½ x 5 or 7½ x 2½)
ISSN: 0084-2957
Ubiquity, Small Changes, Inland, IPD, Fine Print

THE BELLINGHAM REVIEW

Knute Skinner, Editor
The Signpost Press Inc.
1007 Queen St.
Bellingham, WA 98226
(206) 734-9781

Poetry, fiction, reviews, plays, photographs, graphics/artwork.

The focus is primarily on poetry, fiction and drama.

Joanne McCarthy, Carlos Reyes, Gerald Locklin, Marjorie Power, Christianne Balk.

Reading Period: Sept.—Mar. 1.
Payment: 1 year subscription.
Reporting Time: 2–3 months.

Copyright reverts to author upon publication.
1977; 2/yr; 800
$5/yr, $5.50 if agencied; $2.50/ea; 40% on 5 or more
60 pp; 5½ x 8½
Exchange ads only
ISSN: 0734-2934

BELLOWING ARK

Robert R. Ward
P.O. Box 45637
Seattle, WA 98145
(206) 545-8302

Poetry, fiction, essays, graphics/ artwork, novel serializations, short autobiography, plays.

We feature work in the American Romantic tradition, i.e. editorial content is concerned with universal truths and the idea of transcending individual limitation. Content of a work is the primary consideration; form is a distant second, leading to a wryly eclectic mix (we are just concluding the serialization of a 14,000 line epic, for instance).

Nelson Bentley, Susan McCaslin, Irene Culver, Muriel Karr, Harold Witt, Natalie Reciputi, Ray Mizer, Paula Milligan.

Unsolicited Manuscripts Received/ Published per Year: 4,000+/200+.

Reading Period: year–round.
Payment: 2 copies upon publication.
Copyright held by **BELLOWING ARK**; reverts to author upon request.
1984; 6/yr; 800
$15/yr ind, $15/yr inst; $3/ea; 40%; comp to libraries on request
28 pp; 11 x 16
Ad Rates: only in special circumstances.
ISSN: 0887-4115
Ubiquity, Faxon, Popular Subscription Service

THE BELOIT POETRY JOURNAL

Marion K. Stocking
Box 154, RFD 2
Ellsworth, ME 04605
(207) 667-5598

Poetry, reviews.

We publish the best poems we receive without bias as to length, form, subject, or tradition. We especially hope to discover new voices. Occasional chapbooks; recently Afro-American, American Indian, and new Chinese poetry.

Susan Tichy, Sherman Alexie, Alice Jones, Brooks Haxton, Lola Haskins.

Unsolicited Manuscripts Received/ Published per Year: 3,000+/50+.
Reading Period: year–round.
Payment: 3 copies.
Reporting Time: immediately—four months.
Copyright held by magazine; reverts to author upon publication.
1950; 4/yr; 1,800
$12/yr ind, $18/yr inst; $4/ea; 20%
48 pp; 5½ x 8½
No ads
ISSN: 0005-8661
DeBoer, Fine Print, Maine Writer's and Publisher's Alliance, Ubiquity

THE BERKELEY POETRY REVIEW

Connie Vallejo and Kristina Youso
700 Eshleman Hall
University of California at Berkeley
Berkeley, CA 94720

Poetry, fiction, translation, interviews, photographs, graphics/artwork.

THE BERKELEY POETRY REVIEW is a small but longstanding literary journal that publishes primarily poetry. Poets should submit 4 poems maximum; we are always on the lookout for emerging writers.

Victor Hernandez Cruz, Thom Gunn, Heather McHugh, Opal Palmer-Adisa, Ishmael Reed.
Unsolicited Manuscripts Received/ Published per Year: 1,000/100.
Reading Period: year–round.
Payment: 1 copy upon publication.
Copyright held by author.
1973; 1–2/yr; 500–1,000
$10/yr ind, $12/yr inst; $10/ea; 40%
100 pp; 5 x 8
Ad Rates: $55/page (4 x 7); $30/½ page (2½ x 3½)

THE BILINGUAL REVIEW/LA REVISTA BILINGÜE

Gary D. Keller
Hispanic Research Center
Arizona State University
Tempe, AZ 85287-2702
(602) 965-3867

Poetry, fiction, criticism, reviews, scholarly articles.

Devoted to the linguistics and literature of bilingualism, primarily Spanish/English, in the United States. We publish creative literature by and/or about United States Hispanics, literary criticism and reviews of United States Hispanic literature. We do not publish translations.

Leo Romero, Judith Ortiz Cofer, Nash Candelaria, Connie Porter.

Unsolicited Manuscripts Received/ Published per Year: 400/35.
Payment: in copies.
Reporting Time: 30 days.
Copyright held by magazine.
1974; 3/yr; 2,000
$16/yr ind; $28/yr inst; sample copies: $6 ind, $10 inst
96 pp; 7 x 10
Ad Rates: $200/page (5½ x 8½); $125/½ page (5½ x 4)
ISSN: 0094-5366

BLACK BEAR REVIEW

Ave Jeanne & Ron Zettlemoyer
1916 Lincoln St.
Croydon, PA 19021

Poetry, reviews, graphics, market listings, ads.

BLACK BEAR REVIEW is an international literary/fine arts magazine published twice a year. We welcome poetry that shows: knowledge of the craft, depth, the world around us, and human nature. We attempt to get into print as much poetry as possible. Social, environmental, and political topics welcomed.

Tim Peeler, Chuck Barrett, Walt Phillips, Elliot Richman, B.Z. Niditch, Sherman Alexie.

Unsolicited Manuscripts Received/ Published per Year: 3,500/100.
Reading Period: year–round.
Payment: in copy.
Copyright held by magazine; reverts to author upon publication.
1984; 2/yr; 600
$10/yr ind, $12/yr inst; $5/ea; 40%
64 pp; 5½ x 8
ISSN: 8756-0666

BLACK ICE

Mark Amerika, Editor; Associate Editors: Raymond Federman and Kathy Acker
English Dept. Publications Center
Campus Box 494
Boulder, CO 80309-0494
(303) 492-8947

Fiction.

BLACK ICE publishes only fiction, with emphasis on non-traditional fiction. We intend to take risks with the fiction we publish and encourage writers to do the same.

Steve Katz, Erik Belgum, Thomas Glynn, Harold Jaffe, Cris Mazza.

Unsolicited Manuscripts Received/ Published per Year: 350/15–20.
Payment: 2 contributors copies.
Copyright held by magazine; reverts to author upon publication.
1984; 3/yr; 800
$7/ea; 40%
100 pp; 5½ x 8½
Ad Rates: $150/page (5 x 8)
ISSN: 1047-515X

BLACK JACK/VALLEY GRAPEVINE

Art Cuelho
P.O. Box 249
Big Timber, MT 59011

Poetry, fiction, photographs, graphics/artwork; mostly poetry and short stories.

BLACK JACK's focus is on rural America, regional writing; interests are on the the Dustbowl; Okie migration; southern Appalachia; Hoboes; American Indians; the West; American farmer and rancher. **VALLEY GRAPEVINE** focuses on anything in the San Joaquin Valley in Central California.

Bill Rintoul, Gerry Haslam, Wilma McDaniel, Dorothy Rose, Frank Cross.

Payment: in copies.

Reporting Time: 1 week.

Copyright held by Seven Buffaloes Press; reverts to author upon publication.

1973; 1/yr; 750

\$10/yr; \$6.75/ea (post paid); 20%–40%

85 pp; 5¼ x 8¼

BLACK RIVER REVIEW

Deborah Glaefke Gilbert
855 Mildred Ave.
Lorain, OH 44052-1213
(216) 244-9654

Poetry, fiction, critical essay, book review.

BRR presents contemporary writing of diverse styles and genres aimed toward a broad audience. We print work that exhibits originality, craftsmanship, vivid style, by writers both well-known and as-yet-to-be-discovered. More detailed guidelines are available for SASE.

B. Z Niditch, Sandra Nelson, Ioanna-Veronika Warwick, L. E. McCullogh, Paul Weinman, David Mouat, Alysice K. Harpootean.

Unsolicited Manuscripts Received/Published per Year: 1,000+/65+.

Reading Period: Jan.—May. Those received any other time are returned unread. No response without SASE.

Payment: in copies.

Reporting Time: 2 weeks–6 months.

Copyright reverts to author upon publication.

1985; 1/yr; 400

\$4/ea

60 pp; 8½ x 11

Ad Rates: query

THE BLACK SCHOLAR

Robert Chrisman, Editor: JoNina Abron, Managing Editor

P.O. Box 2869
Oakland, CA 94609
(415) 547-6633

Poetry, fiction, sociology, politics, economy, education, book reviews.

A journal of black studies and research, addressing such issues as black culture, black politics, black education, economics, Southern Africa, etc. . . . A journal on the cutting edge of contemporary black thought.

Jesse Jackson, Jayne Cortez, Johnnotta B. Cole, Gwendolyn Brooks, Haki R. Madhubuti, P.P. Sarduy

Unsolicited Manuscripts Received/ Published per Year: 100–150/8–10.

Payment: subscription plus 10 copies.

Reporting Time: 2 months.

Copyright held by Black World Foundation.

1969; 4/yr; 10,000

$30/ind, $50/inst; $6/ea; 20%–40%

64 pp; 7 x 10

$1,000/page; $600/½ page; query

ISSN: 0006-4246

L-S Dist., DeBoer

BLACK WARRIOR REVIEW

Leigh Ann Sackrider
P.O. Box 2936
Tuscaloosa, AL 35486-2936
(205) 348-4518

Poetry, fiction, essays, reviews, translations, interviews.

The **BLACK WARRIOR REVIEW** publishes the best of contemporary writing by the best of contemporary writers.

Andre Dubus, Michael S. Harper, John Ashbery, John Irving, Jorie Graham, Jane Miller, David St. John.

Unsolicited Manuscripts Received/ Published per Year: 20,000/100.

Reading Period: year–round.

Payment: $5–10/page.

Reporting Time: 1–3 months.

Copyright held by magazine; reverts to author upon publication.

1974; 2/yr; 1,800

$11/yr ind, $17/yr inst; $6/ea

165 pp; 6 x 9

Ad Rates: $150/page (5 x 8); $85/½ page (5 x 3½)

ISSN: 0193-6301

BLIND ALLEYS

Michael S. Weaver
Rutgers University
Box 29
Camden, NJ 08102

Poetry, fiction, criticism, essays, reviews, graphics/artwork.

BLIND ALLEYS is a semiannual magazine which has a primary focus on the third world, but it does not limit itself to a specific literary approach or political beat.

Lucille Clifton, Andrei Codrescu, Jerry Ward, Ethelbert Miller, Eric Abrahamson.

Unsolicited Manuscripts Received/Published per Year: 500/40.

Payment: in copies.

Reporting Time: 3 to 4 months.

Copyright reverts to author.

1982; 2/yr; 300

$11/yr ind, $13/yr inst; $5/ea

45 pp; 5¼ x 8⅜

Ad Rates: $100/page; $50/½ page; $25/¼ page

BLIS

Meltem Persion
1096 Casitas Pass Rd.
Ste. 289
Carpinteria, CA 93013

Short fiction, poetry.

BLIS is a quarterly magazine of short fiction and poetry about spiritual living (not religious). We wish to accept stories and poetry that have underlying spiritual ideas such as understanding, acceptance, and kindness.

Linda Healy, William Vernon, Phylis Eichen.

Unsolicited Manuscripts Received/Published per Year: 600/40.

Reading Period: year–round.

Payment: $20 for each poem/story regardless of length.

Reporting Time: up to 6 months (one month average).

Copyright: yes.

1993; 4/yr

$18/yr; $5/ea

24 pp; 8½ x 11

THE BLOOMSBURY REVIEW

Tom Auer, Publisher; Marilyn Auer, Assoc. Publisher
1028 Bannock St.
Denver, CO 80204
(303) 892-0620; Fax (303) 892-5620

Reviews, graphics/artwork, poetry, interviews, photographs, essays.

THE BLOOMSBURY REVIEW is a "Book Magazine" that includes reviews, interviews, essays, poetry, profiles, and previews of new titles, with an emphasis on new titles from small, medium-sized, and university presses.

Harlan Ellison, Gregory McNamee, John Nichols, Linda Hogan, Peter Wild.

Unsolicited Manuscripts Received/Published per Year: 1,000/100.

Reading Period: year–round.

Payment: $15/review; $10/poetry; $20/interviews.

Reporting Time: 4–6 weeks.

Copyright reverts to author.

1980; 6/yr; 50,000
$16/yr; $3/ea; 40%; less discount through distributors.
32 pp; 11¼ x 16
Ad Rates: $3,150/page (9⅞ x 15¼); $1,680/½ page (9⅞ x 7½); $890/¼ page (4⅞ x 7½ or 2⁵⁄₁₆ x 15¼ or 9⅞ x 3⅝)
ISSN: 0276-1564

BLUE LIGHT RED LIGHT

Alma Rodriguez
496A Hudson Street, Suite F-42
New York, NY 10014
(201) 432-3245

Fusion of contemporary writing, magic surrealism, and mainstream writing together with speculative fiction.

BLUE LIGHT RED LIGHT, a periodical of speculative fiction and the arts, welcomes all international writers, poets and storytellers inspired by the literature of personal myth, dream images and folklore.

Gloria Naylor, Harlan Ellison, Peter Wortsman, E. S. Creamer.
Payment: small honorarium, plus issues.
Reporting Time: 8-10 weeks.
Copyright held by magazine; reverts to author.
1988; 1–3/yr
$15/yr; $5.50/ea; 40%
176 pp; 9 x 6
$250/page; $150/½ page
ISSN: 10456-0012

BLUE UNICORN

Ruth G. Iodice, Harold Witt, Daniel J. Langton, Editors; Robert L. Bradley, Art Editor; Ila F. Berry, Contest Chairperson
22 Avon Rd.
Kensington, CA 94707
(415) 526-8439

Poetry, translation, artwork.

We are looking for excellence of the individual poetic voice, whether that voice comes through in form or free verse, rhyme or not. We want originality of image, thought and music, poems which are memorable and communicative. We publish both well-known poets and unknowns who deserve to be known better.

John Ciardi, Charles Edward Eaton, Emilie Glen, Diana O'Hehir, William Stafford.
Unsolicited Manuscripts Received/Published per Year: 35,000/100.
Payment: in copies.
Reporting Time: 3–4 months.
Copyright held by magazine; reverts to author upon publication.
1977; 3/yr; 500
$14/yr, $18/yr foreign; $5/ea
56 pp; 5½ x 8½
ISSN: 0197-7016

BLUELINE

Anthony Tyler
English Dept.
SUNY
Potsdam, NY 13676

Poetry, fiction, essays, reviews, graphics/artwork, oral history, journals.

BLUELINE is dedicated to prose and poetry about the Adirondacks and other regions similar in geography and spirit. We are interested in historic and contemporary writing, from new and established writers, that interprets the region as well as describes it.

Eric Ormsby, Robert Morgan, Annie David, Joan Conner.

Unsolicited Manuscripts Received/Published per Year: 130/31. Previously unpublished mss. need SASE for response.

Reading Period: Sept.—Nov.

Payment: in copies.

Reporting Time: 2–10 weeks.

Copyright held by magazine; reverts to author upon publication.

1993; 300

$6/yr; $6/ea; $4

100 pp; 6 x 9

ISSN: 0198-9901

BOGG

John Elsberg, George Cairncross
422 North Cleveland
Arlington, VA 22201

Poetry, prose poems, criticism, essays, reviews, interviews, graphics/artwork.

Editing is a subjective affair, and we print what takes our fancy. **BOGG** is an Anglo-American literary journal, with contributions from the U.S., Canada, England, Australia/New Zealand and India.

Ann Menebroker, Ron Androla, Harold Witt, Robert Peters, John Millett, Tina Fulker, Richard Peabody, Jon Silkin, Laurel Speer, Charles Plymell, A.D. Winans, Charles Bukowski.

Unsolicited Manuscripts Received/Published per Year: 10,000 poems/100-150 US poems; 3-6 prose pieces; 2-3 interviews; 3-6 essays.

Payment: in copies.

Reporting Time: immediately.

Copyright held by author.

1968; 2–3/yr; 750

$12/3 issues; $4.50/ea; $3.50/sample; 40%

64 pp; 6 x 9

ISSN: 0882-648X

BOHEMIAN CHRONICLE

Emily W. Skinner, Ellen M. Williams
P.O. Box 387
Largo, Fl 34649-0387

Fiction, nonfiction, essays, poetry, humor.
An international newsletter/magazine promoting sensitivity in the arts, **BOHEMIAN CHRONICLE'S** primary focus is to extend an arm to communities worldwide whose voices have been quelled.
Sharon Komlos, author of 'Feel the Laughter'.
Reading Period: Dec.—Sept.
Payment: $5.00 per article; $5.00 per art used.
Reporting Time: 2 months.
Copyright: each issue is copyrighted as a whole (magazine buys first rights; SASE for guidelines.)
1991; 12/yr; 500+
$12/U.S. ea; $15/outside U.S. ea; $1/ea
12 pp; 8½ x 5½
Ad Rates: $25/page; $15/½ page; $5/businesscard

rejected poetry

BOMB MAGAZINE

Betsy Sussler
594 Broadway 212 431-5880
Suite 1002A
New York, NY 10012
(212) 431-3943 FAX 431 5880

Interviews, poetry, fiction, photographs, art.
BOMB MAGAZINE is a spokespiece for new art, fiction, theater and film in New York. Named after Wyndham Lewis's "Blast," it promotes and encourages conversations throughout the arts.
Kathy Acker, Gary Indiana, Ameena Meer, Patrick McGrath, Lynne Tillman.
Unsolicited Manuscripts Received/ Published per Year: 2,000/4.
Payment: $100.
Copyright reverts to author.
1981; 4/yr; 8,500
$16/yr; $5/ea; 40%
100 pp; 10 x 14½
Ad Rates: available on request

BOOKENDS

Chet Hagan
P. O. Box 227
Warnersville, PA 19565
(215) 678-6480

Library news (locally & statewide); book reviews aimed at the local market—Reading & Berks County.
Published six times a year, **BOOKENDS** is totally financed by the Friends of the Reading-Berks (PA) Public Libraries. All writing is volunteered.
John Updike, James L. Holton, Christopher Hinz, Lloyd Arthur Eshbach, Chet Hagan.
Payment: none; all volunteer contributions.

Copyright: authors, if they wish, copyright own material. the magazine is not copyright per se.
1981; 6/yr; 2,000
16+ pp; 8½ x 11
ISSN: 0893-6471.

BORDERLANDS: Texas Poetry Review
Editors rotate from among our permanent board members
P. O. Box 49818
Austin, TX 78765
(512) 444-7320
Original poetry, short reviews, essays on contemporary poetry.
BORDERLANDS publishes outward—looking, accessible poems on society, environment, history, other cultures, landscape, or spiritual life; and essays setting contemporary poetry in some large context, often social or political.
Stephen Dobyns, Ted Kooser, David Romtvedt, Elizabeth Socolow, Naomi Nye, William Stafford, Laurel Speer, Walt McDonald, Patianne Rogers.
Unsolicited Manuscripts Received/ Published per Year: 2,000/200.
Payment: 1 copy.
Reporting Time: 3–4 months.
Copyright: 1st North American Rights only.
1992; 2/yr; 500
14/yr ind, $16/yr inst; $8.50/ea; 50%
100 pp; 5½ x 8½
Ad Rates: no ads at present; may trade ads later with other literary journals.
ISSN: 1065-0342
Fine Print, Ebsco

BOSTON LITERARY REVIEW (BLUR)
Gloria Mindock
Box 357
W. Somerville, MA 02144
(617) 625-6087
Poetry, short fiction (under 3,000 words).
We seek work that pushes form or content, and that has a unique, even idiosyncratic voice. 5–10 poems are welcome, as we prefer to publish several poems by each author.
Eric Pankey, David Ray, Stuart Freibert, Richard Kostelanetz.
Unsolicited Manuscripts Received/ Published per Year: 2,500/35.
Payment: 2 copies.
Reporting Time: 2–4 weeks.
Copyright reverts to author upon publication.
1984; 2/yr; 500
$9/yr; $5/ea
24 pp; 5½ x 13

BOSTON REVIEW

Josh Cohen, Editor
33 Harrison Ave.
Boston, MA 02111
(617) 350-5353

THE BOSTON REVIEW is an award-winning national magazine with the distinctive voice of Boston—unconventional coverage of politics, culture, and all the arts. Meet the next generation of gifted young writers alongside established authors saying what's really on their minds. People like Ralph Nader, Henry Louis Grates, Jr., Sharon Olds, Sven Birkerts, bell hooks, Michael Dorris, Robert Pinsky.

Unsolicited Manuscripts Received/Published per Year: 1,000/40.

Payment: $40–$250/depending on length and author.

Copyright held by Boston Critic, Inc.; reverts to author upon publication.

1975; 6/yr; 20,000

$15/yr ind, $18/yr inst

40–48 pp; 11⅜ x 14½

Ad Rates: $800/page (10 x 14); $550/½ page (10 x 6¾); $250/¼ page (4¾ x 6¾)

ISSN: 0734-2306

Interstate, Ingram, Total

BOTTOMFISH

Robert Scott
DeAnza College
21250 Stevens Creek Blvd.
Cupertino, CA 95014
(408) 864-8538 or 864-8547

Poetry, fiction.

BOTTOMFISH accepts lyric poems and short fiction of 5,000 words or less. We publish some experimental fiction. We are interested only in carefully crafted work.

Naomi Clark, Janice Dabney, William Dickey, Edward Kleinschmidt, Martin Nakell.

Unsolicited Manuscripts Received/Published per Year: 500-1,000/30 poems, 6 stories.

Reading Period: year–round.

Payment: in copies.

Copyright held by magazine; reverts to author upon publication.

1975; 1/yr; 500

$4/ea; 40%

70–80 pp; 17.5 x 21 cm.

No ads

BOULEVARD

Richard Burgin, Editor
P. O. Box 30386
Philadelphia, PA 19103
(215) 561-1723

Poetry, fiction, criticism, essays, translations, interviews, photos, graphics.

BOULEVARD publishes exceptional fiction and poetry and

essays by impressive new talent as well as established literary voices. The editors believe a critical dimension is essential to an outstanding literary publication; thus, each issue publishes essays on literature and the other arts. **BOULEVARD** believes in the school of talent.

John Ashbery, Isaac Bashevis Singer, Joyce Carol Oates, Alice Adams, Kenneth Koch.

Unsolicited Manuscripts Received/Published per Year: 6,000+/75.

Reading Period: Oct.—May.

Payment: \$25–150/poetry; \$50–150/fiction & other prose.

Copyright held by Opojaz Inc. for First North American Serial Rights; reverts to author upon publication.

1986; 3/yr; 2,500

\$12/yr ind, \$9/yr inst; \$6/ea. 40%

200 pp

Ad Rates: Contact CLMP for information.

ISSN: 0885-9337

DeBoer

BOUNDARY 2

William V. Spanos
SUNY/Binghamton
Binghamton, NY 13901
(607) 798-2743

Poetry, fiction, criticism, essays, plays, translation, interviews, photographs, graphics/artwork.

BOUNDARY 2 publishes poetry, fiction and literary criticism that try to break out of the impasse that traditional, including modernist, literature and literary criticism have become stalled in. We are especially interested in providing a forum for experiments in open forms that ultimately interrogate the literary tradition and the dominant culture this tradition supports.

Armand Schwerner, Jerome Rothenberg, John Taggart, Charles Bernstein and the l=a=n=g=u=a=g=e poets.

Payment: none.

Reporting Time: 4–6 months.

1972; 3/yr; 1,000

\$15/yr ind, \$13/yr students; \$25/yr inst; \$8/ea; 40%

300 pp; 9 x 5¾

Ad Rates: \$100/page; \$50/½ page; \$25/¼ page

THE BRIDGE: a journal of fiction & poetry.

Jack Zucker; Helen Zucker, Fiction Editor; Mitzi Alvin, Poetry Editor; Marion Meilgaard, Associate Fiction Editor; Lorene Erickson, Managing Editor.
14050 Vernon St.
Oak Park, MI 48237
(313) 547-6823

Fiction, poetry, reviews (1–2).
Eclectic collection of 48% fiction, 48% poetry, 4% reviews, etc. Our writers run from national to new. We devote about 10% of each issue to Michigan writers.
Grace Bauer, X. J. Kennedy, Ruth Whitman, Daniel Hughes, Barbara Greenberg.
Unsolicited Manuscripts Received/ Published per Year: 1,000+/80.
Reading Period: year–round.
Payment: none.
Reporting Time: 3–4 months.
Copyright: first rights only.
1990; 2/yr; 700
$8/yr; $5/ea; 40%
192 pp; 5½ x 8
Ad Rates: $45/page
ISSN: 1052-1569

BRIEF

Jim Hydock
P.O. Box 33
Canyon, CA 94516
(415) 376-5509
Poetry, fiction, post-modern fiction/poetry.
Subscription only. Sold in select bookstores.
Larry Eigner, Fielding Dawson, August Kleinzahler, Anselm Hollo, Martha King.
Payment: none.
Reporting Time: 2–4 weeks.
Copyright held by magazine; reverts to author upon publication.
1988; 3/yr; 250
$10/yr ind, $12/yr inst; $2.50/ea; 40%
25 pp; 5½ x 8½
No ads

THE BROOKLYN REVIEW

2308 Boylan Hall, Brooklyn College
Brooklyn, NY 11210
(718) 951-5195
Short fiction, poetry.
An annual magazine featuring established writers, while also publishing dynamic emerging voices in both fiction and poetry.
Allen Ginsberg, John Ashbery, Amy Gerstler.
Unsolicited Manuscripts Received/ Published per Year: about 5%.
Reading Period: Sept.—Nov. 15.
Payment: 2 copies.
Reporting Time: 6–10 weeks.
1974; 1/yr; 500
$5/ea
120 pp; digest-sized
No ads.

BRÚJULA/COMPASS

Isaac Goldemberg
Latin American Writers Institute
Hostos Community College

500 Grand Concourse,
Bronx, NY 10451
(718) 518-4195

Devoted to Latino Literature in the U.S. Bilingual (Spanish & English). Publishes fiction, poetry, reviews, personal essays, literary criticism, interviews & information on grants, calls for manuscripts, residencies, other magazines, opportunities for publication, literary contests for Latino writers.

Julia Alvarez, Luis Rafael Sánchez, Iván Silén, Iván Stavans, Magali Alabau, Julio Ortega, Judith Ortiz Coffer.

Unsolicited Manuscripts Received/Published per Year: 300/120.

Reading Period: year–round.

Payment: in-kind.

1987; 4/yr; 5,000

$20/yr; $4/ea

32 pp; tabloid

Ad Rates: $400/page; $250/½ page; $150/¼ page; $100/⅛ page; $75/1/16 page

BRUSSELS SPROUT

Francine Porad
P.O. Box 1551
Mercer Island, WA 98040
(206) 232-3239

Haiku Poetry, senryu, renku, tanka, book reviews dealing with haiku, graphics/artwork.

A journal of contemporary English language haiku and art, with international contributors and subscribers. Seeking haiku and senryu in a variety of styles and forms, from one to four lines; tanka, five lines. Subject matter is open. **BRUSSELS SPROUT** looks for haiku that capture "the haiku moment" in a fresh way.

H. F. Noyes, Marlene Mountain, George Swede, Paul O. Williams, Elizabeth St. Jacques, Yvonne Hardenbrock.

Unsolicited Manuscripts Received/Published per Year: 6,000/600.

Reading Period: year–round.

Payment: none, 3–$10 editor's awards.

Reporting Time: 3 weeks.

Copyright reverts to author upon publication.

1980; 3/yr; 300

$16/yr domestic/Canada, $20 elsewhere; $5.50/ea, $7/ea elsewhere.

48 pp; 8½ x 5½

ISSN: 0897-7356

C

CAFE MAGAZINE

c/o City Books
1111 East Carson St.
Pittsburgh, PA 15203
attn: Frank Carroll

Payment: in copies.
Reporting Time: 8 weeks.
Please do not submit until you have ordered a sample copy.
Copyright held by Solo Press.
1969; 3/yr; 500
$20/yr; $5/ea; 40%
44 pp; 8½ x 11
ISSN: 0773-1796

CAFE SOLO

Glenna Luschei
Box 2814
Atascadero, CA 93422
(805) 243-1058

Poetry, criticism, essays, reviews, translation, photographs, graphics/artwork and letters to the editor.

We seek excellence and the avant-garde: Subconscious navigation in strange waters and Columbus sighting land. We print new writers next to known ones. We emphasize poetry, but encourage imaginative essays and new literary art forms.

Robert Bly, Denise Levertov, Ai, Gene Frumkin, Gary Snyder, Lawrence Ferlinghetti, Thomas McGrath, Brenda Hillman, David Oliveria, and Ioanna Carlson.

Unsolicited Manuscripts Received/Published per year: 3000/50.

Reading Period: Oct.—Feb.

CALIBAN

Lawrence R. Smith
P. O. Box 561
Laguna Beach, CA 92652
(714) 497-7437

Poetry, fiction, translation, interviews, graphics/artwork.

CALIBAN has redefined the literary and artistic avant-garde by cutting across partisan lines, making different writers and artists in serious pursuit of the new aware of each other. **CALIBAN** also insists that the avant-garde is not the exclusive domain of white, middle-class males, bohemian or otherwise.

Berssenbrugge, Vizenor, Komunyakaa, Kingston, Wakoski.

Unsolicited Manuscripts Received/Published per Year: 2,000/20.

Payment: $15–$20, plus 2 copies.

Reporting Time: 1–2 months.

Copyright held by magazine; reverts to author upon publication.

1986; 2/yr; 1,700

$14/yr; $26/2 yr ind; $24/yr inst; $8/ea; 40%, 25% textbook orders
192 pp; 6 x 9
Ad Rates: $100/page (5 x 8)
ISSN: 0890-7269
DeBoer, BookPeople, SPD

CALLALOO

Charles H. Rowell
Department of English
Wilson Hall
University of Virginia
Charlottesville, VA 22903
(804) 924-6616

Bibliography, poetry, fiction, criticism, essays, reviews, plays, translation, photographs, graphics/artwork.

CALLALOO is a quarterly journal which features the arts and literature of Africans, African-Americas and Canadians, and Africans in the Diaspora (the Caribbean, Latin American, Europe, and Southeast Asia & Australia). **CALLALOO** now also features a special section, "Cultural Criticism," which presents challenging essays by critics and theorists on all topics and areas of cultural interest.

Rita Dove, John Edgar Wideman, Maryse Condé, Alice Walker, Derek Walcott, K. Anthony Appiah, Caryl Phillips, Audre Lorde, Yusef Komunyakaa. Recent issues focused on Haitian arts and literature, Puerto-Rican American Literature, the writer Leon Forrest, and the playwright George C. Wolfe.

Payment: (When grants are available from NEA.)

Copyright held by Johns Hopkins University Press; reversion to author depends upon situation.

1976; 4/yr; 800
$25/yr, $50/yr inst; $8/ea ind, $15/ea inst; $33.22/ind Canada; $31.05/ind Mexico; All Others $42.85/ind.
256 pp; 7 x 10
Ad Rates: $225/page (5½ x 8); $155/½ page (5½ x 4); cover 3/$250
ISSN: 0161-2496

CALLIOPE

Martha Christina
Creative Writing Program
Roger Williams University
Bristol, RI 02809
(401) 254-3217

Poetry, fiction.

Interested in both established and emerging writers, but need not have published elsewhere. Prefer concrete to abstract images, work that appeals to the emotions through the senses.

Thomas Lux, Mark Doty, Mark

Cox, Lynne deCourcy, Tim Seibles, Allison Joseph.
Unsolicited Manuscripts Received/Published per Year: about 2,000/about 50.
Reading Period: Aug. 15—Oct. 15; Jan. 15—Mar. 15.
Payment: 2 copies and subscription.
Copyright held by magazine; reverts to author upon publication.
1977; 2/yr; 300
$5/yr; $3/ea; 40%
5½ x 8½

CALYX: A Journal of Art and Literature by Women

Margarita Donnelly, Bev McFarland, Co-Managing Editors; the collective
P.O. Box B
Corvallis, OR 97339
(503) 753-9384; Fax (503) 753-0515
Poetry, fiction, essays, translations, reviews, photographs, visual art, interviews.
Considered one of the finest literary magazines in the U.S., **CALYX** publishes work by women and presents a wide spectrum of women's experience. **CALYX** is committed to publishing work by women of color, working class women, lesbians, politically active women, and older women. Winner of the 1988 OILA, Stewart H. Holbrook Award for literary achievement in Oregon. Two-time winner of the CCLM Editor's Grant (1985 & 1990). Recipient of the American Literary Magazines Award and others.
Gloria Still, Judith Soruberger, Susan Kolodry, Carol Orlock, Eleanora Chiavetta, Lyubov Sirota, Margaret Randall, Sandra Kohler.
Unsolicited Manuscripts Received/Published per Year: 3,500–8,000/75–100.
Reading Period: Oct. 1—Nov. 15; Mar. 1—Apr. 15; however, we are closed Mar.—Apr. 1994.
Payment: in copies & subscription.
Reporting Time: 3–6 months.
Copyright released to authors by magazine.
1976; 3/volume (2/yr); 5,000
$18/yr ind, $22.50/yr inst, $30/yr Canadian, $36/yr foreign; $8/ea + postage; 30%–40%
128+pp.
Ad Rates: $550/page (5¾ x 7); $285/½ page (5¾ x 3⅜)
ISSN: 0147-1627
Small Changes, Inland, BookPeople, Fine Print, Ingram, SPD, Airlift, Armadillo

THE CAPE ROCK

Harvey Hecht
English Department

Southeast Missouri State University
Cape Girardeau, MO 63701
(314) 651-2636

Poetry, photographs.

We have no restrictions on subjects or forms. Our criterion for selection is the quality of the work rather than the bibliography of the authors. We prefer poems under 70 lines. We feature a single photographer each issue.

Laurel Speer, Laurie Taylor, Martin Robbins, Charles A. Waugaman.

Unsolicited Manuscripts Received/Published per Year: 2,500/100.

Reading Period: Aug.—Apr.

Payment: each issue we award $200 for the best poem and $100 for the photography. All contributors are paid in copies.

Reporting Time: 1–4 months.

Copyright held by magazine; reprint rights granted upon request provided reprint credit is given to the magazine.

1964; 2/yr; 700

$5/yr; $3/ea; 40%

64 pp; 5½ x 8½

ISSN: 0146-2199

CAPRICE

James Mechem, Lynne Savitt
229 N. Fountain St.
Wichita, KS 67208-3833
(316) 683-8728

Fiction, poetry, art reviews

Mostly feminist, mostly older writers. Mostly not academic. More short fiction than long fiction. The poems not exceeding a page and a half mostly.

Ai, Sibyl James, Marge Piercy, Ursule Molinaro, Toi Derricotte, Thulani Davis, Naomi Shihab Nye, Cheryl Clarke, Joy Harjo.

Unsolicited Manuscripts Received/Published per Year: 30/8.

Reporting Time: 3 months.

1987; 12/yr

$50/yr; $5/ea

60 pp; 7 x 8 ½

THE CARIBBEAN WRITER

Erika J. Waters
University of the Virgin Islands
RR 02, Box 10,000 Kingshill
St. Croix, VI 00850
(809) 778-0246

Poetry, fiction, reviews, graphics/artwork.

THE CARIBBEAN WRITER is an international magazine with a Caribbean focus. The Caribbean should be central to the work, or the work should reflect a Caribbean heritage, experience, or perspective.

Derek Walcott, Olive Senior, Julia

Alvarez, O. R. Dathorne, Opal Palmer Adisa.
Unsolicited Manuscripts Received/Published per Year: 600/50.
Reading Period: Oct.—Dec. 15.
Payment: 2 copies.
Copyright held by Research Publications Center; reverts to author upon publication.
1987; 1/yr; 1,500
$9/ea; 30%
150–200 pp; 6 x 9
Ad Rates: $250/page (6 x 9); $150/½ page; $100/¼ page
ISSN: 0893-1550

A CAROLINA LITERARY COMPANION

Nellvena Duncan Eutsler, Managing Editor; Michael Parker, Fiction Editor; Patrick Bizzaro, Poetry Editor
Community Council for the Arts
P.O. Box 3554
Kinston, NC 28502-3554
(919) 527-2517

Poetry, fiction.

A CAROLINA LITERARY COMPANION is published twice yearly, and is intended primarily as a vehicle for emerging Southern writers of poetry and short fiction. Primary consideration is given to writers who live in the South or are natives of that region. All selections are made on the basis of artistic merit.
Ron Rash, Becke Roughton, Marion Hodge, R. T. Smith, Ruth Moose.
Payment: in 2 copies of the volume in which contributors are published.
Reporting Time: 2–3 weeks after each deadline (10/15 and 2/15 each year).
Copyright held by Community Council for the Arts; reverts to author upon publication.
1985; 2/yr; 400
$8.50/yr; $5/ea; 40% on 5 or more; 33% on 3 or 4 copies
67 pp; 5½ x 8½
No ads

CAROLINA QUARTERLY

Amber Vogel
Greenlaw Hall CB #3520
University of North Carolina at Chapel Hill
Chapel Hill, NC 27599-3520
(919) 962-0244

Poetry, fiction, reviews.
A literary journal published three times yearly.
Barry Hannah, Denise Levertov, William Harmon.
Unsolicited Manuscripts Received/Published per Year: 4,000/60-80.
Reading Period: year–round.

Reporting Time: 2–4 months.
Copyright held by magazine.
1948; 3/yr; 1000
$10/yr ind, $12/yr inst; $5/ea
80 pp; 6 x 9
Ad Rates: $80/page; $60/½ page; $40/¼ page
ISSN: 000-8-6797

CARTA ABIERTA

Juan Rodriguez
Center for Mexican American Studies
Texas Lutheran College
Seguin, TX 78155
(512) 372-6059
News/notices about the Chicano literary world.
An irregular, off-beat, progressive and at times incisive newsletter (rag) that keeps an eye on the Chicano literary world.
1975; irreg; 1,000
$20/yr; $3/ea
12 pp; 8 ½ x 11
ISSN: 0198-1021

CATALYST MAGAZINE

Pearl Cleage
236 Forsyth St., Suite 400
Atlanta, GA 30303
(404) 730-5785
Fiction, nonfiction, poetry, criticism, essays.
Focuses primarily on Southern writers, but welcomes all submissions in fiction, poetry, drama and criticism. The magazine presents writers in a format designed to stimulate discussion and encourage the exchange of ideas.
Willie Woods, Zaron Burnett, Mari Evans.
Unsolicited Manuscripts Received/Published per Year: 800/500.
Payment: $20–$200.
Reporting Time: 4 months.
Copyright authors.
1986; 2/yr; 5,000
$10/2 yrs; $2.50/ea
96 pp; 7½ x 14
ISSN: 0896-7423

CAT'S EAR

Jim Roland, Founding Editor; Scott Ludtke, Assoc. Editor; Jack Holcomb, Asst. Editor
Galliard Group Publishers
P.O. Box 946
Kirksville, MO 63501
(816) 785-4185
Poetry, fiction.
CAT'S EAR publishes poetry and fiction with an emphasis on the lyrical and metaphorical, always with an eye on future directions of the tradition.
Diane Wakoski, Charles Edward Eaton, Robert Peters, Laurel Speer, Naomi Shihab Nye.

Payment: 2 copies.
Reporting Time: 9 weeks.
Copyright held by Galliard Group Publishers, but reverts to author upon publication.
1992; 3/yr; 250
$10/ind, $12/inst; $4/ea; 40%
48 pp; 5½ x 8½
Ad Rates: $50/page (4 x 7); $30/½ page (4 x 3¼ or 2 x 7); $20/ page (4 x 1 or 1 x 7)
ISSN: 1062-6379

Joy Walsh, Harry Knickerbocker, Paul Weinman.
Unsolicited Manuscripts Received/ Published per Year: 500+/50.
Payment: 1 copy.
Copyright reverts to author upon publication.
1974; 2/yr; 200
$5/yr; $3/ea
28 pp; 5½ x 8½
No ads
ISSN: 0145-8310

THE CATHARTIC

Patrick M. Ellingham
P.O. Box 1391
Fort Lauderdale, FL 33302
(305) 967-9378

Poetry, reviews, photographs, artwork.

THE CATHARTIC is devoted to the unknown poet, with the understanding that most poets are unknown in America. All types of poetry except those that are racist or sexist. Avoid poems over 50 lines or rhyme for the sake of rhyme. Experiment with language and form. Poems that deal with or come from the dark side; intense poems that use words sparingly and forget the poet; poems that jar the reader's sensibilities; darkly erotic poems; poems that show social awareness.

CEILIDH: AN INFORMAL GATHERING FOR STORY & SONG

P.O. Box 6367
San Mateo, CA 94403
(415) 378-2350 or (415) 591-9902

Fiction, poetry, plays, translation, photographs, graphics/artwork.
Patrick Smith, John Moffitt, Traise Yamamoto, Richard Soos, Sarah Bliumis.
$7.50/yr; $2.50/ea; 40%

CEILIDH is taking a Sabattical until April 1994. We will consider no manuscripts until then.

CENTRAL PARK

Stephen-Paul Martin; Richard Royal, Prose and Visuals; Eve Ensler, Poetry
P.O. Box 1446
New York, NY 10023

(212) 691-0890 or (212) 242-0302

Experimental fiction, narrative fiction, theory, graphics/artwork, poetry, photographs, translation, interviews, reviews.

CENTRAL PARK is moving in three main directions: poetry and fiction of an either experimental or aggressively political nature, essays in social or esthetic theory, and visual work that moves the eye to think about how it sees. Prospective contributors are advised to order a sample copy ($5) before submitting.

Marc Kaminsky, Rosmarie Waldrop, Rae Armantrout, Ron Silliman, Jackson Mac Low.

Payment: 1 copy.

Reporting Time: 8 weeks.

Copyright held by magazine.

1981; 2/yr; 1,000

$8/yr; $5/ea; 40%

100 pp; 7½ x 10

Ad Rates: $100/page; $50/½ page; $25/¼ page

Ubiquity, Edge

CHAMINADE LITERARY REVIEW

Loretta Petrie
Chaminade University of Honolulu
3140 Waialae Ave.
Honolulu, HI 96816-1578
(808) 735-4723

Poetry, fiction, criticism, reviews.

CHAMINADE LITERARY REVIEW intends to bring together work from both artists and writers, talented new ones along with those nationally or internationally recognized. We want writing from Hawaii side by side with writing from the mainland to demonstrate how well our local writers compare. We want a magazine at once regional and cosmopolitan. We hope to reflect the diversity of Hawaii's people, their writers, their interests.

Cathy Song, John Unterecker, Phyllis Thompson, William Stafford, Tony Quagliano.

Unsolicited Manuscripts Received/Published per Year: 200/60+.

Payment: 1 year's subscription, upon publication.

Copyright held by Chaminade Press; reverts to author upon publication.

1987; 2/yr; 350

$10/yr; $18/2 yrs (ind & inst); $5/ea; 20%

175 pp; 6 x 9

Ad Rates: $50/page (4 x 7¼); $25/½ page (4 x 3⅞)

ISSN: 0894-6396

CHANTS

Terrell Hunter
R 1 Box 1738
Dexter, ME 04930
(207) 924-3673

Poetry, translations of poetry.

CHANTS publishes the best poetry we can find, regardless of style. We value intensity, originality, involvement—poems that grab you hard and won't let go.

Bill Shields, Connie Voisine, James Laughlin, Michael Kreps, Michael LaBruno.

Unsolicited Manuscripts Received/ Published per Year: 1,000/75–100.

Reading Period: year–round.

Payment: 2 copies

Reporting Time: 2–3 months, sometimes longer.

Copyright reverts to poet.

1989; 2/yr; 500

$12/3 issues; $4/ea; 30–40%

64 pp; 6 x 9

Ad Rates: $25/½ page

THE CHARIOTEER

Pella Publishing Company
337 West 36th St.
New York, NY 10018-6401
(212) 279-9586

Poetry, fiction, criticism, essays, reviews, plays, translation, graphics/artwork.

Purpose: to bring to English-speaking readers information on, appreciation of, and translations from modern Greek literature, with criticism and reproductions of modern Greek art and sculpture.

Unsolicited Manuscripts Received/ Published per Year: 6/none.

Payment: none.

Reporting Time: 3 months.

Copyright held by Pella Publishing Company; reverts to author upon request.

1960; 1/yr; 1,000

$15/yr; $28/2 yrs; $40/3 yrs

200 pp; 5½ x 8½

Ad Rates: $125/page (4⅛ x 7); $75/½ page (4⅛ x 3½)

ISSN: 0577-5574

THE CHARITON REVIEW

Jim Barnes
Northeast Missouri State University
Kirksville, MO 63501
(816) 785-4499

Poetry, fiction, essays, reviews, translation.

Excellence in literature only. We like the old; we like the new.

Jack Cady, Phyllis Barber, Barry Targan, David Ray, Robert Canzoneri, Patricia Goedicke, Gordon Weaver, Steve Heller, Elizabeth Moore.

Unsolicited Manuscripts Received/ Published per Year: 6-8,000/100.
Payment: $5/page.
Reporting Time: 1 week—1 month.
Copyright held by Northeast Missouri State University; reverts to author upon publication.
1975; 2/yr; 700
$9/yr, $15/2yr, $5/ea; $3/sample copy
100 pp; 6 x 9
Ad Rates: $100/page (4 x 7); $50/½ page (4 x 3½)
ISSN: 0098-9452

THE CHARLOTTE POETRY REVIEW

A.A. Jillani, Lisa Kerley
P.O. Box 36701
Charlotte, NC 28236
Poetry, book reviews, short–short fiction, poet interviews.
Regardless of percentages, **CPR** as a rule regularly publishes first-time poets alongside some of the best in the country. Freshness is the key here.
Tony Moffeir, William Walsh, Chuck Sullivan, Harry Brody.
Unsolicited Manuscripts Received/ Published per Year: 3,000/100.
Payment: none.
Reporting Time: 2 months.
Copyright held by DeKalb College; reverts to author upon publication.
1992; 4/yr; 1,500
$18/yr; $4.50/ea
48 pp; 8½ x 11
Ad Rates: $35/business card

THE CHATTAHOOCHEE REVIEW

Lamar York
DeKalb College
2101 Womack Road
Dunwoody, GA 30338-4497
(404) 551-3166
Poetry, fiction, criticism, essays, reviews, interviews.
THE CHATTAHOOCHEE REVIEW promotes fresh writing and encourages as yet unacknowledged writers by giving them space in print next to their acclaimed peers.
Leon Rooke, Fred Chappell, George Garrett, Jim Wayne Miller, Peter Meinke.
Unsolicited Manuscripts Received/ Published per Year: 3,000/100.
Reading Period: year–round.
Payment: none.
Reporting Time: 2 months.
Copyright held by DeKalb College; reverts to author upon publication.
1980; quarterly; 1,250
$20/yr; $4/ea; 30%
100 pp; 6 x 9

Ad Rates: $125/page (4½ x 7); $75/½ page (4½ x 3½)
ISSN: 0741-9155

CHELSEA

Sonia Raiziss, Alfredo de Palchi, Richard Foerster, Caila Rossi, Brian Swann, Andrea Lockett
Box 5880
Grand Central Station
New York, NY 10163

Poetry, fiction, criticism, essays, translations, interviews, art.

Stress on style, variety, originality. No special biases or requirements. Flexible attitudes, eclectic material. Active interest, as always, in crosscultural exchanges, in superior translations. Leaning toward cosmopolitan avant-garde, interdisciplinary techniques, but no strictures against traditional modes. Annual competition (send SASE for guidelines).

Roberta Allen, James Laughlin, Ron Tanner, Len Roberts, Elizabeth McBride, Richard Kostelanetz, Nicholas Samaras, Kenneth J. Emberly, Carolyn Stoloff, Daniel Hecht.

Unsolicited Manuscripts Received/Published per Year: 2,500/50.

Payment: $5/page.

Reporting Time: immediately—4 months.

Copyright held by magazine; reverts to author upon publication.

1958; 2/yr; 1,300

$11/2 issues or 1 double issue; $14/foreign; $6/ea

128 pp; 6 x 9

$125/page (4½ x 7½); $75/½ page (4½ x 3½); exchange ads also available

ISSN: 0009-2185

DeBoer, Faxon, Ebsco

CHICAGO REVIEW

David Nicholls
5801 S. Kenwood
Chicago, IL 60637
(312) 702-0887

Poetry, fiction, criticism, essays, reviews, translation, interviews, photographs, graphics/artwork.

CHICAGO REVIEW is an international journal of writing and cultural exchange published at the University of Chicago.A sure hand, demonstrating originality and precision of language and tone, is the sole requirement for inclusion, overriding formal affiliation, theme, regional basis, or previous history of publication.

Meena Alexander, Barry Hannah, William Olsen, Satyajit Ray, Luis Rodriguez, Juan Carlos Vargas.

Unsolicited Manuscripts Received/ Published per Year: 2,000/70.
Payment: copies/subscription.
Reporting Time: 2 months.
Copyright held by magazine; transfers to author upon request.
1946; 4/yr; 2,500
$20/yr ind, $30/yr inst; $5/ea; 40%
110 pp; 6 x 9
Ad Rates: $150/page (4½ x 7½); $100/½ page (2½ x 7½)
ISSN: 0009-3696

CHIRON REVIEW

Michael Hathaway
Rt. 2 Box 111
St. John, KS 67576
(316) 549-3933

Poetry, fiction, nonfiction, reviews, all press news.
Presents the widest possible range of contemporary creative writing, traditional and off-beat in an attractive, professional tabloid format, including artwork and photos of featured writers.
Charles Bukowski, Robert Peters, Lyn Lifshin, Lorri Jackson, Antler, Joan Jobe Smith.
Unsolicited Manuscripts Received/ Published per Year: 1,825+/100.
Payment: copies.
Reporting Time: 2-6 weeks.
Copyright: author retains rights.
1982; 4/yr; 2,000
$10/ind; $3/ea; 40%
20-48 pp; 10 x 13
Ad Rates: send SASE
ISSN: 1046-8897

CIMARRON REVIEW

Gordon Weaver, Editor; Deborah Bransford, Managing Editor; Paul Bowers, Associate Editor; Thomas Reiter, Jeff Kersh, Sally Shigley, Poetry Editors; Gordon Weaver, Kathy Bedwell, Dennis Bormann, Al Learst, Jill Patterson, Fiction Editors; E.P. Walkiewicz, Nonfiction Editor; Thomas E. Kennedy, European Editor; Mark Pate, Assistant Editor
205 Morrill Hall
Oklahoma State University
Stillwater, OK 74078-0135
(405) 744-9476

Poetry, fiction, essays, reviews.
Seeks well-written material, which emphasizes attempts to find value and purpose in a dehumanized and dehumanizing world. Avoids "easy" answers of extremes and would not publish work which espouses any specific religious or political view or advocates simple escapism. It does not publish children's stories; but does publish stories about children aimed at adult understanding.

Unsolicited Manuscripts Received/ Published per Year: 2,275/12–16.
Payment: $50/prose; $15/poem.
Reporting Time: 6–8 weeks.
Copyright held by magazine.
1967; 4/yr; 450
$12/yr; $3/ea
112 pp; 6 x 9
ISSN: 0009-6849

CINCINNATI POETRY REVIEW

Dallas Wiebe
English Department, 069
University of Cincinnati
Cincinnati, OH 45221
(513) 556-3922

Poetry.

CINCINNATI POETRY REVIEW sets local writers in a national context. One fourth to one third of each issue is local; the rest is national. "Local" means about 150 from the city. All types of poetry considered. Poetry contest each issue.

Alvin Greenberg, X.J. Kennedy, David Citino, Laurie Henry, Walter McDonald.
Payment: none.
Reporting Time: 4–6 weeks.
Copyright held by magazine; reverts to author upon publication.
1985; 2/yr; 1,000
$9/yr; $2/ea (samples); 40%; 50% for direct purchase by dealers
72 pp; 5½ x 8½

CLOCKWATCH REVIEW

James Plath, Editor; Robert, C. Bray, Lynn DeVore, James McGowan, Pamela Muirhead, Associate Editors
Dept. of English
Illinois Wesleyan University
Bloomington, IL 61702-2900
(309) 556-3352

Fiction, poetry, interviews, essays, photographs, graphics/artwork.

CLOCKWATCH REVIEW seeks to present quality work in a format lively enough to attract a popular as well as literary/academic audience. Special feature: an ongoing interview series with contemporary artists and musicians.

Dawn Upshaw, Friz Freleng, Gary Gildner, Pat Hutchings, Peter Wild, Martha M. Vertreace.
Unsolicited Manuscripts Received/ Published per Year: 3,500/40-50.
Payment: 3 copies and a small cash award.
Reporting Time: 2 weeks–3 months.
Copyrighted.
1983; 2/yr; 1,500
$8/yr; $4/ea

80 pp; 5½ x 8½
ISSN: 0740-9311
Ingram

CLUES: A Journal of Detection

Pat Browne
Journals Department
Popular Press
Bowling Green State University
Bowling Green, OH 43403
(419) 372-2981

Articles, reviews.

A magazine focusing upon detective fiction.

Unsolicited Manuscripts Received/Published per Year: 50–60/25.

Reading Period: year–round.

1982; 2/yr; 700

$12.50/yr; $7.75/ea

COLLAGES & BRICOLAGES

Marie-José Fortis
P.O. Box 86
Clarion, PA 16214
(814) 226-5799

Poetry, fiction, criticism, essays, reviews, plays, translation, interviews, photographs, graphics/artwork.

COLLAGES & BRICOLAGES, which has published authors from the five continents, believes in innovative writer who has read the classics. At this point in time we would like to receive less egocentric, more politically engaged, pieces. Our 1993 will focus on *China: The Decade Preceding Tiananmen Square & Luzma Umpierre: Homophobia in Academia.*

Marilou Awiakta, Eric Basso, Susan Onthank Mates, Greg Boyd.

Unsolicited Manuscripts Received/Published per Year: 600/20-25.

Reading Period: Aug.—Nov.

Payment: 1 or 2 copies. Extras: $5/copy.

1987; 1/yr; 400

$6/ea

120 pp; 11 x 18

Ad Rates: $50/page (9 x 16); $30/½ page (5 x 8); $15/¼ page (2½ x 4)

COLORADO REVIEW

David Milofsky, Editor; Robert Olen Butler, George Cuomo, James Galvin, Jorie Graham, Joanne Greenberg, Michael Martone, Dan O'Brien, Carol Oles, Toby Olson, Robert D. Richardson, Jr., Alberto Rios, Contributing Editors.

Department of English
Colorado State University
Fort Collins, CO 80523

Fiction, poetry, essays, and reviews.

Although published in Colorado,

COLORADO REVIEW is more than a regional literary magazine. We seek to print the best fiction, poetry, translations, interviews, reviews, and articles on contemporary literary subjects that we receive from a contributorship that is national and international. We continue to be interested in Magical Realist writing, but any writing that is vital, highly imaginative and highly realized in artistic terms and that avoids mere mannerism to embody important human concerns will find support here.

Reg Saner, Patricia Goedicke, Bin Ranke, Carole Oles, T. Alan Broughton, Rita Ciresi, David Huddle; interviews with Carolyn Forche; Gwendolyn Brooks, Gretel Ehrlich.

Unsolicited Manuscripts Received/Published per Year: 7,000/varies.

Reading Period: Sept.—May.

Payment: when funding permits.

1977; 2/yr 1,000

$15/yr, $28/2 yr; $8/ea; 40%

112 pp; 6 x 9

Ad Rates: $100/page (7½ x 5); $50/½ page

COLUMBIA: A Magazine of Poetry and Prose

Rotating Editors
404 Dodge Hall
Columbia University
New York, NY 10027
(212) 854-4391

Poetry, fiction, essays.

Reading Period: year–round.

Payment: in copies; Editors' awards also.

Reporting Time: 1–2 months.

Copyright reverts to author.

$18/3 issues; $13/2 issues; $7 ea

Approx. 220 pp; 5 x 8

Ad Rates: on request

CONFRONTATION

Martin Tucker
L.I.U. Dept. of English
C.W. Post
Greenvale, NY 11548
(516) 299-2391

Poetry, fiction, criticism, essays, plays, translation, interviews.

We are eclectic in our tastes, preferring a mix of traditional and experimental, of the known and relatively unknown writers. We have no prohibition except that of poor literary quality.

Cynthia Ozick, Wilfrid Sheed, Stephen Dixon, Joyce Carol Oates, Thomas Fleming, Joseph Brodsky.

Unsolicited Manuscripts Received/Published per Year: 5,000/250.
Reading Period: Sept.—May.
Payment: $5 to $100.
Reporting Time: 6 weeks.
Copyright held by Long Island University; reverts to author upon publication.
1968; 2/yr; 2,000
$10/yr ind, $10/yr inst; $6/ea
160–190 pp; 5½ x 8½

CONJUNCTIONS

Bradford Morrow
Bard College
Annandale-on-Hudson, NY 12504
(914) 758-1539

Poetry, fiction, translation, interviews, photographs, graphics/artwork, essays.

CONJUNCTIONS publishes formally innovative writing, with equal emphasis on fiction and poetry; also essays on culture and the arts, special features. Editorial staff: Walter Abish, John Ashbery, Mei-Mei Berssenbrugge, Guy Davenport, Elizabeth Frank, Robert Kelly, Kenneth Irby, William Gass, Susan Howe, Ann Lauterbach, Patrick McGrath, Nathaniel Tarn, Quincy Troupe, John Edgar Wideman.

Unsolicited Manuscripts Received/Published per Year: 5,000+/10.
Payment: in copies, and $150.
Reporting Time: 4–6 weeks.
Copyright reverts to author upon publication.
1981; 2/yr; 7,500
$18/yr; $32/2yr; $10/ea
320 pp; 6 x 9
Ad Rates: $350/page (4⅜ x 7½); $250/½ page
ISSN: 0278-2324

THE CONNECTICUT POETRY REVIEW

Harley More, J. Claire White
P.O. Box 818
Stonington, CT 06378

Poetry, criticism, reviews, translations, interviews, excerpts from verse plays.

Marge Piercy, John Updike, Margaret Randall, Allen Ginsberg, Eugenio de Andrade.

Unsolicited Manuscripts Received/Published per Year: 1,500/18–20.
Payment: $5/poem; $10/review; $20/interview; $20/verse play.
Reporting Time: 3 months.
1981; 1/yr; 500
$3/ea
50 pp; 5¾ x 9¼
ISSN: 0277-7770

CONNECTICUT RIVER REVIEW

Ben Brodinsky, Editor
327 Seabury Dr.

Bloomfield, CT 06002

Poetry.

The **CRR** uses highest quality poetry, in which logic and emotion, picture and sound cohere, making for authentic music. All forms welcome, except haiku. Prefer poems of 40 lines or under; submit no more than 5 poems at a time.

Unsolicited Manuscripts Received/ Published per Year: 800–1,000/90–100.

Reading Period: year–round.

Payment: 1 copy.

Reporting Time: 2–8 weeks.

Copyright held by Connecticut Poetry Society; reverts to author upon publication.

1978; 2/yr; 400

$20/2 yr; $6/ea; 40%

40 pp; 6 x 9

sent √

CONTACT II

Maurice Kenny, J.G. Gosciak
P.O. Box 451, Bowling Green
New York, NY 10004
(212) OR4-0911

Poetry, reviews, criticism, translation, interviews, photographs, graphics/artwork.

Contemporary American poetry.

Janice Mirikitani, Charlotte de Clue, Carolyn Stoloff, Shalin Hai-Jew, Karoniaktatie.

Unsolicited Manuscripts Published per Year: 20%.

Payment: in copies; when payment is cash, $10/poem, $15/review.

Reporting Time: 6 months.

Copyright held by Contact II Publications; reverts to author upon publication with credit.

1976; 2/yr; 2,500

$10/ind, $16/inst; $7/ea; 40%; 50% prepaid on 10 or more.

92 pp; 7¾ x 10½

Ad Rates: $150/page; $80/½ page; $50/¼ page

ISSN: 0197-6796

CONTEXT SOUTH

David Breeden, Craig Taylor, Paul Hadella
Campus Box 4504
Schreiner College
2100 Memorial Blvd.
Kerrville TX 78028-5697

Poetry, fiction, criticism, graphics/ artwork.

A magazine based in the South, but not confined to it, **CONTEXT SOUTH** endeavors to be a collection by artists interested in pushing boundaries.

Wayne Dodd, Andrea Hollander Budy, Diane Glancy, William Greenway.

Unsolicited Manuscripts Received/ Published per Year: 1,000+/50.

Copyright held by author.

300
$12/yr; $5/ea; 40%
65 pp; 5½ x 8½
$100/page; $50/½ page; $25/¼ page
ISSN: 1045-2265

CORNFIELD REVIEW

Stuart Lishan, Editor; Ann Bower, Fiction Editor; Terry Hermson, Poetry Editor; Larry Sauselen, Art Editor
OSU at Marion
1465 Mt. Vernon Ave
Marion, OH 43302
(614) 389-2361

Poetry, short stories, nonfiction essays; original art (black & white) and photography.

A "little" literary magazine showcasing the Midwest experience (but not limited to that topic). Submissions should be of high quality; fiction and nonfiction should not exceed 3,500 words.

Unsolicited Manuscripts Received/Published per Year: 600/20.
Reading Period: Sept.—Jan.
Payment: 2 copies.
Reporting Time: 2–4 months.
Copyright reverts to author.
1976; 1/yr; 1,500
$5/ea
64 pp
ISSN: 0363-4574

COTTONWOOD

George Wedge, Editor; Phil Wedge, Poetry Editor; Ben Accardi & Laurie Carlson, Fiction Editors
Box J, 400 Kansas Union
University of Kansas
Lawrence, KS 66045
(913) 864-3777

Poetry, fiction, reviews, interviews, photographs, graphics/artwork.

COTTONWOOD uses fiction and poetry with clear images and interesting narratives and reviews of books by writers or from publishers in our area. The magazine welcomes submissions from all parts of the country.

Robert Day, Rita Dove, Patricia Traxler, Gerald Early, William Stafford.

Unsolicited Manuscripts Received/Published per Year: 3,000+/50.
Payment: 1 copy.
Reporting Time: 2–6 months.
Copyright held by magazine; reverts to author upon publication.
1965; 3/yr; 500
$15/yr; $6.50/ea; 30%
120 pp; 6 x 9
ISSN: 0147-149X

CPQ

John M. Brander
1200 E. Ocean Blvd., #64

Long Beach, CA 90802
(213) 495-0925
Poetry, translation, graphics/artwork.
Poems may come from anywhere in the country. We like everything we've published in **CPQ**, some of it a lot, but from now on we would like to receive not only poems like those we've printed but also those which are unlike anything we've ever printed.
Jennifer Olds, William James Kovanda, Sylvia Rosxen, Joseph Kent, Aaron Kramer.
Unsolicited Manuscripts Received/Published per Year: 150/30.
Payment: none.
Reporting Time: 2-3 months.
Copyright held by English Department, Chapman College, Orange, CA; reverts to author upon publication.
1972; 3 or 4/yr; 500
$5/ea; 20%
84 pp
No ads
Small Press Traffic, Midnight Special

CRAB CREEK REVIEW

Linda Clifton; Carol Orlock; Fiction
4462 Whitman Ave., N.
Seattle, WA 98103
(206) 633-1090
Poetry, fiction, translation, essays, graphics/artwork.
". . . well-crafted and perceptive works . . . technically proficient and sensitive poems . . . powerfully expressed images . . . tightly controlled narrative . . . diverse enough to appeal to a variety of literary tastes . . ." Literary Magazine Review.
William Stafford, Rebecca Wells, Maxine Kumin, David Lee.
Unsolicited Manuscripts Received/Published per Year: 400/0 until 1994.
Payment: 2 copies.
Reporting Time: 4–8 weeks.
Copyright held by magazine; reverts to author upon publication.
1983; 3/yr; 350
$8/yr; $3/ea; 40%; 50% through distributor
32 pp; 6 x 10
$120/page (6 x 10); $65/½ page (6 x 5); $35/¼ page (6 x 2½); $20/⅛ page (3 x 2½)
ISSN: 07380-7008
Small Changes

CRAZYHORSE

Zabelle Stodola, Managing Editor; Judy Troy, Fiction Editor; Ralph Burns, Poetry Editor; Dennis Vanatta, Criticism Editor.

English Department
University of Arkansas at Little Rock
2801 S. University
Little Rock, AR 72204
(501) 569-3160

Poetry, fiction, criticism, reviews, interviews.

A literary magazine which publishes quality work by established and promising new writers.

Andre Dubus, Bobbie Ann Mason, Raymond Carver, Jorie Graham, John Updike.

Unsolicited Manuscripts Received/Published per year: 20,000/60.

Reading Period: Sept.—Oct. for fiction.

Payment: 2 copies and $10/page.

Annual fiction and poetry awards: $500 each.

Reporting Time: 3 months.

Copyright reverts to author upon request.

1960; 2/yr; 1,000

$10/yr; $5/ea; 25%–40%

135 pp; 6 x 9

Ad Rates: $85/page; $50/½ page

ISSN: 0011-0841

CRAZYQUILT

Jim Kitchen
P.O. Box 632729
San Diego, CA 92163-2729
(619) 688-1023

Poetry, fiction, criticism, essays, plays, photographs, graphics/artwork.

All kinds of poetry; short stories with good character development; nonfiction about writers; literary criticism; one-act plays and black and white photography and art work. Accept translations of poetry. Publish new writers as well as established authors.

Robert K. Johnson, William Jolliff, Nahid Rachlan, Walter Griffin, Teresa Peck.

Unsolicited Manuscripts Received/Published per Year: 500/70-80.

Payment: 2 copies.

Reporting Time: 10–12 weeks.

Copyright held by Crazyquilt Press; reverts to author upon publication.

1986; 4/yr; 180

$14.95/yr (ind & inst); $25/2 yrs; $4.50/ea; 40%

100 pp

ISSN: 0887-5308

CREAM CITY REVIEW

Mark Drechsler, Editor-in-Chief; Brian Jung, Editor
P.O. Box 413
University of Wisconsin-Milwaukee
Milwaukee, WI 53201
(414) 229-4708

Poetry, fiction, reviews, essays, interviews, plays, photographs, graphics/artwork.

The **CREAM CITY REVIEW** is an eclectic literary magazine affiliated with the University of Wisconsin-Milwaukee; it strives to publish the best of traditional and non-traditional work by new and established writers.

Tess Gallagher, Stuart Dybek, Donald Hall, Cathy Song, David Ignatow, Marge Piercy, Maxine Kumin, Amy Clampitt, Derek Walcott, Amiri Baraka, Mary Oliver & William Stafford, Lawrence Ferlinghetti.

Unsolicited Manuscripts Received/ Published per Year: 12,000/226+.

Reading Period: year–round, but response time is longer in the summer.

Payment: varies with funding, usually $5 per page minimum plus 1 yr subscription.

Reporting Time: 2–8 weeks.

Copyright held by the Board of Regents of the University of Wisconsin; reverts to author upon publication.

1975; 2/yr; 2,000

$10/yr; sample $4.50; 40%

300 pp; 5½ x 8½

Ad Rates: inquire with SASE

CREEPING BENT

Joseph P. Lucia
433 West Market St.
Bethlehem, PA 18018
(215) 866-5613

Poetry, reviews, fiction, essays, translation.

Hewing to no orthodoxies but reflecting an awareness of the broad spectrum of current writing and thought about writing, **CREEPING BENT** is an independent, eclectic, and adventurous magazine for serious (but not solemn or humorless) readers and writers of contemporary literature, with emphasis on poetry.

Brigit Kelly, Charles Edward Eaton, Turner Cassity, Robert Gibb, Donald Revell.

Unsolicited Manuscripts Received/ Published per Year: 1,500/varies, 0-100.

Payment: none.

Copyright held by publishers; reverts to author upon publication.

1984; 2/yr; 250

$6/yr ind, $7/yr inst; $3/ea. 40%

No ads

ISSN: 8756-0291

THE CRESCENT REVIEW

Guy Nancekeville
1445 Old Town Road
Winston-Salem, NC 27106-3143
(202) 364-5939

Short stories.
Unsolicited Manuscripts Received/ Published per Year: 1,500/40+.
Reading Period: July—Oct., Jan.—Apr.
Payment: in copies.
Copyright reverts to author.
1983; 2/yr; 500
$10/yr; $5/sample copy
160 pp; 6 x 9
Ebsco, Faxon, Swets

CRITICAL TEXTS: A Review of Theory and Criticism
Joe Childers, Jon Anderson, Richard Moye, Martha Buskirk, James Buzard, Ina Lipkowitz, Susan Fraiman, Gary Hentzi, Eric Lott
602 Philosophy Hall
Columbia University
New York, NY 10027
(212) 854-3215
Articles, reviews, translations and interviews dealing with theory in the humanities.
We are an oppositional journal interested in printing articles and reviews on theoretical issues connected with the humanities and social sciences.
Payment: none.
Reporting Time: 2 months.
Copyright held by magazine.
1982; 3/yr; 850
$9/yr ind; $3.75/ea; $5/back issues
120 pp; 6 x 9
$185/page; $100/½ page
ISSN: 0730-2304
Ubiquity

CROSSCURRENTS
Linda Brown Michelson
2200 Glastonbury Rd.
Westlake Village, CA 91361
(818) 991-1694
Fiction, graphics.
CROSSCURRENTS features previously unpublished, literary short fiction. Select pieces are highlighted by photos and line drawings. Two special issues each year.
Alice Adams, Saul Bellow, Josephine Jacobsen, Joyce Carol Oates, John Updike.
Unsolicited Manuscripts Received/ Published per Year: 5,000/60.
Reading Period: June—Nov. 30.
Payment: varies, $35 minimum/story.
Reporting Time: 6 weeks.
Copyright reverts to author.
1980; 4/yr; 3,000
$18/yr; $6/ea; 40%
176 pp; 6 x 9
ISSN: 0739-2354
Faxon, Ebsco, Boley, L-S Distributors, Ingram

CUMBERLAND POETRY REVIEW

Editorial Board
P.O. Box 120128 Acklen Station
Nashville, TN 37212
(615) 371-9078

Poetry, criticism, interviews.

CUMBERLAND POETRY REVIEW is devoted to poetry and poetry criticism and presents poets of diverse origins to a widespread audience. We place no restrictions on form, subject, or style. Manuscripts will be selected for publication on the basis of the writer's perspicuous and compelling means of expression. We welcome translations of high quality poetry. Our aim is to support the poet's efforts to keep up the language.

Seamus Heaney, Lewis Horne, Emily Grosholz, Francis Blessington, Mairi McInnes.

Payment: in contributor's copies.

Reporting Time: 6 months.

Copyright held by Poetics, Inc.; reverts to author upon publication.

1981; 2/yr; 500

$14/yr ind; $17/yr inst; $7/ea sample back issue

100 pp; 6 x 9

Ads Rates: Only on exchange basis

ISSN: 0731-7980

Faxon, Swets, Ebsco, McGregor

CUTBANK

Editors
Dept. of English
University of Montana
Missoula, MT 59812
(406) 243-5231

Poetry, fiction, essays, reviews, interviews, photographs, graphics/artwork.

CUTBANK is a literary magazine with a national scope and a regional bias, often featuring new writers alongside more well-known names.

Rick DeMarinis, James Galvin, William Kittredge, Pattiann Rogers, Greg Pape.

Unsolicited Manuscripts Received/Published per Year: 1,000/50.

Reading Period: Aug. 15—Feb. 1

Reporting Time: 8-12 weeks.

1973; 2/yr; 400

$12/yr; $6.95/ea; 40%

128 pp; 5 ½ x 8 ½

Ad Rates: $90/page; $45/half page

ISSN: 0734-9963

D

DECEMBER MAGAZINE

Curt Johnson
Box 302
Highland Park, IL 60035

(708) 940-4122
Fiction, nonfiction, poetry.
A magazine of the arts and opinion.
Unsolicited Manuscripts Received/Published per Year: 150/10.
Payment: 2 copies.
Reporting Time: 4-8 weeks.
1958; irreg.; 1,200
$25/4 issues; $6/ea; 20%
6 x 9
ISSN: 0070-3141

DEFINED PROVIDENCE

Gary J. Whitehead
59 Adams St. #1
Somerville, MA 02145
Poetry, reviews of poetry books, interviews with poets, poetics.
DEFINED PROVIDENCE is a perfect–bound biannual poetry magazine devoted to publishing new and unknown poets alongside those poets considered to be the best in America.
Gary Soto, Sarah Patton, Robert Morgan, David Citano, Lewis Turco, Ellen Davis, Neal Bowers, R.T. Smith, David Ignatow.
Unsolicited Manuscripts Received/Published per Year: 1,500/30-40.
Reading Period: year–round, but prefer seasonal material 2 months in advance.
Payment: copies.
Reporting Time: 1–8 weeks.
Copyright reverts to author upon publication.
1992; 2/yr; 500
$8/yr, $15/2yrs; $4/ea; 40%
54-72 pp; digest size
Ad Rates: $100/page (5 x 8); $50/½ page (5 x 4); $10/business card
ISSN: 1066-2197

DENVER QUARTERLY

Donald Revell
University of Denver
Denver, CO 80208
(303) 871-2892
Poetry, fiction, reviews, criticism, essays, interviews.
For over twenty years the **DENVER QUARTERLY** has been publishing work by distinguished as well as promising new writers. The magazine generally publishes material reflecting on modern culture as it has developed over the past century. It is recognized as the premiere literary publication of the Rocky Mountain region.
James Tate, Carl Dennis, Charles Baxter, Jorie Graham, Rachel Hadas.
Unsolicited Manuscripts Received/Published per Year: 3,000/35.
Payment: $5/page for fiction, es-

says, reviews; $5/page for poetry.
Copyright held by magazine.
1966; 4/yr; 900
$15/yr ind, $18/yr inst; $5/ea; 20%
160 pp; 6 x 9
Ad Rates: $150/page (5 x 8½); $75/½ page (5 x 4½)
ISSN: 0011-8869

DESCANT

Karen Mulhallen
379 Adelaide Street West
Toronto, Ontario, M5V 155
CANADA
(416) 603-0223

Short fiction, poetry, essays, plays, visual essays.
Literary magazine interested in all the arts and their interrelationship. Aims to publish works of excellence from established and emerging writers and artists. Quality bound.
Leon Rooke, Isabel Allende, Joseph Skvorecky, Michael Ondaatje, Margaret Atwood.
Unsolicited Manuscripts Received/Published per Year: 700/10.
Reading Period: year–round.
Payment: varies.
Copyright: 1st Canadian Rights
1970; 4/yr; 1,200
$21/yr ind, $29/yr inst; $10–$13
130 pp; 5¾ x 8¾
$225/page 5¾ x 8¾-one issue; $400-two issues (B&W)
ISSN: 0382-909-X
Canadian Magazine Publishers Association

DIMENSION

A. Leslie Willson
P.O. Box 26673
Austin, TX 78755
(512) 345-0622

Poetry, fiction, essays, plays, translation, interviews, graphics/artwork, German literature in the original and translation: post 1945.
DIMENSION concentrates on established and non-established writers from all German-speaking countries, with original works with translations. Few essays.
Friedrich Dürrenmatt, Wolfgang Hildersheimer, Günter Grass, Günter Kunert, Peter Weiss.
Payment: modest, copies for translators.
Reporting Time: varies.
Copyright held by magazine.
1968; 3/yr; 1,000
$20/yr ind, $24/yr inst; $10/ea; 20%
200 pp; 6 x 9

DJINNI (formerly NAHANT BAY)

Kalo Clarke, Kim Alan Pederson
29 Front St. # 2

Marblehead, MA 01945
(617) 639-1889

Essays, poetry, fiction, drawings, B&W photographs.

Literary magazine looking for unique voices and original style.

Unsolicited Manuscripts Received/Published per Year: 350–400/50–60.

Reading Period: June—Dec.

Payment: 1 copy.

Reporting Time: 2–4 months.

Copyright: 1st North American Serieal Rights.

1990; 1/yr

60-100 pp; half sheet

DOG RIVER REVIEW

Laurence F. Hawkins, Allove DeVito
5976 Billings Road
Parkdale, OR 97041-9610
(503) 352-6494

Poetry, fiction, reviews, short plays, black and white art.

Open to all poetic forms. Favorite poets/writers: Whitman, Jeffers, Thomas, Patchen, Cardenal, Bukowski, Celine, Bowles, Miller Burroughs, Whinkla.

David Chorlton, Richard Kostelanetz, Sheila Nickerson, Lyn Lifshin.

Unsolicited Manuscripts Received/Published per Year: 400–450/50–60.

Payment: in copies.

Reporting Time: immediately to 4 months.

Copyright reverts to author of publication.

1981; 2/yr; 300

$7/yr; $3.50/ea; 40%

44-56 pp; 5½ x 8½

ISSN: 0749-260X

THE DRAMA REVIEW

Richard Schechner
MIT Press Journals
55 Hayward St.
Cambridge, MA 02142
(617) 253-2866

TDR is a quarterly journal of performance with a strong intercultural, intergeneric, and interdisciplinary focus. We consider everything from wrestling to ritual, from Peter Brook's Mahabharata to what is going on at "Downtown Beirut." **TDR** borrows from the fields of anthropology, performance theory, ethology, psychology, and politics. We combine scholarship and journalism in the form of essays, interviews, letters and editorials.

Payment: $50–250.

Copyright held by MIT Press.

1955; 4/yr; 6,000

$25/yr ind, $55/yr inst; $7/ea

160 pp; 7 x 10
ISSN: 0012-5962

EARTH'S DAUGHTERS: A Feminist Arts Periodical

Editors: Kastle Brill, Joan Ford, Judi Geer, Bonnie Johnson, Joy Walsh, Joyce Kessel, Robin Willoughby, Ryki Zuckerman
Box 41
Central Park Stn
Buffalo, NY 14215
(716) 837-7778

Poetry, fiction, plays, photographs, graphics/artwork.

EARTH'S DAUGHTERS is a feminist literary and art periodical published in Buffalo, New York. We believe ourselves to be the oldest feminist arts periodical extant, having published our first issue in February, 1971. Our focus is the experience and creative expression of women.

Jimmie Canfield, Lyn Lifshin, Marge Piercy, Kathryn Machan Aal, Susan Fantl Spivack.

Unsolicited Manuscripts Received/Published per Year: 1,000–1,500/200+.

Payment: 2 copies.

Reporting Time: 3 months.

Copyright held by magazine; reverts to author upon publication.

1971; 3/yr; 1,000

$14/yr ind, $22/yr inst; $5/ea; 30%

60 pp; 6 x 9

No ads

ISSN: 0163-0989

Ebsco, Faxon, Burroughs

EARTHWISE REVIEW/ EARTHWISE PUBLICATIONS

Barbara Holley
P.O. Box 680536
Miami, FL 33168
(305) 653-2875

Poetry, fiction, criticism, essays, reviews, translations, interviews, photos, artwork, short stories, black and white artwork.

EARTHWISE REVIEW is a bimonthly tabloid of poetry, fine arts, focuses on poetry and environment. Accepts interviews, critical essays, fiction, children's work and sponsors contests with cash prizes.

The annual **EARTHWISE LITERARY CALENDAR** appears for the twelfth year and includes poetry of over 200 poets, quotes and excerpts from longer poems. We feature an annual Artist, and recently have featured etchings & prints by Joseph Nutt of Staunton, Virginia.

Calendar sells for $9.95. Free copy to members of the Earth Chapter, FSPA, Inc. ($15 annual dues)

Larry Rubin, Carolyn Kizer, and Judson Jerome.

Unsolicited Manuscripts Received/Published per Year: 300-500/50-100.

Payment: $5 and up (poems). More for articles/interviews.

Copyright reverts to author upon publication.

1978; 6/yr; 400

$25/yr ind

60–80 pp; 5½ x 8½

Ad Rates: $100/page (4 x 6); $50/½ page (4 x 4); $30/¼ page (2 x 3½)

ISSN: 0190-1761

ECHOES

Marcia Grant

P.O. Box 7

LaGrangeville, NY 12540

Prose, poetry.

ECHOES is a literary quarterly sponsored by the Hudson Valley Writers' Association. It consists of prose and poetry accompanied by original illustrations, a readership response page, contributors' notes, and quotes by acknowledged masters. It is printed on recycled paper and reflects the work of well-known authors as well as talented beginners.

Robert Cooperman, John Grey, Gayle Ellen Harvey, Father Benedict Auer, Ruth Daigon, Brian Daldorph, R. Nikolas Macioci, and Arnold Lipkind.

Unsolicited Manuscripts Received/Published per Year: 1,000+/125–150.

Reading Period: year–round.

Payment: 1 copy.

Reporting Time: Write for guidelines.

Copyright reverts to author upon publication.

1985; 4/yr; 300

$15/yr; $4.50/ea; $3/back issues

44 pp; 5½ x 8½

1812

Dan Schwartz, Richard Lywch, Joe Todaro

Box 1812

Amherst, NY 14226-7812

Fiction, poetry, art.

The war along the Niagara.

Unsolicited Manuscripts Received/Published per Year: 400/25.

Payment: various/arranged.

Reporting Time: 2 months.

Copyright.
1995; 1/yr; 1,000+
100+ pp; 4½ x 11
Ad Rates: arranged

ELF: Eclectic Literary Forum

C. K. Erbes
P.O. Box 392
Tonawanda, NY 14150
(716) 693-7006

Poetry, short fiction, essays on literary themes, critical reviews, special features.

Professionally printed quarterly, publishing well-crafted contemporary works in an uncluttered, readable format; continuing Native American folklore. ". . . a good choice for any literatures collection,"—Library Journal.

Judson Jerome, William Stafford, John Dickson, Martha Vertreace.

Unsolicited Manuscripts Received/Published per Year: 3,000+/100–125.

Reading Period: year-round.

Payment: 2 sample copies.

Reporting Time: 4–6 weeks.

Copyright: ELF Associates, Inc.

1991; 4/yr; 5,200
$16/yr; $5.50/ea
56–60 pp; 8½ x 11
Ad Rates: inquire for rate sheet.
ISSN: 1054-3376
Ingram, DeBoer

3%

EMBERS

Katrina Van Tassel, Mark Johnston, Charlotte Garrett
Box 404
Guilford, CT 06437
(203) 453-2328

Poetry.

A poetry journal. Editors are poets, interested in poets' voices. New writers encouraged. Submit 3–5 poems.

Yearly chapbook contest. Guidelines available.

Unsolicited Manuscripts Received/Published per Year: 3,000/85.

Payment: 2 copies.

Reporting Time: Continuously.

Copyright held by poets; reverts upon publication.

1979; 2/yr; 500
$11/yr; $6/ea; $3/sample
48 pp; 6 x 9
ISSN: 0731-0382

THE EMRYS JOURNAL

Linda Julian
P.O. Box 8813
Greenville, SC 29604
(803) 294-3151

Poetry, fiction, essays.

Our journal is interested in publishing the work of new writers, especially that of women and other minorities. We are interested in maintaining a high literary standard.

Maxine Kumin, Carole Oles, Linda Paston, Amy Clampitt, Pattiann Rogers.
Unsolicited Manuscripts Received/Published per Year: 800/30.
Payment: in copies.
Reporting Time: 6 weeks.
Copyright held by The Emrys Foundation.
1984; 1/yr; 400
$10/ea; 40%
No ads

EPOCH

Michael Koch
251 Goldwin Smith Hall
Cornell University
Ithaca, NY 14853
(607) 255-3385

Poetry, fiction.
EPOCH is primarily a journal of fiction, poetry and essays. Publish work by a wide range of writers, some established, some just beginning their careers.
Harriet Doerr, Rick DeMarinis, Stuart Dybek, Thylias Moss, Lee K. Abbott, Alice Fulton.
Reading Period: Sept. 15—April 15.
Payment: $5/magazine page (prose); 50¢/line (poetry). These are minimum payments. We pay more when we have the funds.
Reporting Time: 1 month.
Copyright held by Cornell University; reverts to author upon publication.
1947; 3/yr; 1,000
$11/yr; $5/ea
128 pp; 6 x 9
Ad Rates: $180/page (5 x 8); $100/½ page (3 x 8)
ISSN: 0145-1391
DeBoer

EUROPE PLURILINGUE/ PLURILINGUAL EUROPE

Françoise Wuilmart, Editor-in-chief; Nadine Dormoy, Director of Publication; Albert Russo, Assistant Editors.

Nadine Dormoy
44 rue Perronet
92200 Neuilly, FRANCE
(331) 46.24.12.76

Articles, essays, interviews, poetry and short prose, pluridisciplinary.
All material should involve any of the 12 nations of the European community, their culture and languages and must be written in any of its 10 official languages, i.e.: English, French, German, Spanish, Italian, Portuguese, Danish, Dutch, Greek, Gaelic—High specialization in every field is required and excellence.

George Steiner, Umberto Eco, Hugo Claus, Albert Russo, Jacques Darras, Renzo Titone, Jean-Pierre Faye, Henri Adamczewski, Eduardo Lourenco.
Unsolicited Manuscripts Received/ Published per Year: dozens/20.
Payment: 2 copies of the issue.
Reporting Time: 2–3 months—send 3 IRC (international reply coupons) with mss.
Copyright is property of the review, but may be negociated with author.
1991; 4 as of 1993; 1,000
$40/yr; $11/ea; 15%; postage included, checks to be made out and setnt to: Liliane Lazar, 37 Hill Lane, Roslyn Heights, NY 11517, but mss *must* be sent to Nadine Dormoy—44 rue Perronet—92200 Neuilly, FRANCE.
150+ pp; 15cm x 20cm.
Ad Rates: upon request
ISSN: 1161-8884

THE EVERGREEN CHRONICLES

Jim Berg, Susan Raffo, Managing Editors
P.O. Box 8939
Minneapolis, MN 55408
Poetry, prose, visual art.
A journal of gay and lesbian literature.
Lev Raphael, Ruthann Robson, Terri Jewell.
Unsolicited Manuscripts Received/ Published per Year: 300/50.
Payment: in copies.
Reporting Time: 3 months.
Copyright: First run rights only.
1985; 2/yr; ,500
$15/yr; $7.95/ea
80–100 pp; 5¼ x 8½
Ad Rates: Write for rates.
ISSN: 1043-3333
Fine Print, Inland

EXHIBITION

Mary Guterson, Editor
261 Madison Ave. S.
Bainbridge Island, WA 98110
(206) 842-7901
Short fiction, essays, poetry, artwork.
Seek work which is innovative and challenging from Pacific Northwesterners.
Unsolicited Manuscripts Received/ Published per Year: 600/45+.
Payment: 2 copies.
2/yr; 1,000
$5/ea
35 pp; 8½ x 11
Ad Rates: available on request.

EXQUISITE CORPSE

Andrei Codrescu
P.O. Box 25051

Baton Rouge, LA 70894

Poetry, criticism, essays, reviews, translation, photographs, graphics/artwork, polemics, letters, reports from many countries.

A review of books and ideas. We are a print cafe, hopeful that vigorous dialogue on general culture is still possible in Mandarin US. We encourage honesty, combativeness and openness. We have published wide-ranging polemics, as well as essays on various matters of literary interest. Our foreign bureaus report on goings-on in several European and Asian cities. We also publish translations, and reprint important but overlooked texts. Our contributors are both famous and unknown.

Lawrence Ferlinghetti, Hayden Carruth, Maggie Estep, James Laughlin, Laura Rosenthal.

Unsolicited Manuscripts Received/Published per Year: 10,000/500.

Payment: some payment to contributors.

Reporting Time: 1 month.

Copyright held by authors.

1983; 6/yr; 5,500

$20/yr; $3.50/ea

28 pp; 6 x 15½

ISSN: 0740-7815

Inland

EYEBALL

Jabari Asim, Andrea M. Wren
P.O. Box 8135
St. Louis, MO 63108
(314) 947-6313

Poetry, fiction, essays, reviews, interviews, art.

EYEBALL exists to defend and extend the quest of literature to function as a unifying force in a world challenged by disorder and division.

Gwendolyn Brooks, Dennis Brutus, Paul Beatty, Kevin Powell.

Unsolicited Manuscripts Received/Published per Year: 50-100/20+.

Payment: 2 copies.

Reporting Time: within 1 year.

Copyright reverts to author.

1992; 2/yr; 2,000

$7/yr; $3.50/ea

48 pp; 13 x 10¾

Ad Rates: negotiable

ISSN: 1063-9675

F MAGAZINE

John Schultz
1405 West Belle Plaine
Chicago, IL 60613
(312) 281-7642

Fiction, criticism, essays, reviews, translations, interviews.

F MAGAZINE has the contemporary purpose of being devoted to the publication of fiction that is part of a literary movement toward a synthesis of fiction techniques, emphasizing story—content, imagery, character, voice, style, a rich exploration of points of view, forms, dimensions of time, dramatic and self relationships. Award winning fiction.

Andrew Allegretti, Betty Shiflett, Beverlye Brown, Gary Johnson, Shawn Shiflett, John Schultz, Charles Johnson, Harry Mark Petrakis, Cyrus Colter, Paul Carter Harrison.

Reading Period: Sept. 1—May 15.

Payment: varies, from $5/page.

Reporting Time: 4 months.

Copyright held by magazine; reverts to author upon publication.

2/yr; 1,500

$6.95/ea; 40%

210 pp; 6 x 9

Ad Rates: Contact CLMP for information.

ISBN: 0-936959-00-2

Ingram, DeBoer

FAG RAG

John Wieners, Charles Shively, John Mitgel

Box 331
Kenmore Station
Boston, MA 02215
(617) 661-7534

Poetry, fiction, criticism, essays, reviews, plays, translation, interviews, photographs, graphics/artwork, gay autobiography.

Gay male journal in search of the unrestrained aesthetic with emphasis on the striking and astonishing. Prisoners, mental patients, children, pedophiles and other poets.

Payment: in copies.

Reporting Time: 4–6 months.

Copyright held by magazine; reverts to author upon publication.

1971; 1–2/yr; 5,000

$10/yr ind, $20/yr inst; $5/ea; 40%

28–44 pp; quarterfold tabloid

ISSN: 0046-3167

FARMER'S MARKET

Jean C. Lee, John E. Hughes, Lisa Ress, Jim McCurry, Tracy Rose, Romayne Rubinas.

P.O. Box 1272
Galesburg, IL 61402

Poetry, fiction, essays, translation, graphics.

A national, award-winning magazine, publishing quality literary work reflective of Midwestern literary traditions and consciousness.

Walter Bargen, Elaine Fowler Palencia, Mary Troy, David Williams, Edward C. Lynskey, Marjorie Maddox, Joanna Jiggins, Philip Dacey.
Unsolicited Manuscripts Received/Published per Year: 2,000/40.
Payment: 2 copies and author's discount.
Reporting Time: 8–12 weeks.
Copyright held by author.
1982; 2/yr; 500
$10/yr; $6/ea; 40%
100-200 pp; 5½ x 8½
No ads
ISSN: 0748-6022

(FEED.)

P.J. Mark, Editor; Judy Rutkin, Editorial Asst; Steve Wiley, Photography Editor; Tara Eng, Art Director
P.O. Box 1567
Madison Square Station, New York, NY 10003
Poetry, fiction, artwork.
(FEED.) is an affordable paperback arts journal documenting the new movement of writing and art. **(FEED.)** encourages (and is partial to) those underrepresented: queer, feminist, ethnic, etc., but is open to all experience.
Dale Peck, Amudha Rajendran, Gretchen Elkins, Michael J. Mintz, Mark Jacobson.
Payment: 5 copies plus next 2 issues, discount on additional copies.
Reporting Time: prompt.
Copyright held by magazine; reverts to author.
1993; 1,000
$16/yr ind, $22/yr inst; $5/ea; 40%
varies; 6 x 9
Ad Rates: call for rates.
ISSN: 1072-5431
DeBoer, Fine Print

FELL SWOOP

X.J. Dailey
3003 Ponce De Leon St.
New Orleans, LA 70119
(504) 943-5198
Poetry, fiction, essay, drama, art, photographs.
The All Bohemian Revue, **FELL SWOOP** is a guerilla/gorilla venture exploring the edge of 'acceptability' in contemporary writing. We like a good laugh at anyone's expense, especially our own.
Richard Martin, Elizabeth Thomas, Andrei Codrescu, Ed Dorn, Clara Talley-Vincent, R. Speck.
Unsolicited Manuscripts Received/Published per Year: 1,000/25.
Reading Period: year–round.

Payment: in copies.
Reporting Time: immediately.
Copyright reverts to author upon publication.
1983; 3/yr; 1,000
$8/yr; $3/ea
pp varies; 8½ x 11
ISSN: 1040-5607

FICTION

Mark Mirsky, Editor; Allan Aycock, Managing Editor
c/o Dept. of English
The City College
138th & Convent Ave.
New York, NY 10031
(212) 650-6319
Prose fiction, translations.
FICTION represents no particular school of fiction other than the inventive and the innovative. We publish the difficult, the experimental, the unusual, without excluding the well known.
Amdahl, Brodkey, Oates, Minot, Macauley, Mirsky, Cherry.
Unsolicited Manuscripts Received/Published per Year: 2,000–3,000/20–30.
Reading Period: Oct.—May.
Payment: $25 and copies.
Reporting Time: 3–6 months.
Copyright: Fiction, Inc. Reverts to author on request.
1972; 2/yr; 3,000
$20/3 yr; $6.95/ea; 50%

200 pp; 9 x 6
Ad Rates: negotiable
ISSN: 74470 80497
Ingram, DeBoer

FICTION INTERNATIONAL

Harold Jaffe
Department of English
San Diego State University
San Diego, CA 92182
(619) 594-5443 or (619) 594-5469
Fiction, reviews, essays, visuals.
FICTION INTERNATIONAL's twin biases are toward postmodernism and progressive politics, either integrated or apart. We especially welcome writing from the "Third World" (both abroad and at home), and we favor writing that cuts through or fuses or ignores the canonical genres.
Robert Coover, Claribel Alegria, Gerald Vizenor, Michel Serres, Marianne Hauser, Pierre Guyotat, Margaret Randall, Roque Dalton.
Unsolicited Manuscripts Received/Published per Year: 500-700/20-30.
Reading Period: Sept.—Dec. 15.
Payment: copies.
Reporting Time: 1–3 months.
$12/yr ind, $24/yr inst; $6/ea; 40%
McPherson, Blackwell North American, Faxon, Baker & Taylor

THE FIDDLEHEAD

Don McKay
Campus House, UNB P.O. Box 4400
Federiction, New Brunswick, E3B5A3
CANADA
(506) 453-3501

Short fiction, poetry, book reviews. (Canadian books only)

Canada's oldest continuing literary magazine, with a world-wide circulation. Any good writing, from any place, will be welcome here.

Penny Villegas, Mark Sanders.

Unsolicited Manuscripts Received/Published per Year: 2,000/20–25. Include SASE with International coupons or *Canadian stamps.*

Payment: $10/page

Reporting Time: 4–6 months.

Copyright: First serial rights only—copyright remains with author.

1945; 4/yr; 800

$18/yr; $6/ea; 30%

120–128 pp; 6 x 9

Ad Rates: $100/page

ISBN: 015-0630

Canadian Magazine Publishers Association

FIELD

Stuart Friebert, David Young
Rice Hall
Oberlin College
Oberlin, OH 44074
(216) 775-8408

Poetry, criticism, essays, reviews, translation.

We look for the best in contemporary poetry, poetics and translations and emphasize essays by poets themselves on the craft.

Marianne Boruch, Laura Jensen, W. S. Merwin, William Stafford, Charles Simic, James Tate, Sharon Olds, Miroslav Holub.

Unsolicited Manuscripts Received/Published per Year: 16,500/40.

Reading Period: year–round.

Payment: $20–30/page.

Reporting Time: 2 weeks.

Copyright held by Oberlin College; reverts to author upon publication.

1969; 2/yr; 2,500

$12/yr, $20/2 yrs; $6/ea; 20–30%

100 pp; 5½ x 8½

FINE MADNESS

Sean Bentley, Louis Bergsagel, Christine Deavel, John Malek, John Marshall
P.O. Box 31138
Seattle, WA 98103-1138

Poetry, fiction.

We look for poetry that shows wit, imagination, love of language, technical skill and individual style.

Andrei Codrescu, David Ignatow, David Young, Naomi Shihab Nye, Pattiann Rogers, Elton Glaser, David Kirby, Peter Wild.

Unsolicited Manuscripts Received/ Published per Year: 1,500/50.

Payment: copies.

Reporting Time: 3 months.

Copyright held by magazine; reverts to author upon publication.

1980 2/yr; 800

$9/yr; $5/ea

80 pp; 5½ x 8

ISSN: 0737-4704

Small Changes, Ubiquity, Armadillo, Fine Print

FIVE FINGERS REVIEW

John High, Aleka Chase, Thoreau Lovell

P.O. Box 15426

San Francisco, CA 94115

Poetry, fiction, essays.

The **FIVE FINGERS REVIEW** seeks to publish fresh, innovative writing and artwork that is not necessarily defined by the currently "correct" aesthetic or ideology. **FIVE FINGERS REVIEW** welcomes work that crosses or falls between genres. In addition to new fiction and poetry, **FIVE FINGERS REVIEW** presents essays, interviews, and translations. Each issue explores a theme; recent issues have focused on spirituality and the avant–garde, the new lyric and shifting narrative, and new writing from Moscow to San Francisco.

Francisco Alarcon, C. D. Wright, Norman Fischer, Mikhail Epshtein, Leslie Scalapino, Lyn Hejinian, David Levi–Strauss, Thaisa Frank, Keith Waldrop, Rosmarie Waldrop, Peter Gizzi, Aleksei Parschikov.

Unsolicited Manuscripts Received/ Published per Year: 1,000/75.

Payment: in copies.

Reporting Time: 3 months.

Copyright held by magazine; reverts to author upon publication.

1984; 2/yr; 1,000–1,500

$15/yr, $28/2yr, $12 inst; $9/ea; 40%

150–250 pp; 6 x 9

Ad Rates: $150/page (4½ x 7½); $100/½ page (4½ x 3½ or 2 x 7½); $75/¼ page (2 x 3½)

BookPeople, Inland, SPD, L-S Distributors, Spectacular Diseases (UK)

FLOATING ISLAND

Michael Sykes

P.O. Box 516

Point Reyes Station, CA 94956

(415) 663-1181

Poetry fiction, photography in folio format, graphics/artwork.
Expansive, eclectic, very wide-ranging with center on West coast of North America—special interest in photography and graphic arts, lyric poetry and experimental prose. Volumes I-IV, First Series is now complete. Second Series to begin in 1995.
Diane di Prima, Gary Snyder, Michael McClure, Robert Bly, Christina Zawadiwsky, Frank Stewart, Lawrence Ferlinghetti, Joanne Kyger, Sam Hamill, Cole Swensen, Arthur Sze.
Unsolicited Manuscripts Received/ Published per Year: 100/0.
Payment: in copies.
Reporting Time: 4 weeks.
Copyright held by publisher; reverts to author upon publication.
1976; irreg.; 2,000
All issues $15/ea; 40% 5 or more copies, 20% 1–4 copies
160 pp; 8½ x 11
ISSN: 0147-1686
SPD, BookPeople

THE FLORIDA REVIEW

Russell Kesler
English Department
University of Central Florida
Orlando, FL 32816
(407) 823-2038

Poetry, fiction, essays, reviews.
We publish stories with heart that aren't afraid to take risks. Experimental fiction is welcome, so long as it doesn't make us feel stupid. We look for clear, strong poems filled with real things, real people, real emotions, poems that might conceivably advance our knowledge of the human heart.
Stephen Dixon, Jane Ruiter, Liz Rosenberg, Karen Fish, Michael Martone.
Unsolicited Manuscripts Received/ Published per Year: 2,500/40.
Reading Period: year–round.
Payment: small honoraria are awarded when possible.
Reporting Time: 2–3 months.
Copyright held by University of Central Florida; reverts to author upon publication.
1972; 2/yr; 1,000
$7/yr ind, $11/2 yrs ind, $9/yr inst, $13/2 yrs inst; $4.50/ea; 40%
128 pp; 5½ x 8½
Ad Rates: exchange ads only
ISSN: 0742-2466
Fine Print

FOLIO

Department of Literature
American University

Washington, DC 20016
(202) 885-2973

Poetry, fiction, reviews, translations, black & white art & photography.

FOLIO prints quality fiction and poetry by established writers as well as those just starting out. We like to comment on submissions when time permits. Prose limit: 4,500 words. SASE required.

Henry Taylor, Linda Pastan, William Stafford, Jean Valentine, Simon Perchik, Kermit Moyer, Myra Sklarew.

Unsolicited Manuscripts Received/Published per Year: 1,300/6 stories/prose; 30 poems.

Reading Period: Aug.—April.

Payment: prizes of up to $75 awarded for best fiction and poem.

Copyright reverts to author upon publication.

1984; 2/yr; 400

$10/yr; $5/ea; 30%

70 pp; 6 x 9

Chapters, The Writers Center (Bethesda), Politics & Prose, Borders, Bicks

FOOTWORK: The Paterson Literary Review (PLR)

Maria Mazziotti Gillan
Cultural Affairs Department
Passaic County Community College
1 College Boulevard
Paterson, NJ 07505-1179
(201) 684-6555

Poetry, fiction, review, graphics/artwork.

PLR is a high quality literary quarterly.

Laura Boss, William Stafford, Marge Piercy, Daniella Geoseffi, Stanley Barkan.

Unsolicited Manuscripts Received/Published per Year: 10,000/200.

Payment: in copies.

Reading Period: Jan.—Mar.

Reporting Time: 6 months.

Copyright held by Passaic County College; reverts to author upon publication.

1979; 1/yr; 1,000

$8/yr ind, $10/yr inst; $5/ea; 40%

200 pp; 8½ x 11, perfect-bound

Ad Rates: $300/page (8½ x 11); $150/½ page (8½ x 5); $100/¼ page (4 x 2½)

THE FORMALIST

William Baer
320 Hunter Drive
Evansville, IN 47711

Contemporary metrical poetry and translations.

Devoted entirely to formal, metrical verse and publishing contemporary poetry and translations that participate in the great tradition of metrical poetry from Chaucer to Wilbur.

Howard Nemerov, Richard Wilbur, Mona Van Duyn, Derek Walcott, Maxine Kumin, John Updike.

Unsolicited Manuscripts Received/Published per Year: 3,000+/160+.

Reading Period: year–round.

Payment: 2 copies.

Reporting Time: within 2 months.

Copyright: yes.

1990; 2/yr; growing

$12/yr, $22/2 yr; $6.50/ea; contact publisher

128pp; 6 x 9

No advertising

ISSN: 1046-7874

FOR POETS ONLY

L. M. Walsh
P.O. Box 4855
Schenectady, NY 12304

Poetry.

Little "little" publishes sincere, serious poetry—any subject—no pornography.

J. Bernier, C. Weirich, A.M. Swaim, G. Labocetta, J. Frazeur.

Unsolicited Manuscripts Received/Published per Year: Approx. 250/Approx. 120.

Payment: in copies, plus prize money. $3 per poem reading fee.

Copyright held by magazine; reverts to author upon publication.

1985; 4/yr; 150

$3/ea

30 pp; 5½ x 8

ISSN: 0087-0896

THE FOUR DIRECTIONS

Joanna and William Meyer
P.O. Box 729
Tellico Plains, TN 37385
(615) 524-8612

American Indian authors, poets and writers.

To provide a forum for American Indian writers; to provide a positive publishing experience; to assist in development of Indian writers and develop a market and readership for Native American Writers.

Raven Hail, E. James Hillsburg, Whitefeather.

Unsolicited Manuscripts Received/Published per Year: Numerous/100+.

Payment: 2 cents/word for stories and articles; $10/full page poem; $5/half page poem.

Reporting Time: 4—6 weeks.

Copyright: first serial rights.

1992; 4/yr

$21/yr; $6/ea; 40%
64 pp; 8 ½ x 11
Ad Rates: $145/page; $100/½ page; $70/¼ page; inside covers: $170 back, $195 front

FOUR QUARTERS

John J. Keenan, Editor; John P. Rossi, Associate Editor
La Salle Univ.
1900 W. Olney Avenue
Philadelphia, PA 19141
(215) 951-1610

Poetry, fiction, nonfiction, short dramatic pieces.

A magazine of contemporary culture aimed at college-educated readers. Publishes nonspecialized articles, essays, fiction, and poetry.

Seamus Heaney, Joyce Carol Oates, James Merrill, John Lukacs, John Hollander, J.D. McClatchy.

Unsolicited Manuscripts Received/ Published per Year: 350/35+.
Reading Period: Jan.—June 30.
Payment: on acceptance.
Reporting Time: 6 weeks.
Copyright held by La Salle Univ.; assignable to author.
1951; 2/yr
$8/yr; $4/ea; 40%
64 pp; 7 x 10

Ad Rates: $100/page
ISSN: 0015-9107

FRANK: An International Journal of Contemporary Writing and Art

David Applefield, Editor/Publisher
104 rue Edouard Vaillant
93100 Montrevil
FRANCE
(331) 48.59.66.58; Fax (331) 48.59.66.68

Poetry, fiction, translations, interviews, graphics/artwork, essays, photographs.

FRANK is a highly eclectic journal open to both established and emerging talent which emphasizes internationalism. The journal encourages both literary and visual work that takes risks but does not ignore the value of intellectual traditions. Contemporary Chinese, Congolese, Turkish, Nordic, Philippino, Belgian and Pakistani writing.

Vaclav Havel, Samuel Beckett, Italo Calvino, James Tate, Allen Ginsberg, Paul Bowles, Robert Coover, Raymond Carver, Rita Dove, Stephen Dixon, Sony Labou Tansi, Frederick Barthelme, Phillip Glass.

Unsolicited Manuscripts Received/ Published per Year: 1,000/30.

10%

Payment: $5/page plus two copies.
Copyright held by author.
1983; 2/yr; 14,000
$30/4 issues ind, $60/4 issues inst; $9.95/ea; 33%–40%
224 pp; 5½ x 8½
Ad Rates: $1,000/page (5 x 8); $500/½ page (4½ x 3½); $300/¼ page (2½ x 3½)
ISSN: 0738-9299; ISBN: 2-908171-09-0

FREE FOCUS

Patricia D. Coscia
JAF Station
Box 7415
New York, NY 10116-4630

Women's poetry.

FREE FOCUS is a small-press magazine which focuses on the educated women of today and needs stories and poems. The poems can be as long as 2 pages or as short as 3 lines. No X-rated material. Poems should be single-spaced on individual sheets.

Patricia D. Coscia, Ed Janz.
Unsolicited Manuscripts Received/ Published per Year: 500/200.
Payment: 1 copy.
Reporting Time: 6 months.
Copyright held by editor.
1985; 2/yr; 500
$4/yr; $2/ea
20 pp; 8 x 14
Ad Rates: $1/column; $3/page
ISSN: 0447-5667

FREE LUNCH

Ron Offen
P.O. Box 7647
Laguna Niguel, CA 92607-7647

Poetry.

Unsolicited Manuscripts Received/ Published per Year: 2,500/75.
Reading Period: Sept. 2—May 31.
Copyright held by Free Lunch Arts Alliance.
1989; 3/yr; 1,200
Magazine is free to all serious U.S. Poets living in the U.S. send SASE for details. Will not consider more than 3 poems per submission.
Others: $12/yr; $5 ea
32 pp; 5½ x 8½
Ad Rates: $100/page (4 x 8); $60/½ page (4 x 4); $35/¼ page (2 x 2)

FURIOUS FICTIONS

Joseph Lerner
P.O. Box 423665
San Francisco, CA 94102
(415) 431-0461

"Flash" or short-short fiction.

FURIOUS FICTIONS is the

leading literary journal devoted to showcasing the best new short-short or "flash" fiction in the U.S. today.
Molly Giles, Diane Glancy, Tom Whaler, Jacques Servin.
Unsolicited Manuscripts Received/ Published per Year: 6,000/60.
Reading Period: year–round.
Payment: 1 year subscription.
Reporting Time: 2 weeks—2 months.
Copyright: First serial rights.
1992; 3/yr; 1,500
$12/yr; $3.95/ea
36 pp; 8½ x 11
ISSN: 1065-7983
Ubiquity, Desert Moon, Fine Print

G

GAIA: A JOURNAL OF LITERARY & ENVIRONMENTAL ARTS

Robert S. King, Editor-in-Chief
P.O. Box 709
Winterville, GA 30683
(706) 542-0811
Poetry, fiction, essays, graphics/artwork.
GAIA is a quarterly with emphasis on environmental themes.
E.G. Burrows, Stuart Friebert, Paul Grant, Ann Struthers, Martha M. Vertreace.
Payment: 1 year sub.
Reporting Time: 2 months.
Copyright held by Whistle Press, Inc.
1993; 4/yr; 450
$9/yr (ind & inst); $4/ea; 40%
44 pp

THE GALLEY SAIL REVIEW

Stanley McNail
1630 University Ave., #42
Berkeley, CA 94703
(415) 486-0187
Poetry, reviews.
GSR seeks excellence in contemporary poetry, without regard for schools, cliques, or "movements." It values sincerity and honors craftsmanship. It tries to encourage poetry that speaks to the human condition in this modern world, and to develop a wider appreciation of poetry as an essential art in society.
Martin Robbins, Michael Culross, Laurel Ann Bogen, Harold Witt, Carol Hamilton.
Payment: in copies.
Copyright held by magazine; reverts to author upon publication.
1958; 3/yr; 400

$8/yr ind, $15/2 yr ind, $15/2 yr inst; $3/ea; 40%
40 pp; 8½ x 5½
ISSN: 0016-4100

GAS: HIGH OCTANE POETRY

Kevin Opstedal & Tom Clark
3164 Emerson
Palo Alto, CA 94306
(415) 493-5903

Poetry.

GAS prints only premium high-octane poetry guaranteed to rid you of those psychic knocks & pings. Free cranial liposuction with fill-up.

Ed Sanders, Alice Notley, Bukowski, Dorn, Eileen Myles.
Payment: copies.
Reporting Time: 1–2 weeks.
Copyright reverts to individual authors upon publication.
1990; irregular; 100
$30/sub; $10/ea; 40%
130 pp; 9 x 7½
Ad Rates: $100/page; $50/½ page; $25/¼ page
ISSN: 1058-532X
BookPeople, Last Gasp

A GATHERING OF THE TRIBES

Steve Cannon, Gail Schilke
P.O. Box 20693
Tompkins Square
New York, NY 10009

Poetry, fiction, essays, reviews, interviews, graphics/artwork, photographs.

TRIBES is a multicultural, non-academic, literary magazine of the arts which reflects the richness and diversity of America's cultural heritage.

Jessica Hagedorn, Ishmael Reed, Hernandez Cruz, Jayne Cortez, Al Young.
Payment: none.
Copyright held by authors.
1991; 2/yr; 1,000
$15/yr ind, $20/yr inst; $4.50/ea; 40%
40 pp; 8½ x 11
Ad Rates: $275/page (6¼ x 8½); $150/½ page (6¼ x 4¼)
ISSN: 1058-9112

GEORGETOWN REVIEW

Steven Carter, Gwen Curry
Georgetown Review
400 E. College St.
Box 227
Georgetown, KY 40324
(502) 863-7567

Fiction and Poetry.

A literary review looking to publish honest, quality fiction and poetry.

Unsolicited Manuscripts Received/

Published per Year: 800–1,000/30–40.
Reading Period: Sept. 1—May 1.
Payment: 2 copies.
Reporting Time: 2–4 months.
Copyright reverts to author upon publication.
1993; 2/yr; 500
$10/yr; $5/ea; 55%
90–100 pp; 6 x 9
Ad Rates: $75/page; $32.50/½ page.
Fine Print

THE GEORGIA REVIEW

Stanley W. Lindberg
University of Georgia
Athens, GA 30602-9009
(706) 542-3481

Poetry, fiction, essays, reviews, graphics/artwork.

An international journal of arts and letters with a special interest in current American literary writing; seeking interdisciplinary thesis-oriented essays—not scholarly articles—and engaging book reviews, plus the best in contemporary poetry and fiction; authors range from Nobel laureates and Pulitzer Prize winners to the as-yet unknown and previously unpublished.

Rita Dove, Stephen Dunn, Eudora Welty, Fred Chappell, Seamus Heaney, Mary Hood, Louise Erdrich, Wayne Dodd, Emily Hiestand.

Unsolicited Manuscripts Received/ Published per Year: 17,000/100
Payment; $3/line for poetry; $35/printed page for prose.
Reporting Time: 8–12 weeks.
Reading Period: Sept.—May.
Compilation copyright entered by the University of Georgia, which has purchased first serial rights; all other rights are retained by individual authors.
1947; 4/yr; 7,000
$18/yr; $7/ea
208 pp; 6¾ x 10
Ad Rates: $350/page (4¾ x 7½); $225/½ page (4¾ x 3⅝)
ISSN: 0016-8386
DeBoer, Ubiquity, Fine Print

THE GETTYSBURG REVIEW

Peter Stitt
Gettysburg College
Gettysburg, PA 17325-1491
(717) 337-6770

Poetry, fiction, essays, graphics/ artwork.

THE GETTYSBURG REVIEW is an interdisciplinary magazine of arts and ideas, which features the highest quality poetry, fiction, essays, essay-reviews, and graphics by both beginning and established writers and artists. Two special interests are the publication of serial fiction and the inclusion of a full-color graphics section in each issue. Essays are in a variety of disciplines, with a wide range of subject matter.

E.L. Doctorow, Frederick Busch, Philip Levine, Debora Greger, Hayden Carruth, Linda Pastan, Rita Dove, Charles Wright, Kate Wheeler, Richard Wilbur, Joyce Carol Oates.

Unsolicited Manuscripts Received/ Published per Year: 2,500/85.

Reading Period: Year–Round.

Payment: $25/page prose; $2/line poetry; upon publication.

Copyright held by Gettysburg College; reverts to author upon publication.

1988; 4/yr; 2,000

$18/yr ind, $18/yr inst; $32/2 yr; $45/3 yr; $7/ea; 40%

170 pp; 6¾ x 10

Ad Rates: $225/page (5 x 7½)

ISSN: 0898-4557

Eastern News

GIORNO POETRY SYSTEMS

John Giorno
222 Bowery
New York, NY 10012
(212) 925-6372

Poetry.

Magazine in three formats: LP record, Compact Disc, and Cassette. Video Pak series is a magazine in video format.

Laurie Anderson, William Burroughs, Patti Smith, Diamanda Galas, Nick Cave.

Payment: $500 royalty advance, and 12% of the retail price of each record sold.

1972; 4/yr; 10,000

$8.98/single album; $12.98/double album; $8.98/cassette; $13.98/ compact disc; $39.95/video cassette; 40%—55%

GLIMMER TRAIN STORIES

Linda Davis, Susan Burmeister-Brown
812 SW Washington St. #1205
Portland, OR 97205
(503) 221-0836

Quarterly short story magazine printed on acid-free, recycled stock. Each story is illustrated.

Many unknowns as well as Charles Baxter, Ellen Gilchrist, Mary McGarry Morris, Richard Bausch, Ann Beattie.

Unsolicited Manuscripts Received/ Published per Year: 12,000/32.

Payment: $300 upon acceptance.

Reporting Time: 3 months.

Copyright reverts to author upon publication.
1991; 4/yr; 19,500
$29/yr; $9/ea; 40%
168 pp; 5¾ x 9¼
No advertising
Ingram, IPD, Pacific Pipeline, DeBoer, Ubiquity, BookPeople

GRAB-A-NICKEL

Barbara Smith
Alderson-Broaddus College
Philippi, WV 26416
(304) 457-1700

Poetry, fiction, reviews, photographs, graphics/artwork.

GRAB-A-NICKEL is a tabloid journal of poems, fiction, book reviews, photographs and drawings. Open submissions; priority given to Appalachian writers and subject matter. There is encouragement of new writers of any age or background. It is a product of a college community's writers' workshop.

Barbara Smith, John McKernan, Eddy Pendaris, Mark Rowh, T. Kilgore Splake, Llewellyn McKernan, Jim Wayne Miller.

Unsolicited Manuscripts Received/Published per Year: 450–500/200.

Payment: in copies.

Copyright held by author.

1977; 2–3/yr; 1,000
25¢/ea
16 pp; 11½ x 14

GRADIVA

Luigi Fontanella
P.O. Box 831
Stony Brook, NY 11794-3359
(516) 632-7448 or (516) 632-7440

Poetry, essays, reviews, translation, interviews.

GRADIVA is an international journal of modern Italian literature that focuses on literary criticism and theory. All contributions are published in English or Italian. Creative works written in other languages are published with translation.

Umberto Eco, Edoardo Sanguineti, Mario Luzi, Alfredo Giuliani, Andrea Zanzotto.

Unsolicited Manuscripts Received/Published per year: 50+/4.

Payment: in copies, subscription.

Copyright held by magazine; reverts to author upon publication.

1986; 2/yr; 3,000
$25/yr
100 pp; 5½ x 8½
Ad Rates: $100/page (5½ x 8½); $60/½ page (5½ x 4¼); $35/¼ page (2¾ x 4¼)

GRAHAM HOUSE REVIEW

Peter Balakian, Bruce Smith
Box 5000
Colgate University
Hamilton, NY 13346
(315) 824-1000, ext. 262

Poetry, essays, translations, interviews.

We publish the best poetry and poetry in translation we can get. We have just begun an interview series and will publish essays in the future. We pay scrupulous attention to production, and have an international interest in selecting material.

Seamus Heaney, Derek Walcott, Madeline De Frees, David Wagoner, Maxine Kumin, Carolyn Forché.

Unsolicited Manuscripts Received per Year: 10,000.

Payment: in copies.

Reporting Time: 1–2 months.

Copyright held by magazine; reverts to author upon publication.

1976; 1/yr; 1,750

$7.50/yr ind, $7.50/inst; $7.50/ea; 20%

125 pp; 8½ x 5½

GRAIN

Elizabeth Philips, Edna Alford, Judith Drause, Catherine Macaulay
Box 1154
Regina, Saskatchewan, S4P3B4 CANADA
(306) 757-6310; Fax (306) 757-8554

Literary and visual art.

GRAIN publishes the best new previously unpublished fiction, poetry, and other genres from across Canada and around the world.

Unsolicited Manuscripts Received/Published per Year: Hundreds/80.

Reading Period: year–round.

Payment: $30—$100 (Canadian).

Reporting Time: 2—4 months.

Copyright remains with author.

1973; 4/yr; 1,525

$19.95/yr; $6.95/ea; 40%

144 pp; 6 x 9

Ad Rates: $400/page; $250/½ page; $125/¼ page

ISSN: 0315-7423

Canadian Magazine Publishers Association

GRAND STREET

Jean Stein
131 Varick St., Room 906
New York, NY 10013
(212) 807-6548

Poetry, fiction, essays, interviews, art.

Andrei Bitov, Henry Green, Toni Morrison, William T. Vollmann,

Kenzaburo Oe, Terry Southern.
Unsolicited Manuscripts Received/Published per Year: 3,500/10.
Reading Period: year–round.
Payment: inquire.
Reporting Time: 4–6 weeks.
Copyright: one-time first-serial rights only; author retains copyright.
1981; 4/yr; 5,000
$30/yr ind, $40/yr foreign; $10/ea
240 pp; 7 x 9
Ad Rates: $450/page
ISSN: 0734-5496
W. W. Norton

GRASSLANDS REVIEW

Laura B. Kennelly
NT Box 13706
Denton, TX 76203
(817) 565-2050

Poetry and fiction.

Publishes poetry and fiction from known and unknown authors chosen by students in adult learners' creative writing group. Send manuscripts only in October or March.

Jendi Reiter, James Hoggard, Robert Weaver.
Unsolicited Manuscripts Received/Published per Year: 300/64.
Reading Period: Oct. 1—Mar.
Payment: in copies.
Reporting Time: 3–4 months.
Copyright reverts to author.
1988; 2/yr; 300
$8/yr ind, $15/yr inst; $2.50/ea
90 pp; 5 x 9
Ad Rates: $20/½ page, plus subscription

GREAT RIVER REVIEW

Orval Lund
211 West Seventh St.
Winona, MN 55987
(507) 454-6564

Poetry, fiction, criticism, reviews, graphics.

Dedicated to publishing the best in fiction, creative prose, and poetry, and to showcasing the work of new, emerging and established writers. Specially interested in Midwestern writers.

Leo Dangel, Pam Harrison, Madelon Sprengnether.
Unsolicited Manuscripts Received/Published per Year: 1,200/50.
Reading Period: year–round.
Payment: in copies.
Reporting Time: 1–3 months.
Copyright reverts to author.
1977; 2/yr; 1,200
$10/yr; $6/ea
280 pp; 6 x 8
Ad Rates: $100/page; $50/½ page; $25/¼ page
Ebsco, Faxon, Aquinas

GREAT STREAM REVIEW

Penelope Austin, G. W. Hawkes
Lycoming College
Box 66
Williamsport, PA 17701
(717) 321-4114

Poetry, fiction, familiar essays.

GSR provides a forum for writers engaged in evaluating, confronting and offering alternatives to literary modernism and post-modernism; writers who find the source of their imagination in other than despair, disease and alienation. We have published:

Will Baker, Scott Cairns, Pam Houston, Deborah Monroe, Janet Sylvester, Lee Upton.

Unsolicited Manuscripts Received/Published per Year: 300/5%.

Payment: $10/page.

Reporting Time: 8-12 weeks.

Copyright held by magazine.

1989; 2/yr; 1,000

$7.50/yr; $4/ea; 40%

100 pp; 6 x 9

ISSN: 1042-8208

green

Lily Pond
P.O. Box 6508 Berkeley, CA 94706
(510) 644-4188

Essays, poetry, fiction, photography, paintings.

From wilderness to gardening, animals to oceans, we bring our readers a reverent, celebratory exploration of nature through the written and visual arts.

Jane Hirshfield, Mark Doty, Linda Hogan.

Payment: competitive.

Reporting Time: approx. 3 months.

Copyright reverts to author 1 year following publication: we keep non-exclusive reprint, anthology, and electronic rights.

1993; 4/yr

$20/yr; $5/ea

60 pp.; 8½ x 11

Advertising Rates: $1,006.50/page; $522.50/½ page; $352/⅓ page; $258.50/¼ page; $176/⅙ page

ISSN: pending

BookPeople, Inland, Ingram Ubiquity

GREEN FUSE POETRY

Brian Boldt
3365 Holland Dr.
Santa Rosa, CA 95404
(707) 544-8303

Contemporary poetry—generally free verse.

We focus on environmental themes and issues of war and

peace in a 52 page, digest size format. Generally we publish what moves us.

Antler, John Brandi, David Fisher, Dorianne Laux, Denise Levertov, Laurel Speer.

Unsolicited Manuscripts Received/ Published per Year: 2,000/80.

Payment: 1 copy, more to featured poets.

Reporting Time: Within 12 weeks.

Copyright reverts to author upon publication.

1984; 2/yr; 450

3 issues for $14; $4.50

52 pp; digest; perfect-bound

Galway Kinnell, Denise Levertov, Larry Levis, David St. John, Ellen Lesser, David Wojahn.

Unsolicited Manuscripts Received/ Published per Year: 600/40.

Reading Period: year–round.

Payment: in copies.

Reporting Time: 1–3 months.

Copyright held by magazine; reverts to author upon publication.

1987; 2/yr; 1,000

$12/yr; $6/ea; 40%

120+ pp; 6 x 9

$150/page; $75/½ page

ISSN: 0895-9307

Ubiquity

GREEN MOUNTAINS REVIEW

Neil Shepard, Poetry Editor; Tony Whedon, Fiction Editor

Johnson State College

Johnson, VT 05656

(802) 635-2356

Poetry, fiction, essays, reviews, interviews, translations, photographs.

GMR publishes work by promising newcomers and well-known writers from across the country. In addition, each issue features the work of one regional writer—either a suite of poems, extended work of fiction, interview or literary essay.

THE GREENSBORO REVIEW

Jim Clark

Department of English

Univ. North Carolina-Greensboro

Greensboro, NC 27412

(910) 334-5459; Fax (910) 334-3281

Poetry, fiction.

Contemporary and experimental. We want to see the best being written regardless of theme, subject or style.

Ellen Herman, Peter Taylor, Greg Johnson, Peter Meinke, Lane von Herzen, Jere Hoar, Molly Giles, Robert Morgan, Greg Kuzma.

Unsolicited Manuscripts Received/

Published per Year: 1,000–1,200 fictions/12–20.
Payment: in copies.
Reporting Time: 2–4 months.
Copyright held by magazine; reverts to author.
1966; 2/yr; 5–600
$8/yr, $16/2 yrs, $20/3 yrs; $4/ea
120–180 pp; 6 x 9
ISSN: 0017-4084

GULF COAST

Randall Watson, Stewart James
Department of English
University of Houston
4800 Calhoun Rd.
Houston, TX 77204-5641
(713) 749-3640

Poetry, fiction, essays, translation, photographs, graphics/artwork.

GULF COAST encourages submission of high-quality, well-crafted and energetic poetry and fiction, submissions are open to all styles & subjects.

Lisa Zeidner, Charles Baxter, Rosellen Brown, Amy Clampitt, Richard Howard, Rick Bass, Rodney Jones, John Hawkes, Ann Beattie, Padgett Powell, Glen Blake.

Unsolicited Manuscripts Received/Published per Year: 400/60
Payment: copies.
Copyright held by magazine; reverts to author upon publication.
1981; 2/yr; 500+
$10/yr ind, $8/yr inst; $5/ea; $10 Barthelme Memorial
96 pp; 9 x 6
No ads
ISSN: 0896-2251

GULF STREAM MAGAZINE

Lynne Barrett, Editor; Associate Editors: Christopher Gleason, Blythe Nobleman.
FIU, North Miami Campus
North Miami, FL 33181
(305) 940-5599

Poetry, fiction, essays.

GSM publishes high quality fiction, poetry and essays. We are open to experimental and mainstream work. No more than 5 poems. Limit prose to 25 pages.

Gerald Costanzo, Ann Hood, Stuart Dybek, Dara Wier.

Unsolicited Manuscripts Received/Published per Year: 1,000/50.
Reading Period: Sept.—April.
Payment: in copies.
Reporting Time: 1–3 months.
Copyright held by magazine; First North American serial rights.
1989; 2/yr; 350
$7.50/yr; $4/ea; 40%
96 pp; 8½ x 5½

GYPSY

Belinda Subraman, S. Ramnath
10708 Gay Brewer Drive
El Paso, TX 79935
(915) 592-3701

Fiction, reviews, graphics/artwork, essays, poetry.

We are an international family of independent literary and visual artists. We seek to enlarge our family and support. Please write for current themes and guidelines. In general, we are interested in writing of lasting value, usually dealing with human rights and experience. Currently doing double issue book editions. Inquire before submitting. Prices vary.

Peter Wild, Laurel Speer, James Purdy, Albert Huffstickler, Gerald Locklin.

Unsolicited Manuscripts Received/Published per Year: 5,000±/180±.

Reporting Time: 6–12 weeks.

Copyright: Vergin' Press.

1984; 2/yr; 1,000

Ad Rates: $100/page; $55/½ page; $30/¼ page

ISSN: 0176-3148

H

HABERSHAM REVIEW

David L. Greene, Lisa Hodgens Lumpkin, co-editors
Piedmont College
P.O. Box 10
Demorest, GA 30535
(706) 778-3000

Fiction, Poetry

HABERSHAM REVIEW is a general literary journal with a regional focus (Southeastern U.S.) Each issue features an unpublished work by and an interview with a prominent Southern writer.

D.C. Berry, Judith Cofer, Rosemary Daniell, Mary Hood, Frank Gannan

Unsolicited Manuscripts Received/Published per Year: 900/40.

Payment: copies.

Reporting Time: 4 months ±.

Copyright held by Piedmont College; reverts to author upon publication.

1991; 2/yr; 500

$12/yr; $5/ea; 40%

96 pp; 6 x 9

Ad Rates: $400/page (5 x 8+); $200/½ page (2½ x 4±)

ISSN: 1060-0469

HAIGHT ASHBURY LITERARY JOURNAL

Joanne Hotchkiss, Alice Rogoff, Will Walker
558 Joost Avenue
San Francisco, CA 94127
(415) 584-8264

The magazine began with six editors of extremely diverse socio-economic and ethnic backgrounds. The magazine encompasses diversity of viewpoint, racial, sexual as well as style, tending to confront the difficult and painful of human experiences as well as the higher reaches of emotional experiences. The Journal publishes both local writers and other interested writers.

Eugene Ruggles, Mona Lisa Saloy, Peter Plate, Jack Hirschman, Laura del Feugo, Leslie Simon.

Unsolicited Manuscripts Received/Published per Year: 600/100.

Reading Period: Oct.—Dec., Mar.—June

Payment: in copies.

Reporting Time: 2–4 months.

Copyright held by author.

1980; 1½/yr; 2-3,000

$35/lifetime subs; $3/ea by mail; $6/2 issues; $12/4 issues

16 pp; 11 x 17¼

Ad Rates: $150/page (10 x 17); $75/½ page (7½ x 9); $50/¼ page (9 x 5); $40, $30, $20 for smaller ads

HAMMERS

Nat David
1718 Sherman #203
Evanston, IL 60201
(708) 328-7555

Poetry.

An end of the millennium irregular poetry magazine.

Beatriz Badikian, John Dickson, Michael Warr, Luis Rodriquez, Albert Huffstickler.

Unsolicited Manuscripts Received/Published per Year: 1,000/100.

Payment: 1 free copy.

Reporting Time: 1–2 months.

1990; 2/yr; 500

$5/ea; 40%

7 x 8½

THE HAMPDEN-SYDNEY POETRY REVIEW

Tom O'Grady
P.O. Box 126
Hampden-Sydney, VA 23943
(804) 223-8209

Poetry.

A small, carefully-printed correspondence among poets which attempts to print the unknown with the known.

David Ignatow, Robert Pack, Pa-

tricia Goedicke, David Huddle, Lewis Turco.
Payment: in copies.
Copyright held by Tom O'Grady; reverts to author upon publication.
1975; 2/yr; 500
$5/yr ind; $5/yr, $12/3-yr inst; $5/ea; 1990 Anthology 328 pp. $12.95; 40%
60 pp; 5 x 9
No ads

HANGING LOOSE

Robert Hershon, Dick Lourie, Mark Pawlak, Ron Schreiber
231 Wyckoff Street
Brooklyn, NY 11217
(718) 643-9559
Poetry, fiction, translation, graphics/artwork.
Our interests continue to center on finding new writers and then staying with them, often to the point of book publication. (Book mss and artwork by invitation only.)
Paul Violi, Kimiko Hahn, Steven Schrader, Donna Brook, Gary Lenhart.
Payment: some payment to contributors.
Reporting Time: 2–3 months.
Copyright held by magazine; reverts to author upon publication.
1966; 3/yr; 1,500
$12.50/yr ind, $15/yr inst; $5/ea + $1.50 postage; 20%–40%
96 pp; 7 x 8½
ISSN: 0440-2316
Ubiquity, SPD, Fine Print, Book-People, Inland

HANSON'S SYMPOSIUM: Of Literary & Social Interest

Eric Hanson
113 Merryman Court
Annapolis, MD 21401
(410) 626-0744
Poetry, fiction, essays, humor, interviews, dialogues, and various features.
A magazine of general interest, we are striving to combine the traditionally separate aspects of literary and social journals into one magazine.
Unsolicited Manuscripts Received/Published per Year: 2,000/50.
Payment: $30–$100, plus 1 copy.
Reporting Time: 2 weeks.
Copyright held by Hanson Publishing, reverts to author.
1988; 2/yr; 1,500
$5/ea; 40%
80 pp; 8½ x 11
No ads

HAPPINESS HOLDING TANK

Albert Drake
9727 S.E. Reedway

Portland, OR 97266
(503) 771-6779

Poetry, very short fiction, essays, reviews, interviews, etc. . . .

HHT is an eclectic magazine, and publishes a wide variety of poetry—free verse, forms, narrative, lyric, found poetry, visual poetry, etc. . . . Emphasis is on the well-made poem that expresses a sense of humanity.

Earle Birney, Vern Rutsala, William Stafford, William Mathews, Judith Goren, Lee Upton.

Unsolicited Manuscripts Received/ Published per Year: 1,000+/100.

Payment: in copies.

Reporting Time: 2 weeks–2 months.

Copyright held by author.

1970; 1/yr; 300

$2/ea

pp and size varies

Have never had paid ads.

HAWAII REVIEW

Tamara Moan, Editor-in-Chief
UH Mānoa
Department of English
1733 Donaghho Rd.
Honolulu, HI 96822
(808) 956-8548

Poetry, fiction, criticism, essays, reviews, plays, translations, interviews, photographs, graphics/artwork.

Ursule Molinaro, Ian MacMillan, Nell Altizer, John Unterecker, Michael McPherson, William Pitt Root, Frank Stewart.

Unsolicited Manuscripts Received/ Published per Year: 1,000/100.

Payment: $10–75, plus 2 copies; more for cover art.

Reporting Time: 30–120 days.

Copyright held by magazine; reverts to author upon publication.

1973; 3/yr; 2,000

$15/yr; $5/ea

100–180 pp; 5½ x 9

Ad Rates: $100/page

ISSN: 0093-9625

HAYDEN'S FERRY REVIEW

Salima Keegan, Managing Editor
ASU Matthews Center
Tempe, AZ 85287-1502
(602) 965-1243

Poetry, fiction, nonfiction.

Nationally distributed magazine publishing quality literary art. **HFR** promotes work of emerging and established writers of fiction, poetry, and creative nonfiction.

David St. John, Ken Kesey, Maura Stanton, Raymond Carver, Norman Dubie, Rita Dove, Charles Wright, Jean Valentine, Naomi Shihab Nye, John Ashbery.

Unsolicited Manuscripts Received/ Published per Year: 6,000/60.
Reading Period: year–round.
Payment: copies.
Reporting Time: 3–5 months.
Copyright reverts to author.
1986; 2/yr; 1,000
$10/yr; $6/ea
128; 6 x 9
ISSN 0887-5170

THE HEARTLANDS TODAY

The Firelands Writing Center
Nancy Dunham & Larry Smith, Managing Editors
Firelands College,
Huron, Ohio 44839
(419) 433-5560

Photography, personal essays, fiction (4,000 wds), poems.
We feature a theme from the contemporary Midwest—The Heartlands Today—for each volume (annual). The writing must be set in the Midwest, though it need not treat the Midwest. We look for writing of character and place. Theme for 1994; community and what it means in the Midwest.
Gary Snyder, Scott R. Sanders, Carolyn Banks, Antler.
Unsolicited Manuscripts Received/ Published per Year: 400/40.
Reading Period: Jan.—June.
Payment: $10 and 2 copies.
Reporting Time: 2 months.
Copyright: we buy first rights (in some cases second), return rights to author.
1991; 1/yr; 850
$7.50/yr; $7.50/ea
160; 6 x 9
ISBN: 0-933087-25-X (Vol. 2)

HELLAS, A Journal of Poetry & the Humanities

Gerald Harnett
304 South Tyson Avenue
Glenside, PA 19038
(215) 884-1086

Poetry, classics, Renaissance & modern literary studies.
We provide a unique forum for the poetry, theory and criticism of poets working in meter–"The new formalism," or, as our advertising describes that movement, "The New Classicism."
Timothy Steele, Richard Moore, Joseph Malone, Frederick Turner, Dana Gioia.
Unsolicited Manuscripts Received/ Published per Year: 5,000 poems, 100 articles/60-70 poems, 20-25 articles.
Copyright: First North American serial rights only.
1990; 2/yr; 700
$14/yr, $24/2 yrs; $8.75/sample (p.p.) 40%
176 pp; 6 x 9

$175/page (4 x 7); $100/½ page (4 x 3½)
ISSN: 1044-5331
approx. 100 pp; 8½ x 11
BookPeople, Inland, Ingram, Small Changes, Marginal Distribution

HERESIES: A Feminist Publication on Art and Politics

Heresies Collective, Inc.
P.O. Box 1306
Canal Street Station
New York, NY 10013
(212) 227-2108

Essays, experimental writing, short fiction, interviews, poetry; page art, photography, graphic art, all visual arts.

HERESIES is the longest-lived feminist art journal still publishing. Thematic, political focus. "We believe that what is commonly called art can have a political impact and that in the making of art and all cultural artifacts our identities as women play a distinct role . . . A place where diversity can be articulated."

Unsolicited Manuscripts Received/Published per Year: 3,000/25–35.
Reading Period: year–round.
Payment: nominal.
Reporting Time: 8–12 months.
Copyright reverts to author upon publication.
1977; 1–2/yr; 8,000
Four issues - $27/ind, $38/inst; $8/ea

HIGH PLAINS LITERARY REVIEW

Robert O. Greer, Jr.
180 Adams St., Suite 250
Denver, CO 80206
(303) 320-6828

Fiction, essays, poetry, reviews, criticism, interviews.

Designed to bridge the gap between commercial magazines and an outstanding array of academic quarterlies. A handsomely produced literary magazine that is intended to be more broadly based than academia without being commercially "targeted." A journal designed to display the absolute best of craft. O. Henry award winning fiction appeared as early as Vol. 1, No. 1.

Richard Currey, Nancy Lord, Marilyn Krysl, Darrell Spencer, Tony Ardizzone, Julia Alvarez, Rita Dove.

Unsolicited Manuscripts Received/Published per Year: 4,000/85.
Payment: $5/page prose; $10/page poetry.
Reporting Time: 8 weeks.

Copyright held by magazine; reverts to author upon publicaton.
1986; 3/yr; 1,100
$20/yr; $7/ea; 40%
140 pp; 6 x 9
Ad Rates: $100/page; $50/½ page
ISSN: 0888-4153
DeBoer, Ubiquity, Fine Print

HIRAM POETRY REVIEW

Hale Chatfield and Carol Donley
Box 162
Hiram, OH 44234
(216) 569-5330

Poetry, criticism, essays, reviews, interviews. Photographs, graphics, and artwork by invitation only.
Unsolicited Manuscripts Received/Published per Year: 6,000/50.
Reporting Time: 8–16 weeks.
Copyright reverts to author upon publication.
1967; 2/yr; 500
$4/ea; 40%–60%
40 pp; 6 x 9
ISSN: 0018-2036

HOB-NOB

Mildred K. Henderson
994 Nissley Rd.
Lancaster, PA 17601
(717) 898-7807

Short fiction, nonfiction, poetry, reviews, letters, cartoons.
HOB-NOB is a small literary publication of 72+ pages with material from contributors from around the world, of all ages and levels. New contributors may submit during January & February only. Please send SASE for guidelines before submitting.
Fulbright scholar Sanford Pinsker, other college professors.
Payment: free copy on first appearance (at least). Small payment for cartoons & certain artwork.
Reporting Time: A few weeks, especially for rejections—maybe longer for acceptances (or return of material not sent during reading period). Waiting time until publication for new contributors: more than 2 years.
Copyright: Yes—first rights only—all rights revert to author or poet after that.
1969: 2/yr; 400+
$6/yr; $3.50/ea
72–76 pp; 8½ x 11
Ads are free to subscribers, exchangers, or purchasers of issue

THE HOLLINS CRITIC

John Rees Moore
P.O. Box 9538
Hollins College, VA 24020

(703) 362-6317 or 362-8268

Poetry, critical essays, reviews, graphics/artwork.

A non-specialist periodical concentrating on the work of a single contemporary poet, fiction writer or dramatist in each issue. Cover picture, essay of about 5,000 words, brief account of author, check-list of publications, several poems and a section of brief book reviews.

W. H. Mills, Jane Gentry, Elizabeth Murawski, Mark de Foe.

Payment: $200/essay (by permission of editor only); $25/poems.

Copyright held by magazine.

1964; 5/yr; 650

$6/yr; $2/ea—US

20 pp; 7 x 10

ISSN: 0018-3644

HOME PLANET NEWS

Donald Lev and Enid Dame, Editors

P.O. Box 415

Stuyvesant Station

New York, NY 10009

(718) 769-2854

Poetry, fiction, criticism, reviews, translation, interviews, photographs, news.

We publish poetry, reviews of books, art exhibits, theater, news of the literary and small press scene, interviews and fiction. Occasional pull-out section of single poet's work.

Cornelius Eady, Norman Rosten, Will Inman, William Packard, Antler, Lyn Lifshin, Paul Genega, Richard Kostelanetz.

Unsolicited Manuscripts Received/Published per Year: 320 (poetry)/60

Payment: in copies and subscription.

Reporting Time: 2–4 months.

Copyright held by magazine; reverts to author upon publication.

1979; 3–4/yr; 1,000

$8/yr ind, $8/yr inst, $15/2 yrs; $2/ea; 40%

24 pp; 10 x 15

Ad Rates: $150/page (10 x 15); $75/½ page (10 x 7½); $37.50/¼ page (5 x 7½)

DeBoer, Fine Print

HOPEWELL REVIEW

c/o Arts Indiana, Inc.

47 S. Pennsylvania, Suite 701

Indianapolis, IN 46204

(317) 632-7894

Poetry, short fiction, personal essay.

HOPEWELL REVIEW is an annual collection of poetry, short fiction and personal essays by Indiana writers.

Alice Friman, Susan Neville, Scott

Russell Sanders, Mari Adams, Yusef Komunyakaa.
Unsolicited Manuscripts Received/ Published per Year: 1,500/40.
Payment: $35/poem; $150/short fiction, personal essay. 3 $500 awards of excellence.
Copyright held by Arts Indiana, Inc., reverts to author upon publications.
1989; 1/yr; 8,000
$6.95/ea
128 pp
ISSN:1069-6636

HOWLING DOG

M. P. Donovan
8419 Rhode
Utica, MI 48317
(313) 254-5334
Poetry, fiction, graphics/artwork.
Our purpose is to have an effect similar to the howl of a dog with its foot caught in a fence. We desire something that may not be pleasant or permanent, but will still be heard by everyone in the neighborhood.
John Sinclair, M. L. Liebler, Hank Malone, Larry Goodell.
Unsolicited Manuscripts Received/ Published per Year: 5,000/100.
Payment: in copies.
Reporting Time: 6 months or more.
Copyright held by authors.
1985; 2/yr; 500
$10/yr; $5/ea; 40%
64 pp; 6 x 9
Ad Rates: $80/page (4 x 8); $40/½ page (4 x 4); $20/¼ page (2 x 4)
ISSN: 0888-3521

THE HUDSON REVIEW

Paula Deitz, Frederick Morgan
684 Park Ave.
New York, NY 10021
(212) 650-0020
Poetry, fiction, criticism, essays, reviews.
We publish both new and established writers. We have no university affiliation, and we are not committed to any narrow academic aim or to any particular political perspective. We focus on the area where literature and poetry bear on the intellectual life of the time.
Reading Period: nonfiction Oct. 1—Mar. 31; fiction June 1—Nov. 30; poetry Apr.—Sept. 30.
Payment: 2½¢/word for prose; 50¢/line for poetry.
Reporting Time: 1–3 months.
Copyright held only on assigned reviews.
1948; 4/yr; 4,500
$24/yr; $7/ea
160 pp; 6 x 9¼

Ad Rates: \$300/page (4½ x 7½); \$200/½ page (4½ x 3⅝); \$150/¼ page (2⅛ x 3⅝)
ISSN: 0018-702X
Eastern News

page; \$395/¼ page; \$235/⅛ page; \$145/1/16 page
ISSN: 0887-5499
We distribute free of charge to 400 independent bookstores across the U.S. and Canada.

HUNGRY MIND REVIEW

Bart Schneider, Editor
1648 Grand Ave.
St. Paul, MN 55105
(612) 699-2610

Essays, reviews, interviews, and photographs.

HUNGRY MIND REVIEW publishes book reviews, essays, and forums on particular focuses. **HUNGRY MIND REVIEW** reviews large, small, and university presses, focusing on mid- and backlist titles.

Robert Bly, Lewis Hyde, Herbert Kohl, Phillip Lopate, William Stafford, Bill McKibben, Gerald Early, Maxine Hong Kingston, Michael Dorris, Quentin Crisp.

Unsolicited Manuscripts Received/ Published per Year: 600/0.

Payment: varies.

Copyright held by David Unowsky, dba **HMR**.

1986; 4/yr; 30,000

\$10/yr ind; \$13/yr Canada and inst; free/ea

56 pp; 9¾ x 15

Ad Rates: \$1,350/page; \$750/½

HURRICANE ALICE: A Feminist Quarterly

Pat Cumbie, Carolyn Law
Lind Hall
207 Church Street, SE
Minneapolis, MN 55455
(612) 625-1834

Reviews, essays, criticism, fiction, poetry, graphics/artwork.

HURRICANE ALICE provides a feminist review of culture. It prints reviews of books by and about women, critical essays having a feminist perspective—especially essays on literature, film, dance, and the visual arts—fiction, some poetry and graphics.

Alice Walker, Toni McNaron, Peter Erickson, Meridel Le Sueur, Susan Griffin, Pearl Cleage, Beth Brant.

Unsolicited Manuscripts Received/ Published per Year: 750/60.

Reading Period: year–round.

Payment: in copies.

Reporting Time: 1–3 months.

Copyright reverts to author upon publication.

1983; 4/yr; 700
$12/yr; $10/yr students/seniors; $20/yr libraries; $2.50/ea
12–16 pp; 11 x 17
Ad Rates: $75/1/6 page; $45 (3 x 4); $20 (3 x 2)
Ubiquity, L-S Distributor, Olson, Fine Print

HYPHEN MAGAZINE/ Shoestring Press

Eduardo Cruz Eusebio, Editor-in-Chief; M. Lewis, D. Mead, Fiction; J. Boyer, M. Nelson, Poetry; D.S. Mclaughlin, Art.
3458 W. Devon Ave., Suite 6
Lincolnwood, IL 60659

Fiction, poetry, interviews, essays, graphics/artwork.

Chicago's magazine of the arts, publishing short stories, novel excerpts, poems, artwork, photography, art and lit. columns, and interviews with artists, performers, writers, poets, and others of interest to the arts community.

Larry Heinemann, Lisa-Buscani, K.M. Price, Leslie Peace Jubilee, Andrew Allegretti.

Payment: copies and sub.
Reporting Time: 4 months.
Copyright held by Shoestring Publications.
1991; 4/yr; 1,000
$12/yr ind and inst; $3.25/ea; 40%
72 pp; 8½ x 11
Ad Rates: $250/page (7¾ x 10¼); $130/½ page (7¾ x 4¾); $75/¼ page (3¾ x 4¾)
ISSN: 1058-3297
Desert Moon

I

IKON

Susan Sherman
P.O. Box 1355
Stuyvesant Station
New York, NY 10009

Poetry, fiction, essays, translation, interviews, photographs, graphics/artwork.

IKON is a cultural, political, feminist magazine, showing the experiences of third world, lesbian, Jewish and working women, all women in the diversity of our experience. **IKON** is about making connections through the words and images of women themselves in their essays, articles, paintings, photographs, fiction, art, songs and poems.

Audre Lourde, Kimiko Hahn, Beth Brant, Grace Paley, Adrienne Rich.

Payment: subscription and 2 copies.

Reporting Time: 90 days.

Copyright held by magazine; reverts to author upon publication.

1982; 2/yr; 1,750

$10/yr ind, $15/yr inst; $6/ea; 40%

140 pp; 7 x 9

THE ILLINOIS REVIEW (Formerly Illinois Writers Review)

Jim Elledge

4240/Department of English

Illinois State University

Normal, IL 61790-4240

(309) 438-7705

Creative writing of all genres, as well as essays and reviews.

The **ILLINOIS REVIEW** seeks poems, stories, novel excerpts, one act plays, translations, essays, and book reviews. Open to mainstream and alternative, to established and unknown, and to marginalized writers. Our only bias is excellence.

Reading Period: Aug. 1—May 31.

Payment: two copies and year's subscription.

Reporting Time: 1–2 months, SASE required.

Copyright reverts to author upon publication.

1993; 2/yr; 500

Individuals and Institutions may subscribe to the journal in one of two ways: as a member of Illinois Writers, Inc.: $15/yr ind, $20/yr inst; or to the journal itself: $10/yr ind, $15/yr inst; 40%

Ad Rates: $100/page (4½ x 7); $50/½ page (4½ x 4)

ISSN: 0733-9526

Illinois Literary Publishers' Association

IMAGINE: INTERNATIONAL CHICANO POETRY JOURNAL

Mr. Tino Villanueva, editor and publisher

89 Massachusetts Ave., Suite 270

Boston MA 02115

(617) 267-2592

Poetry, mostly; limited number of articles/interviews; book reviews & book notices.

Poetry in any language provided the original language text is accompanied by a English or Spanish translation. Any mode, no restrictions on form, subject or style.

Jimmy Santiago Baca, García Márquez, Gary Soto, Isabel Allende, Bernice Zamora, Frida Kahlo, Rudolfo Anaya, Luis Valdez, Luis Jiménez.

Payment: small fee plus two author's copies.

Reporting Time: 4–6 months.
Copyright reverts to authors, artist, or photographer upon publication.
1984; 2/yr; 1,000
$8/yr ind, $14/2 yr ind, $12/yr inst, $18/2 yr inst; $4.50/ea; newstand price; back issues vary count; 35%
75–99 pp; 6 x 9
ISSN: 0747-489X
SPD

INDIANA REVIEW

Gretchen Knapp, Cara Diaconoff
316 North Jordan Ave.
Indiana University
Bloomington, IN 47405
(812) 855-3439

Fiction, poetry, essays.
We have no prejudices of style or content, but will publish only those poems and short stories which demonstrate: 1) keen sense of craft; 2) insight into the human condition. Writers should send their best work only. We prefer stories of rich texture to those that depend on a gimmick.
Dean Young, Philip Levine, Ann Packer, David Michael Kaplan, Martin Espada, Amy Gerstler, Lane von Herzen, Ursula K. LeGuin, Charles Flowers.
Unsolicited Manuscripts Received per Year: 12,000 (poetry and fiction).
Payment: $5 per page.
Reporting Time: 3 weeks–3 months.
Copyright held by magazine; reverts to author upon publication.
1976; 2/yr; 1,200
$12/yr ind, $15/yr inst; $7/ea
200 pp; 6 x 9
Ad Rates: $150/page (6 x 9); $85/½ page (6 x 4½)
ISSN: 0738-386X
Ingram, DeBoer

THE INKSLINGER'S REVIEW

Mr. Michael W. Eliseuson
212 E. Marcy St.
Radio Plaza 10-C
Santa Fe, NM 87501
(505) 988-2099

Author interviews, book reviews, fiction, poetry.
Publishes the works of New Mexican authors and reviews books about New Mexico.
John Nichols, Larry Frank, Bob Woodford, Renee Gregorio.
Unsolicited Manuscripts Received/Published per Year: c. 200/c. 100.
Payment: contributor's copies.
Reporting Time: 3 months.
Copyright: one-time first & second serial rights.
1992; 6/yr; 1,000
$9/yr; $1.25/ea; 40%
16 pp; 11½ x 16½
Ad Rates: $25/5 x 5

INNISFREE/Softspin Press
Rex Winn, Arlene J. Pollack, Editors
P.O. Box 277
Manhattan Beach, CA 90266
(213) 772-5558; Fax (310) 546-5862
Fiction, poetry, essays, graphics/artwork.
INNISFREE is a home-grown, informal literary magazine of professional quality. All submissions of merit will be considered regardless of subject or theme. New and unpublished writers are welcome. We strive for the rediscovery of the age-old art of storytelling. We rarely publish longer fiction. We avoid political and religious sensationalism, as well as sentimental verse.
Unsolicited Manuscripts Received/Published per Year: 2,000/60.
Reading Period: Jan.—Sept.
Reporting Time: 2 months. Include SASE for response.
Copyright held by author.
1981; 4/yr; 500
$20/yr ind; $5/ea
46 pp; 8½ x 11

INTERIM
A. Wilber Stevens, Editor; John Heath–Stubbs, English Editor; George Bruce, Scottish Editor; Associate Editors: James Hazen, Joe McCullough, Timothy Erwin
Department of English
University of Nevada
Las Vegas, NV 89154
Poetry, fiction.
INTERIM prints the best poetry and short fiction we can find, plus occasional reviews. It is the revival, under its original editor, of the magazine published and edited in Seattle in 1944–55.
William Stafford, John Heath-Stubbs, X.J. Kennedy, Stephen Stepanchev, Gladys Swan.
Unsolicited Manuscripts Received/Published per Year: 3,000-3,400/60.
Reading Period: year–round.
Payment: contributor's copies plus a two-year subscription.
Copyright held by magazine; reverts to author upon publication.
1944; 2/yr; 750
$16/3 yrs; $8/yr; $14/yr inst; $5/ea; 40%
48–64 pp; 9 x 6
ISSN: 0888-2452

INTERNATIONAL POETRY REVIEW
Mark Smith-Soto
Dept. of Romance Lang.
UNC-Greensboro

Greensboro, NC 27412

Unpublished translation with contemporary original language poem. Contemporary English language poetry with international or cross cultural theme preferred, graphics.

Willis Barnstone, Charles Edward Eaton, William Stafford, Pureza Canelo, Ana Lstarú, Clara Janés.

Unsolicited Manuscripts Received/Published per Year: 1,200/100.

Payment: in copies.

1975; 2/yr; 400

$10 ind, $15 libraries; $5/ea; 40%

100 pp; 5½ x 8½

Ad Rates: $50/page; $25/½ page

INTERSTATE

Loris Essary, Mark Loeffler
P.O. Box 7068
University Station
Austin, TX 78713
(512) 928-2911

Poetry, fiction, criticism, essays, reviews, plays, translations, interviews, photographs, graphics/artwork; experimental art in all genres and non-genres.

INTERSTATE has a special focus on non-traditional, experimental writing and art, particularly visual literature, mixed media and work for theatre. There is a strong non-US content.

Charles Brownson, Robert Coover, Brian Eno, Karl Kempton, Dan Raphael.

Payment: in copies.

Reporting Time: immediately, occasionally longer.

Copyright reverts to author upon publication.

1974; 1/2 yrs; 500

$10/2 issues; 40%

92 pp

ISSN: 0363-9991

IN THE COMPANY OF POETS

Jacalyn Robinson
P.O. Box 10786
Oakland, CA 94610
(510) 568-2531

Poetry, short stories, essays, visual art.

E. Donald Two-Rivers, Selma Glasser, Patrick Fitch.

Unsolicited Manuscripts Received/Published per Year: Approx. 350/120.

Payment: 3 copies.

Reporting Time: 3-6 months.

Copyright: US & Int'l.

1991; 6/yr; 20,000

$16/yr

approx. 62 pp; 8 x 10

ISSN: 1055-0038

INVISIBLE CITY

John McBride, Paul Vangelisti
P.O. Box 2853

San Francisco, CA 94126
(415) 527-1018
Poetry, criticism, translation, graphics/artwork, visual poetry.
A book series, formerly tabloid, of poetry, translation, visuals and statements published whenever enough good material is available: focusing on current U.S. writing, some concrete poetry and Italian writing—focused on "the internal tension of language."
Adriano Spatola, Giulia Niccolai, Ernst Meister, John Thomas, Stanislaw Baranczak, Antonio Porta, Emilio Villa; and now DAYBOOK by Robert Crosson, with DIVISION appended, remarks, criticism & such.
Unsolicited Manuscripts Received/ Published per Year: 365/?.
Reading Period: year–round.
Payment: copies and then some.
Reporting Time: 2 months.
Copyright reverts to author upon publication.
1971; 1–2/yr; 1,000
$10/yr ind, $15/yr inst
80+ pp; 5 x 9
ISSN: 0034-2009

THE IOWA REVIEW

David Hamilton
308 EPB
University of Iowa
Iowa City, IA 52242
(319) 335-0462
Poetry, fiction, criticism, essays, reviews, interviews.
We look for new as well as established writers and are usually pleased, on the whole, with what we are able to publish.
Unsolicited Manuscripts Received/ Published per Year: 8,000/100.
Reading Period: Sept.—Apr.
Payment: $1/line for poetry; $10/page for prose.
Reporting Time: 2–3 months.
Copyright held by the University of Iowa; reverts to author upon publication.
1970; 3/yr; 1,500
$18/yr ind, $20/yr inst; $6.95/ea; 30%
200 pp; 6 x 9
Ad Rates: $150/page (5½ x 8½)
ISSN: 0021-065X
Ingram

IOWA WOMAN

Marianne Abel, Editor; Sandra Adelmund Witt, Poetry Editor
P.O. Box 680
Iowa City, IA 52244
(319) 987-2879
Fiction, essays, reviews, interviews, poetry, news briefs, features, ads, memoirs, graphics/artwork.

Rooted in the Midwest, **IOWA WOMAN** publishes award-winning women writers everywhere. National readership. Send SASE for annual writing contest guidelines.

Judy Ruiz, Enid Shomer, Ingrid Hill, Alice Friman, Natalie Kusz.

Unsolicited Manuscripts Received/Published per Year: 4,000+/80+.

Payment: $5/page, copies, ad discounts.

Reporting Time: 3 months.

Copyright held by magazine; reverts to author upon publication.

1980; 4/yr; 2,500

$18/yr, $24/yr Canada & Pan America; $30/yr other; $6/ea; 30%

48 pp; 8⅛ x 10⅞

ISSN: 0271-8227

irresistible impulse

Camille Blanchette
711 Belmont Pl. E., #201
Seattle, WA 98102-4451

Fiction, poetry, essays, humor, interviews, line art

Literary and art magazine. Focus: sharing human experiences, increasing communication and community, providing information about progressive issues, and entertaining. Multicultural, anti-discriminatory.

Unsolicited Manuscripts Received/Published per Year: 150/15

Reading Period: year–round.

Payment: copies.

Reporting Time: 2–3 weeks.

Copyright reverts to author/artist.

1982; 2/yr; 150

$8/yr; $4/ea; 40%

60 pp; 7 x 8½

Small Changes

THE ITHACA WOMEN'S ANTHOLOGY

Editorial Board; Rotating board of editors.

P.O. Box 582
Ithaca, NY 14851

Poetry, fiction, translation, photographs, graphics/artwork, criticism.

THE ITHACA WOMEN'S ANTHOLOGY was originally established as an annual collection of creative work, by, for and about women. The types of work we publish include essays, interviews, criticism, journal entries, translations, fiction, and poetry as well as graphics of all kinds. Our commitment is to provide a medium for women to creatively express their concerns, to coin varied and new voices, while emphasizing the highest in artistic quality.

Unsolicited Manuscripts Received/ Published per Year: 200/30+. From Tompkins and contiguous canties only.
Payment: copies.
Copyright held by magazine; reverts to author upon publication.
1976; 1/yr; 400
$4/ea; 40%

J

JACARANDA REVIEW

Katerine Swiggart
Department of English
2225 Rolfe Hall
University of California
Los Angeles, CA 90024
(213) 825-4173

Poetry, fiction, essays, reviews translation, interviews.
We try to publish the best fiction, poetry, and essays we can find. A potential contributor should read an issue or two to see what we mean by that. We feature in each issue an interview with a major writer and, usually, a supplement featuring work of special interest to us.
Jorge Luis Borges, Carolyn Forché, Allan Gurganus, Zbigniew Herbert, Billy Collins, Graig Raines.
Unsolicited Manuscripts Received/ Published per Year: hundreds/1%.
Payment: three copies.
Copyright held by University of California; reverts to author upon publication.
1985; 2/yr; 1,000
$10/yr ind, $14/yr inst; $6/ea; 40%
120 pp; 5½ x 8
Ad Rates: $75/page (5½ x 8); $50/½ page (5½ x 4); $25/¼ page (2¾ x 4)

JAMES WHITE REVIEW

P. Willkie, C. Mayhood, T. Carlson
P.O. Box 3356
Butler Quarter Station
Minneapolis, MN 55403
(612) 339-8317

Poetry, fiction, criticism, reviews, memoirs, photographs, graphics/artwork.
We are a gay men's literary quarterly.
David Feinberg, Essex Hemphill, Lev Raphael, Assotto Saint, Stan Leventhal.
Unsolicited Manuscripts Received/ Published per Year: 1,000/100.
Reading Period: after deadlines: Feb 1, May 1, Aug 1, Nov 1

Payment: $50/story, $10/poem.
Reporting Time: 6–8 weeks.
Copyright held by magazine; reverts to author upon publication.
1983; 4/yr; 4,500
$12/yr ind, $12/yr inst; $3/ea; 40%
20 pp; 11 x 15
Ad Rates: $400/page; $200/½ page; $120/¼ page

JEOPARDY

John Yuse, Editor; Matt Mathesius, Poetry Editor; Gretchen Lehman, layout
132 College Hall
Western Washington University
Bellingham, WA 98225
(206) 676-3118

Poetry, fiction, essays, art, criticisms.
Annie Dillard, Madeline De Frees, James Bertolino.
Unsolicited Manuscripts Received/Published per Year: 400-700/40.
Payment: Two copies.
Reporting Time: 2 weeks—4 months.
Copyright reverts to author.
1963; 1/yr; 4,000
$4/ea
100-120 pp; book–sized

JORDAN CREEK ANTHOLOGY

Jo Van Arkel
900 N. Benton
Springfield, MO 65802
(417) 865-8731

Fiction, poetry, interviews.
We publish short stories and poetry which are literary, contemporary, experimental, humorous, or regional, with an emphasis on the Midwest to the South. No genre or formula.
John Mort, Paul Ramsey, Debra Thornton, Wilma Yeo.
Unsolicited Manuscripts Received/Published per Year: 300/15–20.
Reding Period: Sept.—May.
Payment: copies.
Reporting Time: 6 weeks.
Copyright: first time rights.
1987; 1/yr; 500
$12/3 yr; $4/ea; $2/resale
80 pp

THE JOURNAL

Kathy Fagan, Poetry Editor; Michelle Herman, Fiction Editor
164 West 17th Ave.
Department of English
The Ohio State University
Columbus, OH 43210
(614) 292-4076

Poetry, fiction, reviews.
THE JOURNAL attempts to provide an outlet for good writing by Ohio writers and writers from around the country. We seek out good work and attempt to attract the best new writers.

The editorial staff works to publish and distribute poetry, fiction, nonfiction, and reviews, the sole criterion for which is excellence.

Maurya Simon, J. R. Hummer, Jonathan Holden, Eric Pankey, and Linda Bierds.

Reporting Time: 4–6 weeks.

Copyright held by Ohio State University.

1972; 2/yr; 1,100

$8/yr; $4.50/ea; 40%

80-100 pp; 6 x 9

ISSN: 1045-084X

JOURNAL OF NEW JERSEY POETS

Sander Zulauf, Editor; Associate Editors: North Peterson, Sara Pfaffenroth.

214 Center Grove Rd.

County College of Morris

Randolph, NJ 07869-2086

(201) 328-5471

Poetry by New Jersey poets, essays, occasional quotations.

A magazine dedicated to the best poetry written by poets who live in New Jersey or who have lived or worked here at some time.

Kenneth Burke, Grace Cavalieri, Lesley Choyce, Alfred Starr Hamilton.

Unsolicited Manuscripts Received/Published per Year: 800-1,000/75-100.

Payment: 2 copies/published poem.

Reporting Time: 6 months.

Copyright: County College of Morris.

1976; 2/yr; 500

$7/yr; $4/ea; 25%

48-64 pp; 5½ x 8½

ISSN: 0363-4205

DeBoer

JUST A MOMENT

Gertrude S. Eiler

P.O. Box 40

Jamesville, NY 13078

(315) 423-9268

Short stories, poetry.

Established to be a vehicle for writers of talent and ability whether previously published or not.

Edwidge Danticat (1st book due out April, 1994), L. E. McCullough, Bradley White, Ann T. Beacham, Edith C. Johnson.

Unsolicited Manuscripts Received/Published per Year: 500/Approx. 56

Payment: Choice of free subscription or 4 free copies of issue in which published + 20% discount on more copies of issue in which published.

Reporting Time: 1–3 months.
Copyright: One time copyright. Rights revert to author.
1990; 4/yr; 500
$18/yr; $5/ea; 40%
73–94 pp; 8½ x 5½

K

KALEIDOSCOPE: International Magazine of Literature, Fine Arts, and Disability

Darshan C. Perusek, Ph.D., Editor-in-Chief; Gail Willmott, Senior Editor
United Disability Services
326 Locust Street
Akron, OH 44302
(216) 762-9755

Poetry, photographs, graphics/artwork, fiction, essays, reviews.

KALEIDOSCOPE Magazine has a creative focus that examines the experience of disability through diverse forms of literature and the fine arts. Works should not use stereotyping, patronizing, or offending language about disability.

Oliver Sacks, Natalie Kusz, Nancy Mairs, Barbara Crooker, and Karen Fiser.

Unsolicited Manuscripts Received/Published per Year: 500/30.
Payment: $25–$100 fiction, up to $25 for body of poetry.
Reporting Time: Acknowledged within 2 weeks; up to 1 month of deadline for rejection or aceptance.
Copyright held by Kaleidoscope; reverts to author upon publication.
1979; 2/yr; 1,500
$9/yr, $17/2 yrs ind; $14/yr, $22/2 yrs inst; $4.50/ea; $4/sample copy (prepaid); 20%–50%
64 pp; 8½ x 11
ISSN: 0748-8742
Ubiquity, Fine Print

KALLIOPE: A Journal of Women's Art

Mary Sue Koeppel
Florida Community College
3939 Roosevelt Boulevard
Jacksonville, FL 32205
(904) 387-8211

Poetry, fiction, essays, reviews, interviews (3 annually), photographs, graphics/artwork.

The purpose of **KALLIOPE** is to offer support and encouragement to women in the arts. We are open to experimental forms of short fiction, poetry, prose and art as well as traditional formats. Editors like to see work that challenges the reader and addresses the complex relationships women have with each other, men, children and society.

Marge Piercy, Elisavietta Ritchie, Edith Perlman, Lola Haskins, Colette Inez, Louise Fishman, Colette.

Unsolicited Manuscripts Received/ Published per Year: 1,000/100.

Reading Period: Sept.—May.

Payment: 3 copies or 1 yr subscription to writers and artists.

Reporting Time: 2–3 months.

Copyright held by magazine; reverts to author upon request.

1978; 3/yr; 1,250

$10.50/yr ind, $18/yr inst; $7/ea last issues; $4/ea early issues; 40%

80 pp; 7¼ x 8½

No ads

ISSN: 0735-7885

Ingram

KANSAS QUARTERLY

Ben Nyberg, John Rees, G. W. Clift, Robt. Grindell
Kansas State University
Manhattan, KS 66506-0703
(913) 532-6716

Poetry, fiction, criticism, translation, interviews, photographs, graphics/artwork.

A cultural arts and literary magazine emphasizing but not restricted to the culture, history, art and writing of Mid-America but with international interests.

David Kirby, John Bovey, Stephen Dixon, Jonathan Holden, Peter LaSalle, Susan Fromberg Schaeffer, Jerry Bumpus, Lex Williford, Annabel Thomas.

Unsolicited Manuscripts Received/ Published per year: 5,000/180.

Reading Period: year–round.

Payment: 2 copies and two series of annual awards.

Reporting Time: 2–6 months.

Copyright held by magazine; reverts to author upon request.

1968; 4/yr; 1,500

$20/yr; $6/ea; 10%–40%

152+ pp; 6 x 9

Ad Rates: $100/page (4½ x 7½); $60/½ page (4½ x 3¾); $35/¼ page (2¼ x 3¾)

ISSN: 0022-8745

KARAMU

Peggy L. Brayfield
Department of English
Eastern Illinois University
Charleston, IL 61920
(217) 581-5614

Poetry, short fiction, creative non-fiction prose, black and white graphics.

Quality writing for a literate audience who enjoy fiction, poetry, and other creative pieces.

Emilio DeGrazia, Ellen Winter, Mary McDaniel, Karen Subach, Jefferson Humphries.

Unsolicited Manuscripts Received/ Published per Year: Approx. 150 stories, 1,400 poems/approx. 6-7 stories, 30-35 poems.

Payment: 1 copy of issue containing work, extras at reduced price.

Reporting Time: 2-3 months, longer if work is under serious consideration.

Copyright: First serial rights.

1966; 1/yr; 400

$5/yr; $4/sample copy, $5/2 sample copies

128 pp; 5 x 8

Ad Rates: inquire

ISSN: 0022-8990

THE KENYON REVIEW

Marilyn Hacker, Editor; Cy Wainscott, Managing Editor; David Baker, Carole Maso, Eleanor Benden, Consulting Editors
Kenyon College
Gambier, OH 43022
(614) 427-3339

Poetry, fiction, essays, reviews, interviews, plays, translations, memoirs.

THE KENYON REVIEW seeks excellent writing more than any particular kind or style. We seek to present a balanced diversity of perspective/orientation. We invite offers to review books and proposals for interviews. First publication rights required. No multiple submissions read. We discourage submissions from writers who have not read a recent issue.

Hayden Carruth, Toi Derricote, Kate Braverman, Adrienne Rich, Herbert Blau, Rafael Campo, Ursula K. LeGuin.

Unsolicited Manuscripts Received/ Published per Year: 5,000/60.

Reading Period: Sept.—Mar.

Payment: $10/page, prose; $15/page, poetry and reviews; $12.50/page, drama; $10(translator) $5 (author)/page, translations.

Reporting Time: 3 months.

Copyright reverts to author.

1939; 4/yr; 5,000

$22/yr ind, $24/yr inst; $7.00/ea; 25%

200 pp; 7 x 10

Ad Rates: $285/page (4⅜ x 8); $175/½ page (4⅜ x 3⅞); exchanges considered

ISSN: 0163-075X

Inland, Ingram, Fine Print, DeBoer, Ubiquity

KIOSK

Mary Obropta, Editor-in-Chief; Robert Rebein, Fiction Editor; A. M. Allcott, Poetry Editor
English Department
302 Clements Hall
SUNY at Buffalo
Buffalo, NY 14226
(716) 636-2575

Poetry, fiction, experimental prose.

KIOSK welcomes submissions of creative prose and poetry. We are interested in originality and craftsmanship. We subscribe to no orthodoxy; quality is our top concern.

Recent issues have included Carol Berge, Charles Bernstein, Raymond Federman. Especially interested in new writers.

Unsolicited Manuscripts Received/Published per Year: 800/25-35.

Reading Period: Sept.—Apr.

Payment: 2 copies.

Author retains all rights.

1986; 1-2/yr; 500

Guidelines with #10 SASE; sample issue with large SASE and 6 1st class stamps, if available.

130 pp; 5½ x 8½

No ads

KUMQUAT MERINGUE

Christian Nelson
P.O. Box 5144
Rockford, IL 61125
(815) 968-0713

Poetry and very short prose.

Dedicated to the memory of Richard Brautigan.

Gina Bergamino, Antler, Lynne Douglass, Ianthe Brautigan.

Unsolicited Manuscripts Received/Published per Year: Thousands/130-180.

Payment: copies.

Reporting Time: 6 to 8 weeks.

1991; 3/yr; 500

$4/ea

32-40 pp; digest

L

LACTUCA

Michael Selender
P.O. Box 621
Suffern, NY 10901-0621

Poetry, fiction, black and white art.

Our bias is toward work with a strong sense of place or experience. Writing with an honest emotional depth and writing that is dark or disturbing are preferred over safer material. Work with a quiet dignity is also desired. Subject matter is wide open and work can be rural or urban in character. We don't like poems that use the poem, the word, or the page as images or writing about being a poet/writer (though work about dead poets/writers is o.k.).

Sherman Alexie, Charles Bukowski, Joe Cardillo, Adrian C. Louis, Sheryl Nelms.

Unsolicited Manuscripts Received/Published per Year: 2,000+/120.

Reading Period: year–round, but Nov.—Feb. is best.

Payment: in copies.

Copyright held by magazine; reverts to author upon publication.

1986; 2–3/yr; 750

$10/3 issues, $17/6 issues; $4/ea; 40% bookstores, 60% distributors

72 pp; 7 x 8½

No ads

LANGUAGE BRIDGES QUARTERLY

Eva Ziem
P.O. Box 850792
Richardson, TX 75085
(214) 530-2363

Poetry, fiction, criticism, essays, reviews, plays, translations, photographs, artwork.

LBQ is the only fully bilingual Polish-English literary magazine in the USA. All texts are printed in Polish with English translation or vice-versa. **LBQ** creates, by presenting American writers as well, a bridge between Polish and American writers, as well as readers for cross cultural dialogue.

Prof. Danuta Mostwin, Prof. Lisowski, Prof. Ewa Thompson, Valeriu Butulescu.

Unsolicited Manuscripts Received/Published per Year: 50/25.

Reporting Time: 2-3 weeks.

Copyright held by magazine.

1988; 4/yr; 250

$20/yr ind; $6/ea

24 pp; 8 x 11 ½

Ad Rates: $100/page; $50/½ page; $25/¼ page

ISSN: 1053-9913

LATIN AMERICAN LITERARY REVIEW

Yvette E. Miller
121 Edgewood Ave., 1st Flr.
Pittsburgh, PA 15218
(412) 371-9023; Fax (412) 371-9025

Criticism, essays, interviews, reviews. We now publish articles in Spanish and Portugese in addition to English.

The Journal in English devoted to the literatures of Latin America.

Payment: varies.

Reporting Time: 3 months.

Copyright held by magazine.

1972; 2/yr + special double issue; 1,200
$20/yr ind, $35/yr inst; $36/yr foreign; $16/ea; 10%
150 pp; 250 pp special issue; 6 x 9
Ad Rates: $215/page (4½ x 7½); $140/½ page (4½ x 3¾); $95/¼ page (4½ x 2¼)
ISSN: 0047-4134
Ebsco, Faxon, Turner

THE LAUREL REVIEW
Craig Goad, David Slater, William Trowbridge
GreenTower Press
Department of English
Northwest Missouri State University
Maryville, MO 64468
(816) 562-1265
Poetry, fiction.
THE LAUREL REVIEW is national in scope and prints the best work received, regardless of style or author's reputation.
Stephen Dunn, Sydney Lea, Katherine Soniat, Carol Bly, Albert Goldbarth.
Unsolicited Manuscripts Received/Published per Year: 3,000/70.
Reading Period: Sept.—May.
Payment: 2 copies and subscription.
Reporting Time: 1 week–4 months.
Copyright held by GreenTower Press; reverts to author upon request.
1960; 2/yr; 800
$8/yr, $14/2 yrs; $5/ea; 40%
124 pp; 6 x 9
Ad Rates: $80/page (6 x 9); $50/½ page (6 x 4½); exchange also
ISSN: 0023-9003

THE LEDGE POETRY & FICTION MAGAZINE
Timothy Monaghan, Editor
64-65 Cooper Ave.
Glendale, NY 11385-6150
Poetry and fiction.
THE LEDGE seeks high-quality poetry and fiction that is gritty, arresting and/or provocative in nature, though we will publish a great poem or story even if it doesn't meet these criteria.
Robert Cooperman, Evan Zimroth, lyn lifshin, Arthur Winfield Knight.
Unsolicited Manuscripts Received/Published per Year: 1,100/50.
Reading Period: year–round.
Payment: 1 copy.
Reporting Time: 6–8 weeks; longer if under serious consideration.
Copyright reverts to author.
1988; 2/yr; 600
$9/yr, $15/2 yr; 40%

80 pp; 5 ½ x 8 ¾
$55/page; $35/½ page
ISSN: 1046-2724

LEFT BANK

Linny Stovall, Editor; Stephen I. Beard, Associate Editor
Blue Heron Publishing
24450 NW Hansen Rd.
Hillsboro, OR 97124
(503) 621-3911

Essays mostly—also art, short stories, poems, photos.

A thematic showcase for Northwest writers on Contemporary issues such as "Extinction," "Sex, Family, Tribe," "Gotta Earn a Living." Includes Literary as well as science writers.

Ursula LeGuin, Barry Lopez, William Stafford, Matt Groening.

Unsolicited Manuscripts Received/Published per Year: 350–500/50–60.

Reading Period: Feb.—Mar., Aug.—Sept.

Payment: $50–$150.

Reporting Time: 8–10 weeks.

Copyright: yes.

1991; 2/yr; 5,000+
$16/yr; $9.95/ea
160pp; 6 x 9
Ad Rates: $300/page (4 x 7); $175/½ page (4 x 3¼)
ISSN: 1056-7429
Consortium, Baker & Taylor, Ingram

LIGHT QUARTERLY

Box 7500
Chicago, IL 60680

Light verse (metrical and non-metrical) satire, humor, cartoons and line drawings.

LIGHT QUARTERLY is the only publication in the United States devoted exclusively to light verse and satire.

John Updike, Donald Hall, X. J. Kennedy, William Matthews, Gavin Ewart, William Stafford, W. D. Snodgrass.

Unsolicited Manuscripts Received/Published per Year: 1,000/2,500.

Payment: 2 copies of issue they appear in; 1 copy for foreign contributors.

Reporting Time: 1–3 months.

1992; 4/yr; 1,200
$12/yr; $4/ea; $3/back issue; 40%
32 pp; 8½ x 11
Write for ad rates.
ISSN: 1064-8186
Ubiquity

LILLIPUT REVIEW

Don Wentworth
207 S. Millvale Ave., #3
Pittsburgh, PA 15224

Poetry

Short poems, ten lines or less.
David Chorlton, Vogn, Steven Doering, Sheila E. Murphy.
Unsolicited Manuscripts Received/Published per Year: 1,100/5% of *all* received
Reading Period: year–round.
Payment: 2 copies of issue in which work appears.
Reporting Time: 4–8 weeks.
Copyright: Magazine uses first rights, reverting back to author upon publication.
1989; 12/yr; 200-250
$5/6; $1 ea. or SASE; 50%
16 pp; 4½ x 3⅝ or 3½ x 4¼

LINDEN LANE MAGAZINE
Heberto Padilla, Belkis Cuza Malé
P.O. Box 2384
Princeton, NJ 08543-2384
(609) 921-7943
Latino-American and American literature and art.
Devoted to promote professional and new talents, both writers and artists. Publish in original language, Spanish and English. No translations.
Severo Sarduy, Alastair Reid, Guillermo Cabrera Infante, Alexander Coleman, Elena Castedo.
Unsolicited Manuscripts Received/Published per Year: 2,000/80.
Payment: copies.
1982; 4/yr; 10,000
$22/yr
28-32 pp; 15 x 10
Ad Rates: $500/page; $250/½ page; $150/¼ page; $100/⅛ page
ISSN: 0736-1084

LIPS
Laura Boss
P.O. Box 1345
Montclair, NJ 07042
(201) 662-1303
Poetry.
LIPS publishes the best contemporary poetry submitted. No biases.
Michael Benedikt, Gregory Corso, Maria Gillan, Allen Ginsberg, Robert Phillips, Marge Piercy, Ishmael Reed.
Payment: in copies.
Reporting Time: 1 month.
Copyright held by magazine; reverts to author upon publication.
1981; 2/yr; 1,000
$10/yr ind, $13/yr inst; $5/ea; 40%
88 pp; 5½ x 8½
ISSN: 0278-0933
Anton Mikofsky

THE LITERARY CENTER QUARTERLY
Ken Smith, Scott Davidson, Neile Graham, Jim Gurley

P.O. Box 85116
Seattle, WA 98145
(206) 547-2503

Reviews, essays, poetry, interviews.

We are a small quarterly hoping to offer a voice for North West writers of all genres.

John Marshall, K. C. Brown, Joseph H. Hudson.

Copyright reverts to authors.

4/yr; 2,000

$15/yr

16–32 pp; 8½ x 11

Write for ad rates and sizes

LITERARY MAGAZINE REVIEW

G. W. Clift, J. E. Roper
Department of English
Kansas State University
Manhattan, KS 66506
(913) 532-6716

Reviews and essays concerning literary magazines.

LITERARY MAGAZINE REVIEW is devoted almost exclusively to objective reviews of the specific contents of issues of magazines which publish at least some short fiction or poetry.

David Kirby, Ben Nyberg, J. B. Hall.

Unsolicited Manuscripts Received/ Published per year: 29/0.

Reading Period: year–round.

Payment: copies.

Reporting Time: queries only, please.

Copyright reverts to author upon publication.

1982; 4/yr; 600+

$12.50/yr; $4/ea; 40%

60 pp; 8½ x 5½

No ads

ISSN: 0732-6637

THE LITERARY REVIEW

Walter Cummins, Editor-in-Chief; Martin Green, Harry Keyishian, William Zander, Editors; Jill Menkes Kushner, Managing Editor
Fairleigh Dickinson University
285 Madison Avenue
Madison, NJ 07940
(201) 593-8564 443-8564

Poetry, fiction, criticism, essays, reviews, translation, interviews, graphics/artwork.

New writing in English and translation. We're looking for a unique blend of craft and insight.

Susan Moon, Tom Hansen, Jane Bradley, T. Alan Broughton.

Unsolicited Manuscripts Received/ Published per Year: 3,500/200.

Reading Period: year–round.

Payment: 2 copies.

Reporting Time: 8–12 weeks.

Copyright held by Fairleigh Dickinson University; reverts to author upon publication.
1957; 4/yr; 2,000
$18/yr; $5/ea; 40%
128 pp; 6 x 9
Exchange ads
ISSN: 0024-4589

LITERATI INTERNATIONALE Original Chicago Blues Annual

L. McGraw Beauchamp, A. C. McGraw-Beauchamp
1133 N. Damen Ave.
Chicago, IL 60622
(312) 862-1313

LITERATI is multi-arts/cultural, featuring: fine art, reproductions, photos, poems and essays. The original Chicago Blues Annual is the same as above with an additional slant toward African American lyrical and musical contribution.

Quincy Troupe, E. B. Rodmund, Henry Miller.
Unsolicited Manuscripts Received/Published per year: 50/3.
Payment: varies.
Reporting Time: 12 weeks before publication.
Copyright reverts to author.
1988; 2/yr; 6,500–25,000
Literati $10/ea; Blues Annual $5/ea; 40%
112 pp; Blues Annual, 8½ x 11; Literati, 6½ x 9½
Ad Rates: please call.
ISBN: (Blues Annual) 0-944802-05-3
ISSN: (Literati) 1054-9404
Ingram

LONG NEWS: In the Short Century

Barbara Henning, Art Editor; Miranda Maher, Contributing Editors: Don David, Lewis Warsh, Paul Buck, Chris Tysh, Michael Pelias
P.O. Box 150-455
Brooklyn, NY 11215
(718) 965-1873

Writing, art, poetry, experimental prose.

LONG NEWS: in the Short Century aims to publish experimental work that challenges the basic tenets of realism and expressionism.

Nicole Brossard, Fanny Howe, Sadeq Muhammad, Lorenzo Thomas.
Unsolicited Manuscripts Received/Published per year: 100/2.
Reporting Time: 60 days.
Copyright reverts to author after publication.
1991; 1/yr; 1,000
$12/2 issues, $22/4 issues; $6/ea; 40%

185 pp; 5 x 8½
CPAD: 74470-80899
DeBoer, SPD, Fine Print, Spectacular Diseases, (UK)

LONG POND REVIEW

Russell Steinke, William O'Brien, Anthony Di Franco
Suffolk Community College
533 College Rd.
Selden, NY 11784
(516) 451-4153

Poetry, fiction, essays, reviews, interviews, photographs, graphics/artwork.

LONG POND REVIEW publishes the finest work submitted by established, emergent, and beginning writers. **LPR** has been recognized as an outstanding small press in **The Pushcart Prize II** (1977–78), **IV** (1979–80), **V** (1980–81), **VI** (1981–82), **VII** (1982–83), and **IX** (1984–85).

Fred Chappell, David Citino, Colette Inez, Linda Pastan, Jim Barnes, William Stafford, Michael Blumenthal.

Payment: 1 contributor's copy.
Reporting Time: 2–6 months.
Copyright held by author.
1975; 1/yr; 500
$3/ea ind, $5/ea inst
72–88 pp; 6 x 9
Ad Rates: $75/page; $40/½ page

LONG SHOT

Jack Wiler, Nancy Mercado, Tom Pulhamus, Danny Shot, Jessica Chosid
P.O. Box 6238
Hoboken, NJ 07030

Poetry, fiction, photographs, graphics/artwork.

"Writing From The Real World."

Charles Bukowski, Allen Ginsberg, Amiri Baraka, June Jordan, Tom Waits, Miguel Algarin.

Unsolicited Manuscripts Received/Published per Year: 3,000/20.
Payment: in copies.
Reporting Time: 8–12 weeks.
Copyright held by magazine; reverts to author upon publication.
1982; 2/yr; 1,500
$20/2 yrs; $6/ea; 40%
144 pp; 5½ x 8½
Ad Rates: $150/page (5 x 8½); $90/½ page (5 x 4¼)
ISSN: 0895-9773
DeBoer, Ubiquity, Fine Print, Desert Moon, Inland

THE LONG STORY

R. Peter Burnham
18 Eaton St.
Lawrence, MA 01843
(508) 686-7638

Fiction.

We are interested strictly in long stories (8,000–20,000 words, or

roughly 20–50 pages)—bias is left wing and concern for human struggle for dignity etc., but quality is the main criterion.
Unsolicited Manuscripts Received/Published per Year: 400/6-7.
Reading Period: year–round.
Payment: 2 copies.
Reporting Time: 2 weeks–2 months.
Copyright held by magazine; reverts to author upon publication.
1983; 1/yr; 900
$5/yr; $5/ea; 40%
160–200 pp; 5½ x 8½
ISSN: 0741-4242
Ingram

LOOK QUICK

Joel Scherzer, Robbie Rubinstein
P.O. Box 222
Pubelo, CO 81002
Poetry, fiction, reviews, photographs.
Emphasis is on free verse, blues lyrics and brief vignettes. We have also published material relating to the Beats. Not reading unsolicited manuscripts.
Payment: in copies.
Copyright held by Quick Books; reverts to author upon publication.
1975; irreg; 200
$3/ea
24–32 pp; 5½ x 8½

LOONFEATHER: A Magazine of Poetry, Short Prose & Graphics

Betty Rossi, Marsh Muirhead, Elmo Heggie
426 Bemidji Avenue
Bemidji, MN 56601
(218) 751-4869
Poetry, Fiction, Graphics.
LOONFEATHER is primarily but not exclusively a regional literary magazine publishing the works of both emerging and established writers. Our purpose is to promote good writing and encourage emerging artists by publishing their work; sponsoring readings, workshops, and exhibits; and supporting fellow artists/writers/organizations. Our regional focus is northern Minnesota, Minnesota, and the surrounding states and Canada.
Lequita–Vance Watkins, Mary Kay Rummel, Wayne Nelsen, Robert Johnson, Marilyn Roe.
Unsolicited Manuscripts Received/Published per Year: 200/65.
Reporting Time: Within four months following deadline for submissions.
Copyright held by magazine, reverts to author upon publication.
1979; 2/yr; 200–250
$7.50/yr; $4/ea; 40%
48 pp; 6 x 9

Ad Rates: $360/page; $180/½ page; $45/¼ page
ISSN: 0734-0699

LOST AND FOUND TIMES

John M. Bennett
137 Leland Ave.
Columbus, OH 43214
(614) 846-4126

Avant-garde, experimental, visual, language, collaborative, and other beyond the pale literature. Also graphics.

More poetry than prose. Any language; emphasizing English and Spanish.

Susan Smith Nash, Al Ackerman, N. Vassilakis, S. Murphy, Jake Berry.

Unsolicited Manuscripts Received/ Published per Year: many/few
Payment: 1 copy.
Reporting Time: immediate.
Copyright retained by authors and artists.
1975; 2/yr; 350
$20/5; $5/ea; 40%
Approx. 56 pp; 8½ x 5½
Small Press Traffic, Printed Matter

LOUISIANA LITERATURE: Literature/Humanities Review

David Hanson, Editor; William Parrill, Norman German, Associate Editors
SLU 792
Southeastern Louisiana University
Hammond, LA 70402
(504) 549-5022

Poetry, fiction, reviews of Louisiana-related books, articles on LA writing and culture.

We are interested in publishing essays and photo articles on Louisiana writing, history or art, but nothing full of jargon. Creative work we will take from anywhere on any topic.

Lewis P. Simpson, Diane Wakoski, Shirley Ann Grau, Kelly Cherry, Louis Gallo.

Unsolicited Manuscripts Received/ Published per Year: 1,500/40.
Reading Period: Sept.—May.
Payment: in copies.
Reporting Time: 1 month.
Copyright held by author.
1984; 2/yr; 650
$10/yr; $5/ea; 40%
100 pp; 6½ x 9½
Query for ad rates
ISSN: 0890-0477

LUZ EN ARTE Y LITERATURA

Veronica Miranda
P.O. Box 571062
Tarzana, CA 91357-1062
(818) 907-1454

Poetry, short stories, translations, art, etc.

LUZ is an international bilingual (Spanish/English) magazine featured mainly creative writing but also articles and interviews of writers and artists.

Laureano Albán, Rima de Vallbona, Ana Rossetti.

Unsolicited Manuscripts Received/Published per Year: 100/20

Payment: 1 copy.

Reporting Time: 3 weeks–1 months.

Copyright reverts to authors after publication.

1992; 2/yr; 500

$25/yr; $14/ea; 50%

100 pp; 8½ x 5½

Ad Rates: $400/page; $200/½ page; $100/¼ page

ISSN: 1067-0084

LYNX

Jane Reichhold, Editor
P.O. Box 1250
Gualala, CA 95445
(707) 882-2226; Fax: (707) 884-1235

Renga, tanka, criticism, essays, reviews, translation, interviews, black and white graphics, features.

LYNX is for linking poets and is the only magazine dedicated to renga and tanka. Renga (linked verse) was an outgrowth of tanka, the oldest poetry form still active in Japan, and has now invaded and captured North America.

Marlene Mountain, Hiroaki Sato, Anne McKay, Lorraine Ellis Harr, David Rice.

Unsolicited Manuscripts Received/Published per Year: 400/120

Payment: copies and/or subscriptions.

Reporting Time: 2–3 months.

Copyright reverts to contributors.

1987; 3/yr; 300

$15/yr

74 pp; 4¼ x 11

ISSN: 1049-4502

LYRA

Lourdes Gil, Iraida Iturralde
P.O. Box 3188
Guttenberg, NJ 07093
(201) 861-1941 or (201) 869-2558

Poetry, fiction, criticism, interviews, essays, photographs, graphics/artwork.

We publish in English, French, Spanish, Italian, as we are committed to raising the level of communication among contemporary writers and artists in North America and other parts of the world.

Mario Benedetti, Elizabeth Macklin, Virgilio Piñera, Alan West, Tom Whalen.

Payment: in copies.

Copyright held by magazine; reverts to author upon publication.
1987; 4/yr; 700
$15/yr ind, $18/yr inst; $4/ea; 40%
32 pp; 8½ x 11
Ad Rates: $200/page; $125/½ page; $70/¼ page. Also, on exchange.
ISSN: 0897-6716
Faxon, Slusa, Giralt

THE LYRIC

Leslie Mellichamp
307 Dunton Drive SW
Blacksburg, VA 24060
(703) 552-3475

Poetry.
We use rhymed verse in traditional forms, for the most part, about 36 lines max. We print only poetry, no opinions, no reviews. Our themes are varied, ranging from religious ectasy to humor to raw grief, but we feel no compulsion to shock, embitter, or confound our readers.
John Robert Quinn, Barbara Loots, R.L. Cook, R.H. Morrison, Neill Megaw, Paul Ramsey, Alfred Dorn, Rhina P. Espaillat.
Unsolicited Manuscripts Received/Published per Year: 2,500/200.
$800 in prizes annually.
$10/yr; $3/ea

M

THE MACGUFFIN

Arthur J. Lindenberg
Schoolcraft College
18600 Haggerty Road
Livonia, MI 48152-2696
(313) 462-4400 ext 5292

Poetry, fiction, essays, photographs, graphics/artwork.
We publish poetry, fiction, and essays of the highest quality. We have no biases with regard to style, but we are committed to seeking excellence. Prose submissions should be less than 4,000 words.
Joe Schall, Tom Sheehan, Wendy Bishop, Jim Daniels, Carol Morris.
Unsolicited Manuscripts Received/Published per Year: 1,200/80.
Reading Period: Aug.—May.
Payment: 2 copies.
Reporting Time: 12 weeks.
Copyright held by Schoolcraft College; reverts to author upon publication.
1984; 3/yr; 500
$12/yr ind, $10/yr inst; $4.50/ea; 40%
144 pp; 5½ x 8½
No ads

MAGAZINE OF SPECULATIVE POETRY

Mark Rich and Roger Dutcher
P.O. Box 564
Beloit, WI 53512

Poetry, reviews, and commentary on poetry.

Speculative poetry is the equivalent to speculative fiction, that confluence of post-modernism and science fiction in the sixties and seventies of the US and UK.

Brian Aldiss, David Memmott, Jane Yolen, Steve Rasnic Tem, Robert Frazier.

Unsolicited Manuscripts Received/Published per Year: 300-400/40.

Payment: 3¢/word; min. $3.00/poem.

Reporting Time: 1–8 weeks.

Copyright: First North American Serial Rights purchased, all rights revert to author.

1984; 4/yr; 200

$11/yr; $3.50/ea

22 pp; 5½ x 8½

ISBN: 8755-8785

THE MALAHAT REVIEW

Derk Wynand, Associate Editor, Marlene Cookshaw
Box 1700
University of Victoria
Victoria, British Columbia, CANADA V8W2Y2
(604) 721-8524

Fiction, poetry.

A "generalist" literary magazine, open to new and celebrated writers. Meticulously edited, eclectic and elegant.

Tim Findley, Michael Ondaatje, Diane Williams.

Unsolicited Manuscripts Received/Published per Year: 1,200/60.

Payment: $20 per magazine page.

Reporting Time: 3 months.

Copyright reverts to author; we buy first rights in English.

1967; 4/yr; 2,000

$20/yr (US); $7/ea (US)

132 pp; 6 x 9

ISSN: 0025-1216

Director

MANHATTAN POETRY REVIEW

Elaine Reiman-Fenton, Editor
FDR Box 8207
New York, NY 10150
(212) 355-6634

Poetry.

MANHATTAN POETRY REVIEW is dedicated to a celebration of excellence in contemporary American poetry, welcomes unsolicited manuscripts, and presents a balance of new and established poets in each issue. It was founded as a community of poets and readers

to demonstrate the diversity of fine poetry in America today.
Unsolicited Manuscripts Received/ Published per Year: 1,200/50.
Reading Period: Sept.—Nov., Jan.—July.
Payment: none.
Reporting Time: 12–16 weeks.
Copyright reverts to author.
1992; $7.50 per issue, no subscriptions (foreign = U.S. $12.50)
52–60 pp; 5½ x 8½
ISSN: 885-9205

THE MANHATTAN REVIEW

Philip Fried
440 Riverside Dr., #45
New York, NY 10027
(212) 932-1854

Poetry, interviews, photographs, reviews.
We try to include American and foreign writers, and we focus on foreign writers with something to offer the current American scene. We like to think of poetry as a powerful discipline engaged with many other fields.
Peter Redgrove, Edmond Jabès, Christopher Bursk, A.R. Ammons, Stanislaw Baranczak, Bei Dao, Duoduo, Adam Zagajewski.
Unsolicited Manuscripts Received/ Published per Year: 400/1-4.
Payment: none.
Reporting Time: 8–10 weeks.
Copyright held by Philip Fried.
1980; 1/yr; 500
$10/ind. per volume (two issues); $14/inst. (2 issues)
64 pp
ISSN: 0275-6889

MANNA

Roger A. Ball, Brad Cutler, Rebecca Bradley
2966 West Westcove Dr.
West Valley City, UT 84119-5940

Short poetry with concise imagery.
Poetry magazine for beginning and intermediate poets publishing shorter poetry with clean imagery, strong content and quality writing. Accepts some rhyme, prefers free verse.
Patricia Higginbotham, Lyn Lifshin, Michael Estabrook, Albert Huffstickler.
Unsolicited Manuscripts Received/ Published per Year: 500+/200+.
Reading Period: year–round.
Reporting Time: under 3 weeks.
Copyright: Magazine copyrighted, first time rights only, reverts to author after publication.
1978; 2/yr; 200
$6/yr; $3.50/ea
35-40 pp; half legal
ISSN: 0886-5957

MĀNOA: A Pacific Journal of International Writing

Robert Shapard, Frank Stewart
English Department
University of Hawaii
Honolulu, HI 96822
(808) 956-3070 or 956-7808

Fiction, poetry, essays, reviews, interviews, translations, art, natural history essays.

US fiction and poetry, not limited to Pacific writers or themes; also features original translations of recent work from Pacific Rim nations.

W. S. Merwin, Kim Chiha, Ann Beattie, Tim O'Brien, Joyce Carol Oates, Barry Lopez, Alberto Ríos, Ai, Norman Dubie.

Unsolicited Manuscripts Received/ Published per Year: 2,800/80.

Payment: copies, plus up to $25 per page prose; more for poetry, reviews.

Reporting Time: 6–8 weeks.

Copyright reverts to author on publication.

1989; 2/yr; 2,150

$15/yr ind, $18/yr inst; 50%

240+ pp; 7 x 10

Ad Rates: $150/page; $95/½ page

ISSN: 1045-7909

THE MASSACHUSETTS REVIEW

Mary Heath, Paul Jenkins, Jules Chametzky
Memorial Hall
University of Massachusetts
Amherst, MA 01003
(413) 545-2689

Poetry, fiction, criticism, translation, interviews, photographs, graphics/artwork.

A quarterly of literature, the arts and current affairs; special art sections and special issues devoted to Feminism, Black literature, Ethnicity, Latin America, contemporary Ireland, etc. ocasionally featured. S.A.S.E. with all mss & inquiries.

Ariel Dorfman, Marilyn Hacker, Seamus Heaney, Joyce Carol Oates, Octavio Paz.

Unsolicited Manuscripts Received/ Published per Year: 3,500–4,000/80–100.

Payment: $50 prose, 35¢/line poetry ($10 min.).

Reporting Time: 3 months.

Copyright held by magazine; reverts to author upon publication when requested.

1959; 4/yr; 1,700

$15/ind, $20/inst; $5/ea + 50¢ postage; 40%

172 pp; 6 x 9

Ad Rates: $125/page (4⅛ x 7); $75/½ page (4⅛ x 3½)

Special university press rate: $100/2 full pages

ISSN: 0025-4878

DeBoer

M/E/A/N/I/N/G

Susan Bee and Mira Schor
60 Lispenard St.
New York, NY 10013
(212) 431-3697

Art criticism and theory, artist statements, art book reviews.

A journal of contemporary art issues and theory; we publish writings by visual artists, art historians, and art critics.

Robert C. Morgan, Richard Tuttle, Nancy Spero, Daryl Chin, Emma Amos, Whitney Chadwick.

Unsolicited Manuscripts Received/ Published per year: 20/1 or 2.

Payment: small fee and issues for authors.

Copyright held by magazine.

1986; 2/yr; 1,000

$12/yr; $6/ea

56 pp; 8 ½ x 11

ISSN: 1040-8576

Ubiquity, SPD, DeBoer

MEN AS WE ARE

Jonathan Running Wind
P.O. Box 150615
Brooklyn, NY 11215-0007
(718) 499-2829

Fiction, poetry, essays, feature stories.

Deeply honest, vulnerable illumination of the masculine experience. A celebration and a lament of who we are today. Compassionate portrayals of our negative characteristics; models of how we can be at our highest.

James Oshinsky, Paul Milenski, David Thorn.

Unsolicited Manuscripts Received/ Published per Year: 1,000/30–50.

Payment: yes.

Reporting Time: 3 months.

Copyright held 90 days, then reverts to author; non-exclusive anthology rights.

1993; 2/yr; 5,000

$12/yr; $3/ea

48 pp; 8 ¼ x 10⅞

Ad Rates: $350/page; ¾, ½, ¼, ⅛, 1/12 page also available.

ISSN: 1067-9707

Bookpeople, Fine Print

METAMORFOSIS

Erasmo Gamboa, Lauro Flores
Chicano Studies Program
American Ethnic Studies Dept.
B523 Padleford Hall, GN-80
University of Washington
Seattle, WA 98195
(206) 543-5401

Poetry, fiction, criticism, essays, reviews, translation, interviews, photographs, graphics/artwork.

METAMORFOSIS welcomes submissions of poetry, drama, critical articles, book reviews, and artwork (black and white 8 x 10 photographs) with SASE.

Shifra Goldman, Pedro Rodriguez, Alfredo Arreguin, Margaret Randall, Bobby Paramo.

Payment: none.

Copyright held by the Center; reverts to author upon publication.

1977; 2/yr; 500

$10/yr ind, $15/yr inst; $5/ea

50 pp; 8 ½ x 10

ISSN: 0273-1606

METROPOLITAIN

J. L. Bergsohn
6307 N. 31st St.
Arlington, VA 22207

Poetry and fiction.

We showcase the talents of Washington-area writers.

Hilary Tham, M. A. Schaffner, Elisavietta Ritchie.

Unsolicited Manuscripts Received/Published per Year: 700/230–50.

Payment: contributor's copy.

Reporting Time: 2–4 weeks.

Copyright reverts to author upon publication.

1991; 4/yr; 250

$8/yr; $2/ea

50 pp; 8 ½ x 5½

MICHIGAN QUARTERLY REVIEW

Laurence Goldstein
3032 Rackham Building
University of Michigan
Ann Arbor, MI 48109
(313) 764-9265

Interdisciplinary essays, fiction, poetry.

A general interest academic journal publishing essays and reviews in all areas, as well as fiction and poetry.

Donald Hall, Margaret Atwood, E.L. Doctorow.

Unsolicited Manuscripts Received/Published per Year: 3,000/40.

Payment: $8-$10/printed page.

Reporting Time: 4-6 weeks.

Copyright reverts to author after first publication.

1962; 4/yr; 1,800

$18/yr; $5/ea; 40%

160 pp; 6 x 9

Ad Rates: $100/page

ISSN: 0026-2420

DeBoer

MID-AMERICAN REVIEW

George Looney, Wayne Barham, Robert Early
English Department
Bowling Green State University
Bowling Green, OH 43403
(419) 372-2725

Poetry, fiction, translations, essays, book reviews, interviews.

MAR publishes poetry using strong, evocative images and fresh language; fiction which is

both character and language-oriented; translations of contemporary writers; essays and book reviews on contemporary authors.
Mark Doty, Stephen Dunn, Diane Glancy, Philip Graham, Frankie Paino, Greg Pape, Alberto Ríos.
Unsolicited Manuscripts Received/Published per Year: 3,500+/90.
Reading Period: Sept.—May
Payment: copies and $10/page, up to $50.
Reporting Time: 1–4 months.
Copyright held by magazine; reverts to author upon publication.
1979; 2/yr; 1,000
$12/yr, $20/2 yrs; $7/ea
200 pp; 5½ x 8½
Exchange ads, 5 x 8
ISSN: 0747-8895

MID COASTER

Peter Blewett
2750 N. 45th St.
Milwaukee, WI 53210–2429
Poetry, fiction.
Unsolicited Manuscripts Received/Published per Year: 500-1,000/25
Payment: in copies.
Reporting Time: up to 8 weeks.
Copyright held by author.
1987; 1/yr; 800
$4.50/ea; 40%
36 pp; 8½ x 11
ISSN: 0892-970X

MIDLAND REVIEW

205 Morrill
Stillwater, OK 74078
(405) 744-9474
Poetry, fiction, photography, artwork, essays.
Journal of contemporary literature, literary criticism, and art.
Fritz Hamilton, Ionna-Veronica Warwick, Mark Cox.
Unsolicited Manuscripts Received/Published per Year: 400/50.
Payment: contributor copy.
1985; 1/yr; 200
$6/ea; $3/5 or more
128 pp; 6 x 9
Ad Rates: $80/page, $50/½ page, $50/¼ page

MILDRED

961 Birchwood Ln.
Niskayuna, NY 12309

MINDPRINT REVIEW

Ron Pickup
P.O. Box 62
Soulsbyville, CA 95372
(209) 532-7045
Poetry, fiction, photographs, translations, graphics/artwork.
We publish quality prose, fiction, poetry, translations, B&W photography and graphics of both well-established and emerging writers, artists and photogra-

phers. Our submission base is Northern California, but our publication reflects a national/international cross section of work. Each issue forms a thematic focus pertaining to humanity or philosophy, but submissions are never limited to any subject, style or persuasion. Quality is our criteria for acceptance.

Rosalie Moore, John Oliver Simon, Lo Fu, Agusti Bartra, Jack Hirschman.

Payment: in copies only, upon publication.

Copyright held by magazine; reverts to author upon publication.

1983; 1/yr; 600

$7/yr ind, $7/yr inst; $6.50/ea, $7.50 by mail; 40%; consignment

128 pp; 6 x 9

Ad Rates: $240/page (4 x 7¾); $120/½ page (4½ x 4); $60/¼ page (4½ x 2½ or 2½ x 3¾)

ISSN: 1040-2233

Bookpeople

THE MINNESOTA REVIEW

Jeffrey Williams
the minnesota review
Dept. of English
East Carolina Univ.
Greenville, NC 27858
(919) 757-6388; Fax (919) 757-4889

Poetry, fiction, criticism, essays, reviews, translations, interviews.

THE MINNESOTA REVIEW is a journal of committed writing. We are particularly interested in new work that is progressive in nature, with special commitment to the areas of socialist and feminist writing.

Jean Franco, Richard Ohmann, Michael Bérubé, Lyn Lifshin, Joan Frank, Bruce Robbins.

Unsolicited Manuscripts Received/Published per Year: 1,500-2,000/50–75.

Payment: in copies.

Reporting Time: 60–90 days.

Copyright held by magazine; reverts to author upon publication.

1960; 2/yr; 1,600

$12/yr ind, $24/yr inst; $7.50/ea

200 pp; 5½ x 8 ½

Ad Rates: $100/page (5 x 7); $150/2 pages; $60/½ page (5 x 3½); $30/¼ page (2 x 3)

ISSN: 0026-5667

MISSISSIPPI MUD

Joel Weinstein
1336 SE Marion St.
Portland, OR 97202
(503) 236-9962

Poetry, fiction, photographs, graphics/artwork.

MISSISSIPPI MUD presents lucid, elegant writing and art from the *ne plus ultra* of the American scene.

Katherine Dunn, Joyce Thompson, Fred Pfeil, Todd Grimson, Christina Zawadiwsky, Tom Spanbauer.

Unsolicited Manuscripts Received/ Published per Year: 150/20.

Payment: cash, on publication, depending on length or scale.

Reporting Time: 6–8 months.

Copyright held by magazine; reverts to author upon publication.

1973; 2–3/yr; 1,500

$19/4 issues, $6/ea

48 pp, 11 x 17

MISSISSIPPI REVIEW

Frederick Barthelme
Southern Station, Box 5144
Hattiesburg, MS 39406
(601) 266-4321

Fiction, poetry, criticism, translation, interviews.

MISSISSIPPI REVIEW is a nonregional literary magazine published by the Center for Writers at the University of Southern Mississippi. The editors combine solicited and unsolicited works of well-known and new writers in an innovative format, producing three numbers a year. Although **MR** publishes mostly fiction and poetry, the editors are interested in literature in translation, interviews, and literary criticism.

Elizabeth Tallent, William Gibson, E.M. Cioran, Amy Hempel, Tama Janowitz.

Unsolicited Manuscripts Received/ Published per Year: 1,200/30-40.

Reading Period: Sept.—May.

Payment: in copies.

Reporting Time: 8–12 weeks.

Copyright held by magazine; reverts to author upon publication.

1976; 2/yr; 2,000

$15/yr; $12/ea

120 pp; 5½ x 8½

Ad Rates: $100/page; $50/½ page; exchange

ISSN: 0047-7559

DeBoer, Fine Print

MISSISSIPPI VALLEY REVIEW

John Mann, Tama Baldwin
Department of English
Western Illinois University
Macomb, IL 61455
(309) 298-1514

MVR publishes poetry, fiction, and essays without regard to any special slant of theme. Special issues (such as "the literature of witness" issue of Spring '92) are published occasionally.

We encourage work by both new and experienced writers.
Recent contributors include Edward Allen, David Ray, Ronald Wallace, Ralph J. Mills, Michael Water, Martha Vertreace, Christopher Davis, and Patricia Henley.
Unsolicited Manuscripts Received/Published per Year: 1,500/75.
Reading Period: Sept.—May.
Payment: in copies.
Reporting Time: 3 months.
Copyright held by author.
1971; 2/yr; 500
$12/yr; $6/ea
96 pp; 9 x 6
ISSN: 0270-3521

O

MISSOURI REVIEW

Speer Morgan, Greg Michalson
University of Missouri
1507 Hillcrest Hall
Columbia, MO 65211
(314) 882-4474
Poetry, fiction, essays, reviews, interviews, special features of literary interest, cartoons.
Reading Period: year–round.
Payment: $20/page; (average) up to $500.
Reporting Time: 10–12 weeks.
Copyright held by the University of Missouri; reverts to author upon request.
1978; 3/yr; 6,000
$15/yr; $6/ea; 40%
224 pp; 6 x 9
Ad Rates: $250/page
ISSN: 0191-1961

MOBIUS

Fred Schepartz
1149 E. Mifflin
Madison, WI 53703
(608) 255-4224
Short fiction, poetry, occasional essays.
Fiction and poetry which uses social change as a primary or secondary theme. Doesn't have to be overtly political as long as it has something to say. Otherwise anything goes.
William Steigerwaldt, Gay Davidson, R. Russell, Bonnie Brown, Andrea Musher.
Payment: Copies.
Reporting Time: 4-6 weeks.
Copyright: Reverts to author upon publication.
1989; 4/yr; 200
$12/yr ind, $3.50/ea; 40%
32pp; 8 ½ x 11
Ad Rates: $90/page (7 ½ x 10); $50/½ page (3 x 9)

MODERN HAIKU

Robert Spiess
P.O. Box 1752
Madison, WI 53701

(608) 233-2738

Haiku, essays, reviews.

We publish only quality haiku in which felt-depth, insight and intuition are evident. Good university and public library subscription list includes foreign.

Paul O. Williams, Geraldine Little, William J. Higginson, Corvan den Heuvel, Wally Swist, Patricia Neubauer, James Kirkup.

Unsolicited Manuscripts Received/ Published per Year: 14,000/850.

Payment: $1/haiku on acceptance; $5/page for articles.

Reporting Time: 2 weeks.

Copyright held by Robert Spiess; reverts to author upon publication.

1969; 3/yr; 700

$14.25/yr; $5/ea

108 pp; 5½ x 8½

ISSN: 0026-7821

THE MONOCACY VALLEY REVIEW

William Heath, Editor
Dept. of English
Mount Saint Mary's College
Emmitsburg, MD 21727
(301) 447-6122

Fiction, poetry, photographs, graphics, artwork, criticism, interviews, essays.

Holly St. John Bergon, Roser Caminals, Mary Noel, John Grey, Roberta Bevington, Barbara Petoskey, Maxine Combs.

Reading Period: Dec.—Jan.

Payment: $10-25 for each poem, story, or artwork accepted (funds permitting).

$8/2 issues; $5/ea

MONOGRAPHIC REVIEW/ REVISTA MONOGRAFICA

Genaro J. Pérez, Janet Pérez
Box 8401
U.T. Permian Basin
Odessa, TX 79762
(915) 367-2249; Fax (915) 367-2115
E-Mail; Perez__G @UTPB.PB. UTexas.Edu

Literature and criticism of the Hispanic world.

A professional journal of criticism in the Hispanic literatures, monographic in character, devoted to areas neglected by mainstream journals. Recent topics: The Erotic, The Comics, Women Poets, Science Fiction, Detective Fiction

David W. Foster, John Dowling, Manuel Andújar, Noel Valis, Paul Ilie.

Unsolicited Manuscripts Received/ Published per Year: 50/25.

Reading Period: Aug. and Sept.

Payment: complimentary copy.

Reporting Time: 2 months.

Copyright: Perez & Perez

1985; 1/yr
$35/yr
pp varies
ISSN: 0885-7512

MOSAIC: A Journal for the Interdisciplinary Study of Literature

Dr. Evelyn J. Hinz
208 Tier Building
University of Manitoba
Winnipeg, Manitoba, R3T 2N2 CANADA
(204) 474-9763; Fax (204) 261-9086

Interdisciplinary study of literature.

MOSAIC is a scholarly journal dedicated to the "interdisciplinary study of literature"—the examination of literary works from antiquity to the present from the perspective of other disciplines.

Unsolicited Manuscripts Received/Published per Year: 200/30–32.

Payment: none.

Reporting Time: 4 months.

Copyright held by magazine.

1967; 4/yr; 1,000

$22/yr, $38/2 yr, $53/3 yr (US/CANADA); $10/sample

138 pp; 6 x 9 ¼

Ad Rates: $150/page; $90/half page B/W

ISSN: 0027-1276

Hignell Printers (CANADA)

MR. COGITO

John M. Gogol, Robert A. Davies
Humanities
Pacific University
Forest Grove, OR 97116
(503) 226-4135 or 233-8131

Poetry, photographs, graphics/artwork.

Poetry in English, including translations; photographs, graphics. We like poems that surprise and move us with their language, sound and invention.

Barbara LaMorticella, Norman Russell, Patrick W. Gray, William Ferrell, Ann Chandonnet.

Manuscripts Published per Year: 1%.

Reading Period: year–round.

Payment: 1 copy.

Reporting Time: 1–3 months.

Copyright held by magazine; all but anthology rights revert to author upon publication.

1973; irregular; 500

$9/3 issues; $3/ea

24–28 pp; 4¼ x 11

ISSN: 0740-1205

Ebsco, Faxon, Dawson

N

NASSAU REVIEW

Dr. Paul A. Doyle, Managing Editor
English Dept.
Nassau Community College
State University of New York
Garden City, NY 11530
(516) 532-7186

Poetry, fiction, criticism, essays.
Unsolicited Manuscripts Received/Published per Year: 500–600/30–35.
Reading Period: Sept.—Dec.
Payment: none.
Reporting Time: 4–6 months.
Copyright held by Nassau Community College; reverts to author upon publication.
1964; 1/yr; 1,200
Free.
92–95 pp; 6½ x 9½

THE NEBRASKA REVIEW

James Reed, Fiction Editor; Susan Aizenberg, Poetry Editor
212 FA
University of Nebraska, Omaha
Omaha, NE 68182-0326
(402) 554-2771

Poetry, fiction.
TNR publishes quality literary fiction and poetry, material that transcends mere technical proficiency.
Carolyne Wright, Stephen Dixon, Joan Joffe-Hall, Elizabeth Evans, David Hopes, Vern Rutsala, Cris Mazza, Roger Weingarten, Rosemarie Kinder, Philip Dacey, Michael C. White
Unsolicited Manuscripts Received/Published per Year: 1,500/6-10 fiction; 45-50 poetry.
Reading Period: Sept.—May.
Payment: 1 year subscription plus contributer's copies.
Reporting Time: 3–5 months (longest for poetry.)
Copyright held by magazine; reverts to author upon publication.
1972; 2/yr; 500
$6/yr; $3.50/ea; 40%
80 pp; 5½ x 8½
Ad Rates: $45/page (3⅝ x 6¼); $25/½ page (3⅝ x 3)
ISSN: 8755-514X

NEGATIVE CAPABILITY

Sue Brannan Walker, Ron Walker
62 Ridgelawn Dr., East
Mobile, AL 36608
(205) 343-6163

Poetry, fiction, essays, reviews, interviews, photographs, graphics/artwork, original music, bagatelles. Annual poetry &

fiction contest: $1,000 award for each.

NEGATIVE CAPABILITY is a creative journal whose emphasis is joy—not merely laughter, though we encourage humor, but the joy that arrives through insight into oneself and others, the world and our all too human condition.

Richard Eberhart, John Brugaletta, X.J. Kennedy, Denise Levertov, Marge Piercy, William Stafford, John Updike, Diane Wakoski.

Unsolicited Manuscripts Received/ Published per Year: 4,000/400.

Reading Period: Sept.—May.

Payment: in copies.

Reporting Time: 6 weeks.

Copyright held by magazine; reverts to author upon publication.

1981; 3/yr; 1,000

$15/yr ind, $20/yr inst; $5/ea; 40%

180 pp; 5¼ x 8¼

Ad Rates: $100/page (4½ x 8); $50/½ page (4 x 4); $25/¼ page (4 x 2½)

ISSN: 0277-5166

NEW AMERICAN WRITING

Maxine Chernoff, Paul Hoover
2920 West Pratt
Chicago, IL 60645
(312) 764-1048

Poetry, fiction, essays, plays, graphics.

Nathaniel Mackey, Lyn Hejinian, Charles Simic, Ron Padgett, Bob Perelman, Robert Creeley, John Ashbery, Wanda Coleman.

Unsolicited Manuscripts Received/ Published per Year: 1,500/50.

Reading Period: Sept.—Dec. and Mar.—June.

Payment: $5/page, when available.

Reporting Time: 1–3 months.

Copyright held by OINK! Press, Inc.; reverts to author upon publication.

1971; 2/yr; 5,000

$18/3 issues; $7/ea; libraries and foreign orders: $24/3 issues, $9/ea; 40%

150 pp; 5½ x 8½

Ad Rates: $150/page (5 x 8); $100/½ page (2¼ x 4)

ISSN: 0893-7842

Ingram, SPD, Ubiquity, Total

NEW DELTA REVIEW

Nicola Mason, Catherine Williamson, Editors; Juliette Busby, Poetry Editor; Matt Clark, Fiction Editor
c/o Department of English
Louisiana State University
Baton Rouge, LA 70803-5001
(504) 388-4079

Poetry, fiction, essays, interviews.

NDR is a literary journal published by the Creative Writing Program at LSU. We are are most interested in new writers and exploring new directions in poetry and fiction. We offer the Eyster Prizes, which honor Warren Eyster, teacher, author, and faculty advisor to **NDR**'s predecessors.

James English, Julie McCracken, Virgil Suarez, Mircea Cartarescu, and an interview with Pulitzer Prizewinner Robert Olen Butler.

Unsolicited Manuscripts Received/Published per Year: 2,000/45.

Reading Period: year–round.

Payment: in copies; Eyster Prize awarded to 1 poet and 1 fiction writer per issue.

Copyright: First North American; reverts to author upon publication.

1984; 2/yr; 500

$7/yr; $4/ea; 40%

100 pp; 6 x 9

Ad Rates: from other literary magazines.

NEW ENGLAND REVIEW

David Huddle, Acting Editor; Associate Editors: William Lychack, Devon Jerslid

Middlebury College

Middlebury, VT 05753

(802) 388-3711 ext 5075

Fiction, poetry, essays, reviews, translation, interviews—open to strong writing of all kinds.

NEW ENGLAND REVIEW has been a mainstay of the American literary community for twelve years. Now located in Middlebury College, under new editorship, and newly affiliated with University Press of New England, **NER** is beginning a new series, *MIDDLEBURY SERIES,* to reflect its energy and direction, its recommitment to the art, craft, and politics of writing.

Arnost Lustig, Ann Beattie, Stephen Dunn, Bridget Pegeen Kelley, Edward Hirsch, W. D. Wetherell, Miroslav Holub, Samuel F. Pickering.

Reading Period: Sept.—June.

Payment: $10/minimum.

Reporting Time: 5–7 weeks.

Copyright held by author.

1978; 4/yr; 3,000

$23/yr ind, $30/yr inst; $7/ea; 40%

128 pp; 6 x 9

Ad Rates: $300/page (7 x 10); $150/½ page (7 x 5); $100/¼ page (3½ x 5)

ISSN: 0736-2579

NEW HOPE INTERNATIONAL

Gerald England

20 Wereth Ave.,

Geecross, Hyde, Cheshire
SK14 SNL ENGLAND
061-351-1878

Poetry, short fiction, b & w artwork

NHI writing publishes poetry from traditional to avant-garde, including translations. **NHI** reviews cover books, mags, cassettes, pc-software, etc.

Lisa Kucharski, B. Z. Niditch, Mary Rudbeck Stanro.

Unsolicited Manuscripts Received/ Published per Year: 3,500/100

Payment: in copies only.

Reporting Time: usually within 2–3 months.

Copyright: First British Serial Rights.

1980; 2–6/yr; 1,500

$30/yr; $5/ea ($10 cheque)

36 pp

ISSN: 0260-7958

NEW LAUREL REVIEW

Lee Meitzen Grue
828 Lesseps St.
New Orleans, LA 70117
(504) 947-6001

Poetry, fiction, criticism, essays, reviews, translation, interviews, graphics/artwork, whatever is interesting.

NEW LAUREL REVIEW publishes poetry, fiction, translation, articles; work of sound scholarship which is alive. We hope to continue showing the best writing by nationally accepted writers with that of fresh new talent not seen before.

Enid Shomer, Sue Walker, Martha McFerren, James Nolan, Nahid Rachlin.

Reading Period: Sept.—May.

Reporting Time: varies.

Copyright held by author.

1971; 500

$9/yr ind, $11/yr inst.

125 pp; 6 x 9

ISSN: 0145-8388

NEW LETTERS

James McKinley, Editor; Robert Stewart, Managing Editor; Glenda McCrary, Administrative Assistant
University of Missouri, Kansas City
Kansas City, MO 64110
(816) 235-1168 or 235-1120

Poetry, fiction, reviews, photographs, graphics/artwork.

NEW LETTERS, an international literary quarterly, publishes contemporary writing, including that of well-known writers and fresh, new talents and interviews with Nobel Laureates and Pulitzer Prize Winners. Also publishes photographs and graphics; notable discoveries of

overlooked gems. e.g., Theodore Roethke interview, Countee Cullen memoir, and Richard Wright, archival material.
Jim Harrison, Jorie Graham, William H. Gass, Tess Gallagher, Luisa Valenzuela, William Stafford, Thomas Berger, William Burroughs, Rosellen Brown, Lisel Mueller, Amiri Baraka.
Unsolicited Manuscripts Received/Published per year: 5,000/100.
Reading Period: Oct. 15—May 15.
Payment: small honorarium and copies.
Reporting Time: 6 weeks.
Copyright held by magazine; reverts to author upon publication.
1934; 4/yr; 2,500
$17/yr ind, $20/yr inst; $5/ea; 40%–50%
128 pp; 6 x 9
Ad Rates: $150/page (4 x 6⅞); $100/½ page (4 x 3⅛)
Ingram, Ubiquity

NEW MYTHS: MSS

Robert Mooney
SUNY Binghampton
Box 530
Binghampton, NY 13901
(607) 777-2168

Poetry, fiction, essays, photographs, graphics.
Special emphasis on publishing the best work of young and unestablished writers with the work of well-known writers.
Andrew Hudgins, Dianne Benedict, Gerald Stern, William Stafford, Linda Pastan.
Payment: whenever funds allow.
Reporting Time: 2–8 weeks.
Copyright reverts to author upon publication.
1961; 2/yr; 1,000
$8.50/yr ind, $14/yr inst; $5.50/ea
Ad Rates: $500/page; $250/½ page

NEW ORLEANS REVIEW

John Mosier, John Biguenet
Box 195
Loyola University
New Orleans, LA 70118
(504) 865-2294

Poetry, short fiction, translations, literary & film criticism, artwork.
Payment: please inquire
Reporting Time: 3 months
1968; 4/yr; 1,000
$25/yr; $9/ea.
100 pp; 8½ x 11
ISSN: 0028-6400

THE NEW PRESS

Robert Dunn, Editor; Bob Abramson, Publisher
53-35 Hollis Ct. Blvd.

Flushing, NY 11365
(718) 229-6782

Poetry, short stories, essays, line drawings.

A literary quarterly that stresses poetic vision and voice. For the literate mind. Work should be accessible and enjoyable to an intelligent reader.

Joe Malone, Ken Di Maggio, Lawrence Ferlinghetti, Karen Swenson, Ann Chandler.

Unsolicited Manuscripts Received/ Published per Year: 400/80.

Payment: 3 copies; $15 for prose. Poetry, essay, and short story contests.

Reporting Time: 2 months.

Copyright: First time serial rights; reverts to author.

1984; 4/yr; 1,500

$15/yr; $4/ea; 40%

40 pp; 8½ x 11

$100/page; $60/½ page; $40/¼ page; $20/business card

ISSN: 0894-6078

DeBoer, Ubiquity

the new renaissance

Louise T. Reynolds, Harry Jackel, Stanwood Boltron, Patricia Michaud
9 Heath Road
Arlington, MA 02174

Fiction, poetry; lead articles; stories & poetry in bilingual translations; reproduction of paintings, sculpture, mixed media, photographs; commentary, graphics, illustrations, essays, reviews.

We offer a forum for idea/opinion pieces on political/sociological pieces, and publish a wide variety of styles, statements, tones, and visions in our fiction, poetry and art sections. Since we take a classicist position, we avoid the trendy and the fashionable, for the most part, but our range is so broad it includes contradictory statements within a single issue. There is, however, an emphasis on the human condition.

Phillip Greene, Kurt Kusenberg, (Lauren Hahn translation), V. Robin Grice, Jay Griswold, Frank Finale, Kevin Kearney, Gina Labriola (Ruth Feldman translations).

Unsolicited Manuscripts Received/ Published per Year: 1,000+/60-78.

Reading Period: Jan.—June 30.

Payment: After publication.

Reporting Time: 8–26 weeks, poetry; 40–60 weeks, prose. One month for queries. No submissions any year after July 1st. Currently overstocked in poetry—no submissions in 1994; oversubmitted in prose and delayed in readings/reportings.

Guidelines sent ONLY w/sample copy ($5.50) on request.
Copyright held by magazine.
1968; 2/yr; 1,500
$19.50/3 issues; $21/3 issues (CANADA); $23/3 issues (other); $8.50/sample of most recent issue.
144–192 pp; 6 x 9
ISSN: 0028-6575

minimum for poems, upon publication.
Copyright held by magazine, and individual writers; reverts to author upon publication.
1979; 3/yr; 3,000
$15/yr; $6/ea; 50% w/no return discount on back issues w/subscriptions.
160–200 pp; 6½ x 10
No ads
ISSN: 0-939233-00-2

NEW VIRGINIA REVIEW

Mary Flinn, Editor; Margaret Gibson, Poetry Editor.
1306 East Cary St., 2A
Richmond, VA 23219
(804) 782-1043
Poetry, fiction, essays.
NEW VIRGINIA REVIEW: a trice yearly collection of new poetry, fiction, and essays that strives to publish the best possible work being done by contemporary authors both unknown and widely recognized. Special issues forthcoming. Nature and poetry at the end of the century; New Russian prose in translation.
Richard Bausch, Peter Taylor, Mandy Sayer, Mona Van Duyn, Rachel Hadas.
Unsolicited Manuscripts Received/ Published per Year: 6,000+/40.
Payment: $10/printed page, $25

NEXT PHASE

Kim Means, Editor; Ken Rand, Asst. Editor
33 Court St.
New Haven, CT 06511
(203) 772-1697; fax same
Fiction, sci-fi, fantasy, commentary.
Whether your interest lies in innovative ways to save our planet, social science fiction, or winning poetry, **NEXT PHASE** offers a unique compilation of the best of the small press in a well designed format.
D.F. Lewis, Wade Tarzia, Greg Nyman.
Unsolicited Manuscripts Received/ Published per Year: 150/20.
Payment: 3 contributors copies.
Reporting Time: 3 weeks.
Copyright reverts to author.
1989; 3/yr; 1,000

$10/yr; $3/ea
32 pp; 8½ x 11
Ad Rates: $100/page; $60/½ page; $40/¼ page
Fine Print, Inland, Ubiquity, Desert Moon, Bear Family

NIGHT ROSES

Allen T. Billy, Sandra Taylor
P.O. Box 393
Prospect Heights, IL 60070
(708) 392-2435

Poetry, some art.
We like to publish romance poetry, flower poetry, ghost images of past or future and odds and ends of interest.
Genoa, Mary R. De Maine, Ken Stone, Jane Camron.
Unsolicited Manuscripts Received/Published per Year: 1,500/150.
Reading Period: Sept.—July.
Payment: copy of issue.
Reporting Time: 4–12 weeks. Write for guidelines before submitting work.
Copyright belongs to authors.
1986; 2–4/yr; 250
$8/3 issues; $3/ea
44–56 pp; 5⅜ x 8½

NIMROD: International Journal of Prose & Poetry

Francine Ringold
Arts and Humanities Council of Tulsa
2210 South Main
Tulsa, OK 74114
(918) 584-3333

Poetry, fiction, prose, translation, photographs, graphics/artwork, interviews.
NIMROD seeks vigorous writing that is neither wholly of the academy nor of the streets. Fall issues feature the winners and finalists of the Nimrod Hardman Literary Awards Competition and spring issues are thematic. Past thematic issues include "Arabic Literature," "China Today," "India: A Wealth of Diversity," "from the Soviets," "Oklahoma Indian Markings," "Clap Hands and Sing: Writers of Age" and "Australian Literature: Then and Now."
Wendy Stevens, Tess Gallagher, Denise Levertov, Gish Jen, Sharon Sakson, Alvin Greenberg, Janette Turner Hospital.
Unsolicited Manuscripts Received/Published per Year: 500-800 fiction and poetry/1%.
Reading Period: year–round.
Payment: $5/page up to $25 plus two copies; also $1,000 to first place winners in our fiction and poetry competition, $500 for second place.
Reporting Time: 3 weeks–3 months.
Copyright of entire magazine held

by the Arts & Humanities Council of Tulsa. Rights to individual stories revert to authors.
1956; 2/yr; 4,000–4,500
$11.50/yr; $6.90/ea
160 pp; 6 x 9
Ad Rates: $150/page; $75/½ page
ISSN: 0029-053X

96 INC

Vera Gold and Julie Phipps, Editors
P.O. Box 15559
Boston, MA 02215
(617) 267-0543; Fax (617) 267-6725

Fiction, poetry, interviews, graphics/artwork.

96 INC, the parent organization of the Kenmore Writers Group, was formed to foster the publication of original literary works, with an emphasis on new writers; to sponsor public and private readings; and to train students of high school and other ages.

Payment: none.
Copyright reverts to author upon publication.
1992; 2/yr; 3,000
$10/yr; $4/ea; 40%; consignment
50 pp; 8½ x 11
Ad Rates: $100/page (8½ x 11); $75/½ page (4¼ x 5½); $50/¼ page (2⅛ x 2¾)
DeBoer

NIT & WIT

Harrison McCormick, Marie Aguirre
P.O. Box 627
Geneva, IL 60134
(312) 232-9496

Poetry, fiction, essays, reviews, interviews, photographs, graphics/artwork.

NIT & WIT is a full-spectrum cultural arts magazine with regular features on art, music, dance, theatre, film, architecture, photography, reviews, essays, fiction and poetry.

Philip Graham, June Brinder, Gordon Lish, Sharon Sheehe Stark.

Payment: none.
Reporting Time: 2–3 weeks.
Copyright held by author.
1977; 6/yr; 6,000
$12/yr; $2/ea; 40%–50%
68 pp; 8½ x 11
Ad Rates: $750/page (7⅛ x 10); $390/½ page (4 11/16 x 7⅜); $210/¼ page (3½ x 4 15/16)

NO ROSES REVIEW

Carolyn Koo, Natalie Kenvin, Juanita Garza
P.O. Box 597781
Chicago, IL 60659

Poetry, fiction, solicited essays.

Contemporary high quality work, all styles and genres from writers known and unknown. Fiction 20 pages double spaced maximum.

Elaine Equi, David Trinidad, Caroline Knox, John Traiter, Susan Wheeler, Rosmarie Waldrop, Carolyn Forché.

Payment: in copies.

Reporting Time: 2–3 months.

Copyright reverts to author upon publication.

1992; 2/yr; 500

$10/yr; $6/ea

96 pp

ISSN in application.

THE NORTH AMERICAN REVIEW

Robley Wilson
University of Northern Iowa
Cedar Falls, IA 50614
(319) 273-6455

Poetry, fiction, criticism, essays, reviews, graphics/artwork.

Oldest magazine in North America, publishing fiction and nonfiction, poetry and reviews. Winner in 1981 and 1983 of National Magazine Award for fiction. Nonfiction frequently has ecological/environmental slant.

Unsolicited Manuscripts Received/Published per Year: 20,000 poetry, 3,000 prose/30-35 poems, 55-65 prose.

Reading Period: Jan.—Apr. 1, Fiction.

Payment: $10/published page; 50¢/line for poetry, minimum.

Reporting Time: 1–3 months.

Copyright by University of Northern Iowa; reverts to author upon publication.

1815; 6/yr; 4,700

$18/yr; $4/ea

48+ pp; 8⅛ x 10⅞

Ad Rates: $500/page (7 x 10); $200/⅓ page (2¼ x 10)

ISSN: 0029-2397

Eastern News

NORTH ATLANTIC REVIEW

John Gill
15 Arbutus Lane
Stony Brook, NY 11790-1408
(516) 751-7886

Poetry, Fiction, Essays.

General fiction and poetry, with a special section in each issue devoted to literary or social issues.

Lewis Turco, Burton Raffel, Walter Cummins, Richard Eberhart, David Ignatow, Archibald MacLeish, James Dickey, May Swenson, David Slavitt, Richard Wilbur.

Unsolicited Manuscripts Received/Published per Year: 1,400/35.

Reading Period: year–round.

Reporting Time: 4–5 months.

Copyright held by author.

1989; 1/yr; 1,000

$10/yr; 40%

300; 7 x 9½
$200/page; $125/½ page; $75/¼ page
ISSN: 1040-7324

NORTH CAROLINA LITERARY REVIEW

Alex Albright
English Dept., ECU
Greenville, NC 27858
(919) 757-4876 or (919) 757-6041

Articles, essays, interviews, reviews, photos, w/NC focus.
For serious readers found as often in bookstores and libraries as in universities. Definition of NC writers/literature as broad as writers make it.
Fred Chappell, A.R. Ammons, Leon Rooke, Janet Lembke, James Applewhite.
Unsolicited Manuscripts Received/Published per Year: 75/10.
Payment: $50–$500.
Reporting Time: 6 weeks.
Copyright: First rights held by magazine; returned to author on request.
1992; 2/yr; 1,200 paid
$15/yr; $8/ea; Returnable/NR 30–40%
196 pp; 7½ x 10
Ad Rates: $200/page; $125/½ page; $75/¼ page
ISSN: 1063-0724
Ebsco, Faxon, Cox

NORTH DAKOTA QUARTERLY

Robert W. Lewis, Editor; William Borden, Fiction Editor; Jay Meek, Poetry Editor
University of North Dakota, Box 7209
Grand Forks, ND 58202
(701) 777-3322

Poetry, fiction, criticism, essays, reviews, graphics.
An interdisciplinary journal in the arts and humanities. Recent and forthcoming special issues on Columbus' quincentenary, nature writing/writers, Yugoslav culture.
Sherman Paul, Peter Nabokov, Kathleen Woodward, Philip Booth, Donald Hall, Alane Rollings.
Unsolicited Manuscripts Received/Published per Year: 1,000/125.
Payment: in copies.
Reporting Time: 1–3 months.
Copyright by University of North Dakota.
1909; 4/yr; 1,000
$15/yr; $5/ea; $10 for special issues; 20%
200 pp; 6 x 9
ISSN: 0029-277X

NORTHEAST ARTS

Mr. Leigh Donaldson
J.F.K. Station

P.O. Box 6061
Boston, MA 02114
Poetry, reviews, fiction.
NORTHEAST ARTS is an arts literary journal, featuring original poetry, short fiction, essays, photography, black & white art and reviews.
Martina Fischer, Thomas Wilock, Jennifer E. Smith
Unsolicited Manuscripts Received/Published per Year: 2,000/100.
Payment: 2 copies.
Reporting Time: 2–3 months.
Copyright: one-time use, rights revert to creator.
$10/yr; $4.50/ea
26-32 pp; 6½ x 9½
Ad Rates: $75/page (5 x 8); $45/½ page (5 x 4½) or $50/½ page (2½ x 8)

THE NORTHLAND QUARTERLY

J. Namio
Published by Rio Salado Books
1522 E. Southern Ave.
Box 2161
Tempe, AZ 85282
Poetry, fiction, criticism, essays, reviews, plays, interviews, photographs, graphics/artwork.
Jennifer Lagier, Mark Vinz, Mitchell Tomfohrde, Tom Padgett, Mark Maire.
Payment: in copies, upon publication.
Reporting Time: 8–10 weeks.
Copyright held by magazine; reverts to author upon publication.
1988; 4/yr; 500
$20/yr ind & inst; $4.95/ea; 40%; 20% to college bookstores; 30% on ind. orders over 100
Ad Rates: $300/page/5½ x 8½; $150/½ page/5½ x 4¼; $75/¼ page/2¾ x 4¼; advertising accepted on barter system
ISSN: 0899-708X

NORTHWEST REVIEW

John Witte, Hannah Wilson
369 PLC
University of Oregon
Eugene, OR 97403
(503) 346-3957
Poetry, fiction, criticism, essays, reviews, translation, interviews, graphics/artwork.
NORTHWEST REVIEW is a tri-annual publishing poetry, fiction, artwork, interviews, book reviews and comment. We have no other criterion for acceptance than that of excellence. We are devoted to representing the widest possible variety of styles and perspectives (experimental, feminist, political, etc.), unified within a humanist framework. "A publica-

tion to which the wise and honest, and literate, may repair!"—William Stafford.

Joyce Carol Oates, Madeline DeFrees, Alan Dugan, Morris Graves, Raymond Carver.

Unsolicited Manuscripts Received/Published per Year: 4,000/90.

Payment: in copies.

Reporting Time: 8–10 weeks.

Copyright held by magazine; reverts to author upon request.

1957; 3/yr; 1,100

$11/yr; $4/ea; 20%–40%

160 pp; 6 x 9

Ad Rates: $160/page/6 x 9

ISSN: 0029-3423

NOTUS new writing

Pat Smith

2420 Walter Dr.

Ann Arbor, MI 48103

Poetry, fiction, reviews, translations.

NOTUS is a semi-annual magazine focusing on experimental and non-traditional writing. Its emphasis is two-fold: to publish new work from writers who already have an audience and to help introduce the work of younger writers. We also have a special interest in publishing translations.

Ed Sanders, Robert Kelly, Nathanial Tarn, Gerrit Lansing, Leslie Scalapino.

Unsolicited Manuscripts Received/Published per Year: 400/1 or 2.

Payment: none.

Copyright held by OtherWind Press, Inc.; reverts to author upon publication.

1986; 2/yr; 500

$12/yr ind, $15/yr inst; $6/ea (foreign add $3); 40%

96 pp; 6 x 9

No ads

ISSN: 0889-0803

SPD, Small Press Traffic

LA NUEZ

Rafael Bordao, Celeste Ewers

P. O. Box 1655

New York, NY 10276

(212) 260-3130

Poetry, fiction, criticism, essays, interviews, plays, reviews, photographs and artwork.

LA NUEZ is an international quarterly magazine of literature and art published entirely **in Spanish**. We publish established as well as new and emerging writers and artists.

Reinaldo Arenas, Clara Janes, José Triana, Antonio Benítez-Rojo, César Leante, Frank Dauster.

Unsolicited Manuscripts Received/Published per year: 200/60.

Payment: 2 copies.

Reporting Time: 6–8 weeks.
Copyright reverts to author upon publication.
1988; 4/yr; 500
$12/ind, $15/inst; $18/foreign; $3/ea; 40%
32 pp; 8½ x 11
Ad Rates: $200/page; $115/½ page; plus smaller
ISSN: 0898-1140

Payment: in copies.
Reporting Time: 6–8 weeks.
Copyright: bluestone Press, reverts to author on publication.
1990; 2/yr; 300
$10/yr; $5/ea
300 pp; 5½ x 8½, perfect bound
Ad Rates: $50/page (8 x 5); $35/½ page (4½ x 5½); trades avail.
ISSN: 1061-429X (issued 1–7; 1 pending issue 8+)

O

OBJECT LESSON/ Bluestone Press
Joshua S. Beckman, John C. Horoschak, Andrew Pollock
P. O. Box 1186
Hampshire College
Amherst, MA 01002
Fiction, poetry, one act plays, essays, essays on art, interviews, black and white artwork, artists books, letters.
OBJECT LESSON is open to all styles of writing no length requirements. Annual poetry and fiction contests.
Alice Mattison, Louis Phillips, Harry Brody, Paul Beckman.
Unsolicited Manuscripts Received/ Published per Year: 1,200/50.
Reading Period: year–round.

O-BLEK, a journal of language arts
Connell McGrath
P.O. Box 1242
Stockbridge, MA 01262
Poetry, art, translation.
O-BLEK publishes formally innovative poetry and large art portfolios. Fiction is published infrequently. **O-BLEK** prides itself on its informative representations of contemporary French poetics.
Robert Creeley, Rosmarie Waldrop, Michael Gizzi, Bernadette Mayer, Emmanuel Hocquard.
Payment: $25 (when available).
Reporting Time: 1–3 months.
Copyright reverts to author upon publication.
1987; 2/yr; 1,000
price varies.
200 pp; 5½ x 7

ISSN: 0896-303
SPD, Fine Print, Inland

Ad Rates: \$200/page (4½ x 7⅛); \$100/½ page (4½ x 3½)
ISSN: 0888-4412

OBSIDIAN II: Black Literature In Review
Gerald Barrax, Joyce Pettis
Box 8105
Department of English
North Carolina State University
Raleigh, NC 27695-8105
(919) 737-3870
Poetry, fiction, criticism, essays, reviews.
OBSIDIAN II is a biannual review for the study and cultivation of creative works in English by Black writers worldwide, with scholarly critical studies by all writers on all aspects of Black literature, book reviews, poetry, short fiction, interviews, bibliographies, bibliographical essays, and very short plays in English.
Houston A. Baker, Jr., Gayl Jones, Wanda Coleman, Raymond R. Patterson, Gerald Early.
Payment: none.
Copyright held by Department of English, North Carolina State University; reverts to author upon publication.
1986; 2/yr; 500
\$12/yr ind, \$12/yr inst; \$5/ea; 40%
130 pp; 6 x 9

ODESSA POETRY REVIEW
Jim Wyzard
RR 1, Box 39
Odessa, MO 64076
Poetry.
Ester Leipen, Rod Kessler, Rochelle Lynn Holt, Marian Park.
Payment: varies with quality of work.
Copyright held by Jim Wyzard; reverts to author upon publication.
1984; 4/yr; 500–700
\$16/yr; \$4/ea; 40%
150 pp; 5½ x 8½
No ads

THE OGALALA REVIEW (formerly EPIPHANY)
Gordon Grice, Editor
P.O. Box 2699
University of Arkansas
Fayetteville, AR 72701
Fiction, poetry, translations, creative nonfiction.
TOR specializes in literary fiction, nonfiction, and poetry.
Alicia Ostriker, R. S. Gwynn, Enid Shomer, David Citino, Trent Busch.
Unsolicited Manuscripts Received/Published per Year: 2,000/24.

Reading Period: year–round.
Payment: 2 copies, small honorarium when funds permit.
Reporting Time: 1–2 months.
Copyright: One time publishing right—copyright reverts to author.
1990; 2/yr; 400
$10/yr; $5/ea; 10% to bookstores
100 pp; 8½ x 5½
Ad Rates: $100/page (5 x 8); $60/½ page (5 x 3¾)

THE OHIO REVIEW
Wayne Dodd
209 C Ellis Hall
Ohio University
Athens, OH 45701-2979
(614) 593-1900
Poetry, fiction, essays, reviews.
THE OHIO REVIEW publishes the best in contemporary American poetry, fiction, book reviews, and essays.
Galway Kinnell, Jane Miller, John Haines, Gladys Swan, William Matthews.
Unsolicited Manuscripts Received/ Published per Year: 2,000/20.
Reading Period: Sept.—May 31.
Payment: $1/line (poetry), $5/page (prose).
Reporting Time: 90 days.
Copyright held by magazine; reverts to author upon request.
1971; 3/yr; 2,700
$16/yr, $40/3yrs; $6/ea; 40%
144 pp; 6 x 9
Ad Rates: $175/page (4¼ x 7¼); $100/½ page (4¼ x 3¼)
ISSN: 0360-1013
Ingram, DeBoer, Ubiquity, Michiana News Service

ONTARIO REVIEW
Raymond J. Smith, Joyce Carol Oates
9 Honey Brook Dr.
Princeton, NJ 08540
Poetry, fiction, essays, interviews, photographs, graphics.
Maxine Kumin, Albert Goldbarth, Russell Banks, Alicia Ostriker, Tom Wayman.
Unsolicited Manuscripts Received/ Published per Year: 1,500/25.
Payment: $10/page.
Reporting Time: 6 weeks.
Copyright held by magazine; reverts to author upon publication.
1974; 2/yr; 1,100
$10/yr; $4.95/ea; 40%
112 pp; 6 x 9
Ad Rates: $125/page (4¼ x 7); $75/½ page (4¼ x 3¼); $50/¼ page (2 x 3¼)
ISSN: 0316-4055
Ingram, Ubiquity

ONTHEBUS
Jack Grapes
6421 1/2 Orange St.

Los Angeles, CA 90048
(213) 651-5488

Poetry, fiction, translations, essays, interviews, book reviews.

Open to all kinds, experimental to neo-narrative to Bohemian-language-confessional haiku! 6-10 poems max, fiction 1,500 max.

Joyce Carol Oates, Charles Bukowski, Ai, David Mura, Wanda Coleman, Kate Braverman, Norman Dubie.

Unsolicited Manuscripts Received/Published per Year: 3,500/200.

Reading Period: Feb.—May.

Payment: 1 copy.

Reporting Time: 2–6 months.

Copyright reverts to contributors.

1989; 2/yr; 3,200

$24/3 issues; $9/ea ($13.50 for double issue); 20-40%

336 pp; 8 ½ x 5 ½

Ad Rates: $300/page (7 ¼ x 4 ¼); $200/½ page; $125/¼ page

ISSN: 1043-884X

DeBoer, Bookpeople, SPD, Fine Print

ON THE ISSUES (The Progressive Woman's Quarterly)

Merle Hoffman, Beverly Lowy
97-77 Queens Blvd.
Forest Hills, NY 11374
(718) 275-6020

Women's issues.

For ideas and opinions too controversial for the mainstream media, **ON THE ISSUES** discusses feminism, politics, health, social reform, animal rights, ecology, global humanism and more with thoughtful, unexpurgated insight. Kate Millet, Rep. Pat Shroeder, Andrea Dworkin, Flo Kennedy, Petra Kelly, bell hooks, Elayne Rapping, Elayne Clift, Norine Dworkin, Phyllis Chesler, Rebecca Chalker, Laura Flanders.

Unsolicited Manuscripts Received/Published per year: 200/10.

Payment: 5¢/word; book reviews, $35.

1991; 4/yr

$14.75/yr, add $10/inst; $3.95/ea; 30%

64 pp; 8½ x 11

Ad Rates: $800/page, B/W only

ISSN: 0895-6014

Ingram, Inland, Bookpeople, Ubiquity, Fine Print

OPEN MAGAZINE

Greg Ruggiero, Paul Pinkman
P.O. Box 2726
Westfield, NJ 07091

Fiction, poetry, essays, photographs, graphics/artwork, plays, interviews.

OPEN works with uninhibited

forms of writing and art that inspire change—be they targeted at social processes or the consciousness of the individual. We are fast to accept work that pioneers form, questions the given, risks discussing the intimate or proposing the radical. New emphasis on essays. Special interest in dissident writing, women's issues, media, information & culture.

Margaret Randall, Noam Chomsky, Sylvia Plachy, John Cage, Claribel Alegria, Sesshu Foster.

Payment: copies and up to $50, depending upon presence of grant money.

Reporting Time: 1 month.

Copyright held by magazine; reverts to author upon publication.

1985; 2/yr; 1,000

$15/3 issues/ind, $20/3 issues/inst; $5/ea; 40%

60 pp; 8½ x 11

Ad Rates: $400/page (8½ x 11); $200/½ page (7½ x 5); $100/¼ page (3¾ x 5)

Ad & issue swaps with other CLMP publications.

ISSN: 0894-265X

DeBoer

ORO MADRE

Loss Pequeño Glazier
P.O. Box 143
Getzville, NY 14068-0143

Poetry, fiction, criticism, reviews, graphics.

ORO MADRE seeks to present writings with attention to details of the poem's status and the uncertain edges of the poetic act; of interest also, electronic poetries and the language of electronic communication; it also focuses on coverage of the small press world through reviews, interviews, and articles on small press activities and trends.

Alejandro Muguia, Jack Hirschman, Robert Anbian.

Reading Period: year–round.

Payment: in copies.

Reporting Time: 2 months.

Copyright held by author.

1981; irreg; 500

$14/yr ind, $20/yr inst; $3.50/ea; 40%

48 pp; 5½ x 8

Ad Rates: $40/page (5 x 7½); $25/½ page (5 x 3¾)

OSIRIS

Andrea and Robert Moorhead
Box 297
Deerfield, MA 01342
(413) 774-4027

Poetry, photographs, graphics/artwork.

OSIRIS is a multi-lingual poetry journal publishing contemporary work in English, French, Italian and German. Poetry in other languages such as Hungarian, Portuguese, and Danish appears in a bilingual format.

Robert Marteau, Hélène Dorion, Eugenio de Andrade, Ingrid Swanberg, Simon Perchik.

Unsolicited Manuscripts Received/ Published per Year: 150-200/6-8.

Payment: in copies.

Reporting Time: 4 weeks.

Copyright reverts to author upon publication.

1972; 2/yr; 500

$10/yr; $5/ea

40 pp; 6 x 9

Ad Rates: $125/page (5½ x 8½)

ISSN: 0095-019X

OSTENTATIOUS MIND

Patricia D. Coscia, Editor

JAF Station Box 7415

New York, NY 10116-4630

Poetry; all types except x-rated.

OSTENTATIOUS MIND is designed to encourage the intense writer, the cutting reality. The staff deals in the truth of life: political, social, and psychological. SASE for submission guidelines.

Payment: 4 copies.

Reporting Time: as soon as possible.

1987

$2/ea

10 pp; 7 x 8

OTHER VOICES

Lois Hauselman, Sharon Fiffer, Editors

University of IL at Chicago

Dept. of English (M/C 162)

601 S. Morgan St.

Chicago, IL 60607-7120

(312) 413-2209

Fiction, interviews.

A Prize-winning (IAC), independent market for quality fiction, we are dedicated to original, fresh, diverse stories and novel excerpts. We've won 13 IAC awards in 6 years, plus a CCLM/GE Younger Writers Award in 1988.

David Evanier, Rolaine Hochstein, Edith Pearlman, Stephen Dixon, Karen Karbo.

Unsolicited Manuscripts Received/ Published per Year: 1,000/40-50.

Reading Period: Oct.—April 1.

Payment: gratuity plus copies.

Reporting Time: 10–12 weeks.

Copyright held by magazine; reverts to author upon publication.

1985; 2/yr; 1,500

$20/yr ind, $24/2 yr inst; $7/ea; 40%, 50% to distributors

225 pp; 7 x 9

Ad Rates: $100/page (7 x 9); $75/½ page (3½ x 4½)

ISSN: 8756-4696

OUTERBRIDGE

Charlotte Alexander
112 E. 10th St.
New York, NY 10003

Poetry, fiction.

Craft first. Regular special themes, i.e., urban, rural, Southern. Slight bias to new voices and less published writers. Personal replies. Anti pure polemic. Theme projects: interdisciplinary (biology, physics, music, astronomy, etc.); the city, immigrant, migrant experience, best humor wit, nature, children's stories.

Stuart Ackerman, Walter McDonald, Candida Lawrence, Linda Bierds, Susan Astor.

Unsolicited Manuscripts Received/ Published per Year: 500+/30+.

Payment: 2 copies.

Reporting Time: 2–2½ months, except July–Aug.

Copyright held by magazine; reverts to author upon publication.

1975; 1/yr; 800

$5/yr; $5/ea

120 pp; 8½ x 5

ISSN: 0739-4969

OWEN WISTER REVIEW

(Editors rotate yearly)
P.O. Box 4238, University Station
University of Wyoming
Laramie, WY 82071
(307) 766-3819

Prose (to 4,000 words), B & W artwork, poetry (no line limit).

Student produced magazine, but publishes a mixture of student and small press authors. Perfect-bound, slick paper, high quality printing. Built to last.

Gerald Locklin, Richard Kostelanetz, W.D. Ehrhart, Cathy Lynn, Laurel Speer, Rane Arroyo.

Unsolicited Manuscripts Received/ Published per Year: 500+/75-100.

Reading Period: Sept.—Mar.

Payment: 1 copy, 10% off additional copies.

Reporting Time: 1–4 months. Do not read over the summer.

Copyright reverts to author upon publication.

1978; 2/yr; 500

$10/yr; $5/ea; Inquire

approx. 100 pp; digest

Poetry O

THE OXFORD AMERICAN

Marc Smirnoff
115½ South Lamar
Oxford, MS 38655

THE OXFORD AMERICAN is a general interest literary magazine originating from the south. We appeal to the intellegent, but non–academic, general reader.

John Grisham, Larry Brown, Eu-

dora Welty, John Updike, Donna Tartt.
Payment: $100–150 per essay, review, story; $60–75 per poem.
Reporting Time: 1–2 months.
Copyright held by magazine, but reverts to author upon publication.
1992; 4/yr; 8,000
$16/yr; $4.50/ea; 40%
72 pp; 8½ x 11
Ad Rates: $675/page (7½ x 10); $435/½ page (7½ x 4¾); $175/¼ page (3¾ x 4¾)
Ingram, Ubiquity

OYEZ REVIEW

Sarah L. Kisar
Roosevelt University
430 S. Michigan Ave.
Chicago, IL 60605
(312) 341-2017

Poetry, fiction, photographs.

OYEZ REVIEW is an award-winning, university-based magazine in its 27th year of publication. Each issue contains a number of poems and short stories written by people from various parts of the country and many different walks of life. The writings are diverse in content; all have universal appeal.

Ronald Wallace, David Martin, Barry Silesky, John Jacob, Brooke Bergan.
Payment: none.
Reporting Time: 6 months.
Copyright held by magazine; reverts to author upon publication.
1967; 1/yr; 400
$4/ea; 40%
110 pp; 5½ x 8½
No ads

P

THE PACIFIC REVIEW

James Brown, Faculty Editor
Department of English
California State University
5500 University Pkwy.
San Bernardino, CA 92407-2397
(714) 880-5824; (714) 880-5894

Poetry, fiction, essays, plays, translation, interviews.

THE PACIFIC REVIEW is an academic-based journal of the verbal and visual arts, edited by graduate and undergraduate students at CSUSB. An annual publication now in its eleventh year, **THE PACIFIC REVIEW** attempts to reflect aspects of its unique position in Southern California whenever possible, but without compromising its goal to serve as a vehicle for both emerging and established

creative voices—from and about any area.
Unsolicited Manuscripts Received/Published per Year: 200-300/15.
Reading Period: Sept.—Feb. 1.
Payment: in copies, upon publication.
Copyright held by magazine; reverts to author upon publication.
1983; 1/yr; 750
$6/yr ind, $7/inst; $4/ea; 40%
102 pp; 6 x 9
Ad Rates: $150/page (5 x 7½); $100/½ page (5 x 3¾); $50/¼ page (2½ x 3¾)

PAISLEY MOON PRESS/OPEN UNISON STOP

Michael Spring, P. Notzka
P.O. Box 95463
Seattle, WA 98145
Poems, prose, reviews.
Joyce Odam, Stephen Kessler, Judson Crews, Carolyn Stoloff.
Payment: 1 copy.
Reporting Time: 1 day–3 months.
300
$10/yr; $3/ea
5½ x 8½
No ads

PAINTBRUSH: A Journal of Poetry, Translations, and Letters

Ben Bennani
Division of Language and Literature
Northeast Missouri St. University
Kirksville, MO 63501
(816) 785-4185
Poetry, criticism, essays, reviews, interviews, translation, photographs, graphics/artwork.
Publishes serious but innovative poetry, translations from any language—especially neglected ones—interviews and book reviews. The focus is always on quality and novelty.
William Stafford, Richard Eberhart, Colette Inez, Kathleen Spivack, Charles Edward Eaton.
Unsolicited Manuscripts Received/Published per Year: 300/50.
Payment: in copies or $10/page when available.
Reporting Time: 4–6 weeks.
Copyright held by magazine; reverts to author upon publication.
1974; 2/yr; 500
$9/yr ind, $12/yr inst; $7/ea; 40%
65 pp; 5½ x 8½
Ad Rates: $150/page
ISSN: 0094-1964

PAINTED BRIDE QUARTERLY

Brian Brown, Marion Wrenn, Kathy Volk Miller
230 Vine Street
Philadelphia, PA 19106
(215) 925-9914
Poetry, fiction, criticism, essays,

reviews, plays, photographs, graphics/artwork.

PAINTED BRIDE QUARTERLY is a journal of literary and visual arts associated with the Painted Bride Art Center in Philadelphia. We publish both local and national writers and artists; the emphasis is on quality. We like crafted, articulate writing in any genre.

Naomi Shihab Nye, Eugene Howard, Etheridge Knight, Tina Barr, Robert Bly, Marnie Mueller.

Reading Period: Sept.—June.

Payment: copies and 1 year subscription.

Reporting Time: 2 weeks–2 months.

Copyright reverts to author.

1973; 4/yr; 1,000

$12/yr ind, $16/yr inst; $5/ea; 50%

80 pp; 5 x 8½

Ad Rates: $75/page; $50/½ page; $25/¼ page

PANDORA

Meg MacDonald, Editor
2063 Belford
Holly, MI 48442

Poetry, fiction, graphics/artwork.

Character-oriented science fiction and fantasy by new and established writers. We emphasize character intensive fiction rather than nuts and bolts SF or stock-plot fantasy. Avoid themes that are racist, sexist, or x-rated. *No horror* or glorification of violence, sex or vulgar language. Give us work about characters we can care about!

Sara Wojceinowski, Thomas Wiloch, Roger Dutcher, Michael Kucharski, D. Lopes Heald.

Unsolicited Manuscripts Received/Published per Year: 1,500-2,000/20-30.

Payment: 1¢-2¢/word; $10 and up on illus; $3.50 and up on cartoons and fillers.

Guidelines available for SASE. Closed to unsolicited manuscripts at this time.

Reporting Time: 6–10 weeks.

Copyright held by author. We buy First North American serial rights usually.

1978; 2/yr; 500

$10/2, $5/ea (US); $14/2, $7/ea (CANADA); $20/2, $10/ea (overseas); *US funds please!*

72 pp; 5½ x 8½

Ad Rates: $40/page (4½ x 7½); $25/½ page (4½ x 3¾); $16.50/¼ page (2¼ x 3¾); $11/⅛ page; ($10 per 25 words non-display)

ISSN: 0275-519X

Faxon

PANHANDLER

Laurie O'Brien, Michael Yots, Stanton Millet
English Department
University of West Florida
Pensacola, FL 32514-5751
(904) 474-2923

Poetry and short fiction.

THE PANHANDLER is a magazine of contemporary poetry and fiction. We want poetry and stories rooted in real experience in language with a strong colloquial flavor. Works that are engaging and readable stand a better chance with us than works that are self-consciously literary. Annual poetry chapbook competition: Winner receives $100 plus 50 copies. Send SASE for details.

Walter McDonald, Malcolm Glass, Enid Shomer, David Kirby, Joan Colby.

Unsolicited Manuscripts Received/ Published per Year: 4,000+/70-80.

Reading Period: year–round, slower in summer.

Payment: in copies.

Reporting Time: 2–3 months.

Copyright held by University; reverts to author upon publication.

1976; 2/yr; 500

$10/yr, $18/2yr–both include winning chapbook; 40%

64 pp; 6 x 9

ISSN: 0738-8705

Ebsco

PAPER BAG

M. Brownstein
P. O. Box 268805
Chicago IL 60626-8805

Guidelines included.

Literary arts publication: all forms of poetry—looking for original and strong images, black-and-white illustrations, and short short fiction (under 500 words).

Claudette Bess, Jean Townes.

Unsolicited Manuscripts Received/ Published per Year: 500/30.

Payment: 1 copy.

Reporting Time: 2 minutes–1 month.

Copyright: no.

1988; 4/yr; 200+.

$10/yr; $2.50/ea

20–30 pp; 5½ x 4¾

THE PAPER SALAd Poetry Journal

R. L. Moore
627 E. 100 S. #A
Salt Lake City, UT 84102
(801) 355-6430

Poetry.

Digest sized, flat spined about 100 pages about 30 poets, sometimes color cover, annual.

Rich Cronshey, Glenn Parker.
Unsolicited Manuscripts Received/ Published per Year: 500/30+.
Reading Period: year–round.
Payment: 1 copy upon publication.
Reporting Time: about 2 months.
Poets retain copyright.
1990; 1/yr; 200
$6.50/ea
100 pp; digest
Ad Rates: contact me and we'll work something out.

PARABOLA: The Magazine of Myth & Tradition
Virginia Baron, Ellen Dooling Draper
656 Broadway
New York, NY 10012
(212) 505-6200
Essays, reviews, interviews, retellings of traditional myths and stories, photographs, graphics/ artwork.
PARABOLA's focus is on myth and the world's cultural and spiritual traditions. Accordingly, **PARABOLA**'s approach to literature involves an emphasis on myths, legends, folktales, and oral transmission. **PARABOLA** primarily publishes articles and interviews which deal with mythology, comparative religion, and contemporary spirituality. Each issue focuses on a central theme.
P.L. Travers, Peter Brook, Eknath Easwaran, Frederick Franck, Robert Lawlor, Rhich Nhat Hanh, Chinua Achebe.
Payment: sliding scale.
Reporting Time: 6 weeks.
Copyright held by author.
1976; 4/yr; 41,000
$20/yr; $6/ea; 40%
128 pp; $6\frac{3}{4}$ x 10
Ad Rates: $815/page ($5\frac{1}{16}$ x $8\frac{5}{16}$); $545/½ page ($5\frac{1}{16}$ x $4\frac{1}{8}$); $310/¼ page ($2\frac{7}{16}$ x $4\frac{1}{8}$)
ISSN: 0362-1596

THE PARIS REVIEW
George Plimpton, Fiction Editor; Richard Howard, Poetry Editor
541 E. 72nd St.
New York, NY 10021
Fiction, poetry, literary nonfiction.
Focus on best of emerging and established poets, writers and artists. Always on the look-out for lively newcomers.
Joseph Brodsky, Carolyn Kizer, Rick Bass, E.L. Doctorow, Alice Munro, Roy Lichtenstein.
Unsolicited Manuscripts Received/ Published per Year: 20,000/35.
Payment: varies.
Reporting Time: 8–10 weeks.
Copyright held by Paris Review Inc.; reverts to author upon publication.

1953; 4/yr; 12,000
$24/yr; $7/ea
250 pp; 5 x 8
Ad Rates: $500/page
ISSN: 0031-2037
Eastern News

PARIS TRANSCONTINENTAL

Claire Larriere
Institut du Monde Anglophone
Sorbonne Nouvelle,5
Rue de L'Ecole de Medecine
75006 Paris, FRANCE

Short stories exclusively.

A forum for writers of excellent stories whose link is the English language, wherever spoken. **PARIS TRANSCONTINENTAL** hopes to introduce the best among today's authors, wherever they hail from, for non literatures are evolving which enrich our common space and actual understanding.

Stephen Dixon, Jayan Ya Mahapatra, Joyce Carol Oates, Albert Russo, Alan Sillitoe, Michael Wilding.

Unsolicited Manuscripts Received/ Published per Year: 100/25.
Reading Period: Oct.—June.
Payment: 2 copies of issue.
Reporting Time: 2–3 months.
Copyright is in name of individual authors.
2/yr; 1,000
FF 120/yr; FF 65/ea (postage included)
128 pp
Ad Rates: none
ISSN: 1146-5948

PARNASSUS

Herbert Leibowitz
41 Union Square West, Room 804
New York, NY 10003
(212) 463-0889

Criticism, essays, poems, reviews, photographs, graphics/artwork.

Devoted to the in-depth analysis of contemporary books of poetry. **PARNASSUS** seeks essays and reviews that are themselves works of art. The ideal reviewer is a poet with his or her own particular point of view. **PARNASSUS** publishes special issues on music, poetry in translation, the long poem; includes paintings, illustrations and photographs.

Seamus Heaney, Ross Feld, Alice Fulton, William Logan, Helen Vendler, Mary Karr.

Unsolicited Manuscripts Received/ Published per Year: 250–300/1–2.
Payment: $25–$250.
Reporting Time: varies.
Copyright held by Poetry in Review Foundation; reverts to author upon request.

1972; 2/yr; 2,500
$23/yr ind, $44/yr inst; $10/ea
350 pp; 6 x 9¼
Ad Rates: $250/page (6 x 9¼); $150/½ page (5 x 4)
ISSN: 0048-3028
Spectacular Diseases (UK)

PARTING GIFTS

Robert Bixby
3413 Wilshire Dr.
Greensboro, NC 27408

Poetry, fiction.
Unsolicited Manuscripts Received/ Published per Year: 2,000/80-100.
Reading Period: Jan.—May, but Mss. welcome anytime.
Payment: 1 copy.
Copyright held by March Street Press; reverts to author upon publication.
1988; 2/yr; 100
$8/yr; $4/ea; 40%
40 pp; 5½ x 8½
ISSN: 1043-3325

PARTISAN REVIEW

William Phillips
236 Bay State Rd.
Boston, MA 02215
(617) 353-4260

Essays, criticism, reviews, fiction, poetry, translation, interviews.
PARTISAN REVIEW examines the central issues of contemporary culture and social thought. It publishes critical essays on the arts and politics, new fiction and poetry, and book reviews.
Octavio Paz, Cynthia Ozick, Slavenka Drakulić, Doris Lessing, Joseph Brodsky.
Unsolicited Manuscripts Received/ Published per Year: 1,000/5 (fiction); 1,000/10-15 (poetry).
Reading Period: year–round.
Payment: varies.
Reporting Time: 2 months.
Copyright held by Partisan Review, Inc; reverts to author upon publication.
1937; 4/yr; 8,150
$18/yr ind, $28/yr inst; $5/ea; 15%
160 pp; 6 x 9
Ad Rates: $200–$250 page (4¼ x 7⅜); $120/½ page (4¼ x 3½); $75/¼ page (2 x 3½)
ISSN: 0031-2525
Eastern News

PASSAGES NORTH

Michael Barrett, Editor; Conrad Hillberry, Poetry Editor
Kalamazoo College
1200 Academy
Kalamazoo, MI 49007

Fiction, poetry, creative nonfiction, interview, visual art and photography.

PASSAGES NORTH publishes high quality writing and art by established and emerging writers and artists. Perfect bound, semiannual.

Tony Hoagland, Thomas Lux, Jim Daniels, Tess Gallagher, Richard Jackson, Alison Baker, Roger Brown, Mary Whalen.

Payment: copies.

Reporting Time: 6–8 weeks.

Copyright held by magazine; reverts to author upon publication.

1979; 2/yr; 1,000

$10/yr; $18/2 yr; $5/sample copy

Ad Rates: $200/page; $100/½ page; $50/¼ page

ISSN: 0278-0828

PASSAIC REVIEW

Richard Quatrone
Forstmann Library
195 Gregory Avenue
Passaic, NJ 07055

Poetry, fiction, plays, photographs, graphics/artwork.

PASSAIC REVIEW is an independent magazine that publishes the best work submitted to it. Emphasis is on strong, clear, direct writing.

Antler, Ronald Baatz, Amiri Baraka, Allen Ginsberg, Eliot Katz, Wanda Phipps.

Payment: none.

Reporting Time: 1–52 weeks.

Copyright held by magazine; reverts to author upon publication.

1979; 2/yr; 500

$6/yr ind, $10/yr inst; $3.75/ea; 40%

48–54 pp; 5 x 8½

Ad Rates: $80/page (5 x 8½); $40/½ page (2¾ x 4¼); $20/¼ page (1⅜ x 2⅛)

ISSN: 0731-4663

PEMBROKE MAGAZINE

Shelby Stephenson
Box 60, PSU
Pembroke, NC 28372
(919) 521-4214, ext. 433

Poetry, fiction, criticism, reviews, plays, interviews, graphics/artwork.

Open to poetry, fiction, essays, interviews, and artwork.

A.R. Ammons, Fred Chappell, Barbara Guest, Robert Morgan, Betty Adcock.

Payment: none.

Reporting Time: up to 3 months.

Copyright held by magazine; reverts to author upon publication.

1969; 1/yr; 500–800

$5/yr; $5/ea; (surface mail add .50 to each rate)

250 pp; 6 x 9

Ad Rates: $40/page; $25/½ page

THE PENNSYLVANIA REVIEW

Julie Parson-Nesbitt, Editor/Poetry Editor; Kellie Wells, Fiction Editor
English Department, 526 CL
University of Pittsburgh
Pittsburgh, PA 15260
(412) 624-6506

Poetry, fiction, criticism, essays, reviews, translations, interviews, graphics/artwork, photos (b&w).

Publishing the finest contemporary fiction, poetry, nonfiction and illustrations, *Choice* calls **THE PENNSYLVANIA REVIEW** a "fine small literary magazine . . . highly recommended".

Edward Abbey, Linda Pastan, Maxine Kumin, Paul West, Dorothy Barresi.

Unsolicited Manuscripts Received/Published per year: 800–1,000/20–25.

Payment: in copies.

Reporting Time: 8–12 weeks.

Copyright held by Univ. of Pittsburgh; reverts to author upon publication.

1990; 2/yr; 500; 1992; Vol. 5 #1, Vol. 5 #2 forthcoming Fall/Winter '92.

$10/yr; $5/ea; 40%

100 pp; 7 x 10

Ad Rates: $150/page (6 x 9); $70/½ page (6 x 4)

ISSN: 8756-5668

PEQUOD

Mark Rudman
N.Y.U. English Dept., 2nd floor
19 University Pl.
New York, NY 10003

Poetry, fiction, criticism, essays, translation.

Past issues of **PEQUOD** have featured Irish, Scandinavian, Russian, Israeli, Ukranian, and British poetry. Recent issues have included a special issue on literature and the visual arts, a focus on the long poem, and two issues on the subject of mourning. A forthcoming issue will focus on the topic of the desert.

Thomas Bernhard, Louise Glück, Donald Hall, Jane Kenyon, Joyce Carol Oates, Charlie Smith, David St. John, John Updike.

Unsolicited Manuscripts Received/Published per Year: 2,600/varies.

Reading Period: Oct.—Apr.

Payment: some payment to contributors.

Copyright held by magazine.

1974; 2/yr; 1,000–2,000

$12/yr ind, $20/2 yrs ind; $18/yr inst, $34/2 yrs inst; $10/ea

200 pp; 5½ x 8½

Ad Rates: $150/page (5½ x 8½); $200/2 pp

ISSN: 0149-0516

DeBoer

PEREGRINE: The Journal of Amherst Writers & Artists

Pat Schneider, Editor
P.O. Box 1076
Amherst MA 01004
(413) 253-3307

Poetry, fiction, cover graphics/artwork.

PEREGRINE is the journal of Amherst Writers & Artists, an organization dedicated to the belief that good writing is honest and unpretentious. We believe literature is related to the speech of home and workplace, and to the meanings discovered in ordinary lives without the bias of sex, race or class.

Jane Yolen, Barbara Van Noord, Steven Reil.

Unsolicited Manuscripts Received/ Published per Year: 500/15.

Payment: in copies upon publication.

Copyright held by Amherst Writers & Artists Press, Inc.; reverts to author upon publication.

1983; 1/yr; varies

$5 plus $2 postage/ea; 40%

Back issue; $3 plus $2 postage

64 pp; 5½ x 8¼

Ad Rates: contact magazine for information

ISSN: 0890-662X

PERMAFROST

203 Fine Arts Building
University of Alaska
Fairbanks, AK 99775
(907) 474-5247

Poetry, fiction, essays, creative nonfiction, photographs, graphics/artwork.

PERMAFROST seeks to promote excellence in contemporary literature and welcomes submissions in this vein. Although the magazine is regionally based, material need not refer to Alaska. Manuscripts from the lower 48 states, Hawaii, and international submissions (in English) are welcomes.

Reading Period: year–round.

Payment: 2 copies.

Reporting Time: 4 months, 6 months for mss. received in Summer.

Copyright held by author.

1975; 2/yr; 250

$7/yr; $3/ea; 30%

80 pp; 5 x 8

No ads

PIEDMONT LITERARY REVIEW

Gail White
Piedmont Literary Society
1017 Spanish Moss Ln.
Breaux Bridge, LA 70517
(804) 384-2027

Poetry, fiction, graphics/artwork, newsletter.

We publish mainly poetry, short stories; approximately 40 poems, 2 short stories. We need short stories of around 1,500 to 2,000 words. Traditional to free verse—we publish established poets and many first timers.

Wm. Stafford, X.J. Kennedy, Martha Bosworth, Barbara Loots, Judson Jerome.

Unsolicited Manuscripts Received/Published per Year: 500/75.

Payment: in copies.

Reporting Time: 5 days–3 months.

Copyright held by magazine; reverts to author upon publication.

1976; 4/yr; 300

$12/yr; $3/ea

50 pp; 5½ x 8½

ISSN: 0257-357X

PIG IRON

Jim Villani
P.O. Box 237
Youngstown, OH 44501
(216) 783-1269

Poetry, fiction, essays, translation, interviews, photographs, graphics/artwork.

Special emphasis on popular culture, genres, and new literature in a highly visual and cerebral format. Publishes issues around special themes: recent issues have featured Third World, Humor, Psychological Literature, Viet Nam Era, Surrealism, Science Fiction, Baseball, Labor, the epistolary form. Most recent volume is "Environment: Essence and Issue." Back issues available.

James Bertolino, Warren Woessner, Helen Ruggieri, Claudia Ricci, Ralph Braver, Wayne Hogan, Coco Gordan, Barbara Kasselmann.

Unsolicited Manuscripts Received/Published per Year: 6,000/85.

Payment: $5/page.

Reporting Time: 3 months.

Copyright held by editors; reverts to author upon publication.

1975; 1/yr; 1,500

$8/1 issue; $15/2 issues

$9.95/ea; 40%

128 pp; 8½ x 11

ISSN: 0362-5214

THE PIKESTAFF FORUM

Robert D. Sutherland, James R. Scrimgeour, James McGowan, Curtis White
P.O. Box 127
Normal, IL 61761
(309) 452-4831

Black and white photographs; line-drawings; small-press book reviews. Poetry, fiction, commentary on contemporary literature and the small-press scene.

A literary magazine eclectic in its tastes, publishing the best poetry and fiction that comes its way; sets a standard in tabloid design and format.

Gayl Teller, Jeff Gundy, Enid Dame, J. W. Rivers, R. Cooperman.

Unsolicited Manuscripts Received/ Published per Year: 2,500/58.

Payment: 3 free copies of issue in which work appears; 50% discount on extras.

Reporting Time: 3 months.

Copyright remains with authors and artists.

1978; 1/yr; 1,000

$10/6 issues; $2/ea

40 pp; tabloid

ISSN: 0192-8716

THE PITTSBURGH QUARTERLY

Frank Correnti, Editor; James Deahl, Canadian Editor; Lyn Ferlo, Art Editor

36 Haberman Ave.

Pittsburgh, PA 15211-2144

Canadian address: P.O. Box 20

99 Kimberley Ave

London, Ontario, N5Z 5A1

(412) 431-8885

Per issue: short short stories (up to 4,000 words), poetry, interview, reviews, features, (essays, etc).

THE PITTSBURGH QUARTERLY is a community writing project which networks (publishes) writers from all parts of the US, Canada, and overseas. We emphasize personal expression and craft over ideology.

Judith R. Robinson, Daryl Palmer, Ellen Smith, Rina Ferrarelli, Bill Ryan Richard Dillon.

Unsolicited Manuscripts Received/ Published per Year: 400/100.

Payment: 2 copies.

Reporting Time: 3 months.

Copyright reverts to author upon publication. Acknowledge **TPQ** in future publication.

1991; 4/yr; 600

$12/yr; $14/overseas; $4/ea; 10 or more 40%

76 pp; 5½ x 8½

Ad Rates: $100/full page (4½ x 7½); $50/½ page; $25/¼ page

ISSN: 1054-6340

Central Wholesale (Pittsburgh PA 15203)

PIVOT

Martin Mitchell

250 Riverside Dr. #23

New York, NY 10025

(212) 222-1408

Poetry.

Now in its 43rd year, **PIVOT**

publishes the work of both seasoned and new poets. It has a reputation for "firsts" of admirable performance.

Philip Appleman, Eugene J. McCarthy, William Matthews, Craig Raine, W. D. Snodgrass, Robert Wrigley.

Unsolicited Manuscripts Received/Published per Year: 500/25.

Reading Period: Jan. 1—June 1.

Payment: in copies.

Reporting Time: 2–4 weeks.

Copyright held by Sibyl Barsky Grucci; reverts to author upon publication.

1951; 1/yr; 1,500–3,000

$5/ea

76 pp; 6 x 9

Ad Rates: $125/page; $70/½ page; $40/¼ page

PLAINS POETRY JOURNAL

Jane Greer
P.O. Box 2337
Bismarck, ND 58502

Poetry, essays.

PLAINS POETRY JOURNAL is a forum for poetry using traditional poetic conventions: meter, rhyme, alliteration, assonance, painstaking attention to sound. No prosaic, conversational "free verse." No Hallmark verse. Will publish one essay per issue: humorous or serious essays on poetry. Widely published and unpublished poets receive same consideration.

Rhina Espaillat, Jack Butler, Johnny Wink, Gail White, Frederick Feirstein, Frederick Turner.

Unsolicited Manuscripts Received/Published per Year: 2,000+/100.

Reading Period: year–round.

Payment: 2 copies.

Reporting Time: 1 month.

Copyright held by magazine; reverts to author upon publication.

1982; 2/yr; 500

$9/yr; $18/5 issues; $4.50/ea; negotiable

60 pp; 5½ x 8½

ISSN: 0730-6172

PLAINSWOMAN

Elizabeth Hampsten
P.O. Box 8027
Grand Forks, ND 58202
(701) 777-8043

Essays, fiction, reviews, interviews, poetry, photographs, graphics/artwork.

PLAINSWOMAN publishes articles, interviews, fiction, poetry and graphics. We encourage clear writing by both academic and unpracticed writers, and we work with prospective contributors.

Emily Rhoads Johnson, Enid Shomer, Susan Strayer Deal.

Payment: $5 to $50, or more if funds allow.

Reporting Time: 1 week–1 month.

Copyright held by magazine; reverts to author upon publication.

1977; 10/yr; 600

$20/yr; $2/ea; 40%

20 pp; 8 x 11

ISSN: 0146-902X

PLOUGHSHARES

DeWitt Henry, Don Lee, David Daniel

Emerson College

100 Beacon St.

Boston, MA 02116

(617) 578-8753

Poetry, fiction, non-fiction, reviews, translation.

A magazine of new writing edited on a revolving basis by professional poets and writers to reflect different and contrasting points of view.

Sue Miller, Al Young, Tobias Wolff, Marie Howe, Christopher Tilghman, Alberto Ríos, Carolyn Forché.

Unsolicited Manuscripts Received/Published per Year: 5,000/200

Reading Period: Aug. 1—Apr. 1.

Reporting Time: 3-5 months.

Copyright reverts to author upon publication.

1971; 3/yr; 3,800

$19/yr ind, $22/yr inst; $8.95/ea; 20%–40%

280 pp; 5½ x 8½

Ad Rates: $250/page (4½ x 7); $150/½ page (4½ x 3¼); $100/¼ page (2¼ x 3¼)

ISSN: 0048-4474

DeBoer, L-S Distributors

THE PLUM REVIEW

M.Hammer, Christina Daub

P.O. Box 3557

Washington, DC 20007

Poetry, poetry book reviews, interviews.

All-poetry magazine featuring the best in contemporary poetry by both established and emerging poets from around the world.

Joseph Brodsky, Mark Strand, Marge Piercy, Robert Bly, Donald Hall, Linda Pastan, Jane Hirshfield.

Unsolicited Manuscripts Received/Published per Year: 3,000+/50–60.

Reading Period: Sept.—May.

Payment: 1 copy.

Reporting Time: 1 month.

1991; 2/yr; 1,000

$12/yr; $6/ea

120 pp; 6 x 9 flat-spined

Ad Rates: $200/page; $125/½ page

DeBoer

POEM

Nancy Frey Dillard
English Department
University of Alabama in Huntsville
Huntsville, AL 35899
(205) 895-6320

Poetry.

High quality mature poetry. No bias as to form or theme. Particular regard given to less well known poets.

Charles Edward Eaton, John Ditsky, Stephen Lang, R.T. Smith, Alison Reed.

Unsolicited Manuscripts Published per Year: 100-120.

Payment: in copy.

Reporting Time: 1 month.

Copyright held by Huntsville Literary Association.

1967; 2/yr; 400

$10/yr; $5/ea

70 pp; 4½ x 7½

No ads

POET AND CRITIC

Neal Bowers
203 Ross Hall
Iowa State University
Ames, IA 50011
(515) 294-2180

Poetry, criticism, reviews.

POET AND CRITIC publishes poems, essays on contemporary poetry and/or poetics (3,000 words or less), and reviews of current poetry books. We try to be receptive to all types of poetry, asking only that the work display a sense of language.

Brendan Galvin, Jean Burden, Albert Goldbarth, Ann Struthers, Malcolm Glass, Ron Offen.

Unsolicited Manuscripts Received/Published per Year: 6,000 poems/60 poems.

Reading Period: Sept.—May.

Payment: 1 copy.

Reporting Time: 3 days–2 weeks.

Copyright held by Iowa State University; reverts to author upon publication.

1964; 3/yr; 400

$18/yr ind, $18/yr inst; $8/ea; 40%

48 pp; 6 x 9

Ad Rates: exchanges with other magazines

ISSN: 0032-1958

POET LORE

Sunil Freeman, Managing Editor
Poet Lore, The Writer's Center
4508 Walsh St.
Bethesda, MD 20815
(301) 654-8664

Poetry, criticism, essays, reviews, translation, graphics/artwork.

POET LORE publishes original poems of all kinds. The editors continue to welcome narrative poetry and original translations of contemporary world poets. **POET LORE** publishes reviews of poetry collections and critical essays of contemporary poetry.

Walter McDonald, Sharon Olds, Leonard Nathan, Peter Wild, Albert Goldbarth.

Unsolicited Manuscripts Received/ Published per Year: 1,500/150.

Payment: 2 copies.

Reporting Time: 3 months.

Copyright held by The Writer's Center; reverts to author upon publication.

1889; 4/yr; 600

$15/yr ind, $24/yr inst; $4.50/ea; 40%

80 pp; 6 x 9

Ad Rates: $100/page (5½ x 8); $55/½ page (5½ x 4)

ISSN: 0032-1966

Faxon, Ebsco, McGregor, Boley

POET'S SANCTUARY

Hollee Donavan
P.O. Box 16720
Seattle, WA 98116

Poetry, very short stories, reviews, visual poetry and more.

POET'S SANCTUARY contains diversified literature, social/environmental information, poetry education, interesting facts, humorous segments, reviews, and a pen pals section. Artwork compliments material throughout magazine.

A. D. Winans, Erroll Miller, Nancy Henderson.

Unsolicited Manuscripts Received/ Published per Year: 100%/80–160.

Payment: 2 copies.

Reporting Time: 2–3 weeks.

Copyright reverts back to author upon publication.

1993; 4/yr; appx. 75–100

$12.50/yr; $3.50/ea; $3.00

35+ pp; 8½ x11

Ad Rates: $40/6 x 6; $30/4 x 6; $20/2 x 6; $10/1 x 6

POETIC SPACE: POETRY AND FICTION

Don Hildenbrand, Editor; Thomas Strand, Fiction Editor
P.O. Box 11157
Eugene, OR 97440

Poetry, fiction, reviews, interviews, graphics/artwork, theater and film reviews. Chapbook and Anthology now available; for information send SASE.

Patty McDonald, Albert Huffstickler, William Meyer, Crawdad Nelson, Arthur Winfield Knight, Spenser Reese, Sesshu Foster.

Unsolicited Manuscripts Received/ Published per Year: 500+/50.
$10/yr, $18/2 yr; $3/ea, $4/back issues.

POETICS JOURNAL

Lyn Hejinian, Barrett Watten
2639 Russell St.
Berkeley, CA 94705
(510) 548-1817

Criticism, essays, reviews.

POETICS JOURNAL is an irregularly published journal of contemporary poetics by poets and prose writers as well as by other artists, critics, linguists, and political theorists. It features essays, articles, and investigatory reviews. Individual issues focus on topics including "close reading", "poetry and philosophy", "women and modernism", "non-narrative", etc.

Ron Silliman, George Lakoff, Rae Armantrout, Kofi Natambu, Leslie Scalapino.

Unsolicited Manuscripts Received/ Published per Year: 40-50/3.
Payment: in copies.
Reporting Time: 2–4 weeks.
Copyright held by author.
1982; irreg.; 600
$10/ea; 25%–40%
144 pp; 6 x 9
ISSN: 0731-5236
SPD, Sun & Moon

POETPOURRI

Comstock Writer's Group; Kathleen Bryce Niles, Coordinator; Jennifer B. MacPherson, President
907 Comstock Ave.
Syracuse, NY 13210
(315) 475-0339

Poetry only.

Perfect-bound 100 pp, put out twice yearly. We accept poetry on the basis of quality, not reputation. We do not accept porno, sentimental, greeting card verse and very few haikus or religious verse. Well crafted poetry, free or formal, written in understandable, grammatically correct English—metaphor, fresh, vivid imagery enjoyed.

Gayle Elen Harvey, Robt. Cooperman, R. Nikolas Macioci, Kathryn Howd Machah, Michael Bugeja.

Unsolicited Manuscripts Received/ Published per Year: thousands/200.
Payment: copy, prize money.
Reporting Time: usually 2–4 weeks, with comments.
Copyright reverts to author.
1986; 2/yr; 500
$8/yr; $15/2 yrs; $4/ea
75–100 pp; 5½ x 8½

POETRY

Joseph Parisi
60 West Walton St.
Chicago, IL 60610
(312) 280-4870

Poetry, reviews, essays.

For over 80 years **POETRY** has been the most widely read monthly of verse. From Auden to Ashbery, Pound to Pinsky, Stevens to Soto—voices famous and new.

Adrienne Rich, A.R. Ammons, Richard Kenney, J.D. McClatchy, Sharon Olds.

Unsolicited Manuscripts Received/Published per Year: 75,000/300±.

Reading Period: year–round.

Payment: $2/line for verse; $20/page of prose.

Reporting Time: 8–10 weeks.

Copyright held by Modern Poetry Association; reverts to author upon request.

1912; 12/yr; 7,600

$25/yr ind, $27/yr inst; $2.50/ea

64 pp; 5½ x 9

Ad Rates: $280/page (3¾ x 7); $174/½ page (3¾ x 3½); $111/¼ page (1¾ x 3½)

ISSN: 0032-2032

DeBoer, Ingram, Fine Print, Michiana News Service, Ubiquity

POETRY CANADA

Barry Dempster, Poetry Editor; Bob Hilderley, Prose Editor
P.O. Box 1061, 221 King St. E.
Kingston, Ontario K7L 4Y5
CANADA
(613) 548-8429 Fax: (613) 548-1556

Poetry essays on poetry, reviews of poetry books.

Bill Bissett, Maggie Helwig, Daniel David Moses.

Unsolicited Manuscripts Received/Published per Year: 2,400/20.

Payment: after publication.

Reporting Time: 4 months.

Copyright: We retain first North American Serial Rights.

1980; 4/yr; 700

$16/4; $4.55/ea

36 pp; tabloid

Ad Rates: available upon request.

ISSN: 0709-3373

POETRY EAST

Richard Jones
802 W. Belden
English Department
DePaul University
Chicago, IL 60614
(312) 362-5114

Poetry, translations, fiction, art, interviews, reviews.

POETRY EAST publishes issues dedicated to particular poets or topics. We are also interested in reading essays on poetics, the relationship between art and the world. We are also looking for translations and ideas for feature/symposia.

Gerald Stern, Ruth Stone, Jack Grapes.

Unsolicited Manuscripts Received/Published per Year: 5,000/200–300.

Payment: in copies, honoraria.

Reporting Time: 3 months.

Copyright reverts to author, but we reserve the right to include work in anthologies.

1980; 2/yr; 1,500

$12; $8

200 pp; 5½ x 8½

Ad Rates: $100/page; $50/½ page

ISSN: 0197-4009

DeBoer, Fine Print

POETRY FLASH

Joyce Jenkins, Editor; Richard Silberg, Associate Editor

P.O. Box 4172

Berkeley, CA 94704

(510) 525-5476

Criticism, essays, reviews, interviews, photographs, poetry.

POETRY FLASH, A Poetry Review and Literary Calendar, publishes the most complete literary calendar of the West available. Also reviews of books, magazines, readings, and events, as well as interviews, occasional essays, photos, general commentary and information on submissions and publications for poets.

Keith Abbott, Marilyn Chin, Ivan Arguelles, Jack Marshall, Jack Foley, Dorianne Laux, Tony Burnstone.

Unsolicited Manuscripts Received/Published per Year: 1,500/50.

Reading period: year–round.

Payment: subscription to $25; $50 to $100 maximum.

Reporting Time: 3 months.

Copyright held by author.

1972; 12/yr; 19,000; free to public places

$15/yr ind, $16/yr inst

24–32 pp; 11½ x 15

Ad Rates: $500/page (10 x 13¾); $250/½ page (10 x 7); $125/¼ page (6½ x 5) or $130/5 x 7

ISSN: 0737-4747

THE POETRY MISCELLANY

Richard Jackson, Michael Panori

University of Tennessee at Chattanooga

Department of English

Chattanooga, TN 37402

(615) 624-7279 or 755-4629

Poetry, essays, reviews, translation, interviews.

We are very much a miscellany in the traditional sense of that

word; we publish a variety of "types" of poetry.
John Ashbery, Marvin Bell, Carolyn Forché, William Stafford, Mark Strand.
Payment: none.
Reporting Time: 6 weeks.
Copyright held by magazine; reverts to author upon publication.
1971; 2/yr; 1,100
$3/yr ind; $2/yr inst; $3/ea
130 pp; 6 x 9
Ad Rates: $100/page (5 x 8); $65/½ page (5 x 4½); $40/¼ page (5 x 2)

POETRY MOTEL

Jennifer Willis Long, Bud Backen, Patrick Mckinnon
1619 Jefferson
Duluth, MN 55812
(218) 728-3728
Poetry.
General poetry magazine open to all from "beginners" to "pros."
Todd Moore, Linda Wing, Robert Peters.
Unsolicited Manuscripts Received/Published per Year: 1,000/100
Reading Period: year–round.
Payment: 1 copy.
Reporting Time: 1 month.
Copyright: yes.
1984; varies; 1,000
$15.95/3 issues; $5.95/ea; 40%
52 pp; 8 x 7
No ads

POETRY NEW YORK: A Journal of Poetry and Translation

Burt Kimmelman, Tod Thilleman
P.O. Box 3184
Church St. Station
New York, NY 10008
Poetry, translations of poetry, artwork.
About 9 x 6, perfect bound, about 80 pp.
Bonnefoy, Bronk, Creeley, Di Prima, Heller, Mac Low, Rothenberg.
Unsolicited Manuscripts Received/Published per Year: 400/5–10.
Reading Period: Spring
Payment: 1 copy.
Reporting Time: 4 months or more.
Copyright belongs to author.
1985; 1/yr; 1,500
$5/ea; 500
80 pp; 9 x 6
Ad Rates: swap ads
DeBoer

POETRY PROJECT NEWSLETTER

Jordan Davis
The Poetry Project
St. Mark's Church
131 E. 10th St.

New York, NY 10003
(212) 674-0910
Poetry, criticism, essays, reviews, listings.
Bernadette Mayer, Anselm Hollo, Robert Creeley, Kofi Natambu, Paul Violi, James Schuyler, Nicole Brossard.
Reading Period: Sept.—May.
Payment: none.
Reporting Time: 4 weeks.
Copyright held by author.
1967; 4/yr; 3,000
$20/yr
24 pp; 8½ x 11
Ad Rates: $200/page (7 x 10); $130/½ page (7 x 5 or 3½ x 10); $100/⅓ page (3½ x 5 or 7 x 2½); $60/⅙ page (3½ x 2½); $40/1/12 page; Discounts for nonprofits.

POETS ON

Ruth Daigon
29 Loring Ave.
Mill Valley, CA 94941
(415) 381-2824
Poetry.
POETS ON is a semi-annual poetry magazine. Theme-oriented, exploring basic human concerns through insightful, significant, well-crafted poetry. We publish recognized poets as well as unknown poets.
Sue Walker, Michael Bugeja, Marge Piercy, Lyn Lifshin, Barbara Crooker, James Broughton.
Unsolicited Manuscripts Received/Published per Year: 5,000+/85.
Reading Period: Sept.—Dec. 1, Feb.—May 1.
Payment: in copies.
Reporting Time: 2–3 months.
Copyright reverts to author.
1977; 2/yr; 500
$8/yr; $5/ea
48 pp; 5½ x 8½

THE PORTABLE LOWER EAST SIDE

Kurt Hollander, Arthur Nersesian
P. O. Box 30323
New York, NY 10011
Fiction, poetry, photography, essays.
PORTABLE LOWER EAST SIDE is a literary magazine involved with New York City. Strong emphasis on ethnic and cultural diversity, and on social issues. Latest issue: "Queer City." Forthcoming: Drugs.
Hubert Selby, Margaret Randall, Luisa Valenzuela, Willie Colon, Edward Limonov.
Payment: in copies and small sums.
Reporting Time: 2 months.
Copyright reverts to author.
1984; 2/yr; 2,000.
$11/yr ind, $20/yr inst; $7/ea; 40%
175 pp; 5½ x 7

Ad Rates: $100/page; $75/½ page
SPD, Inland, DeBoer

PORTLAND REVIEW

Kala Rounds
P.O. Box 751
Portland, OR 97207
(503) 725-4468

Fiction, poetry, essays, plays, photographs, graphics/artwork.

The **PORTLAND REVIEW** is the biannual Arts and Literature Magazine of Portland State University. It draws material mainly from the Pacific Northwest, but is open to submissions from outside the region.

Unsolicited Manuscripts Received/Published per Year: 700/100.
Payment: 1 copy.
Reporting Time: 1–2 months.
Copyright held by author.
1953; 2/yr; 1,000
$10/yr; $5/ea + $1 postage
80 pp; 9 x 12

POTATO EYES

Roy Zarucchi, Carolyn Page
Nightshade Press, P.O. Box 76
Troy, ME 04987
(207) 948-3427

Canadian and US poetry, short stories, reviews of poetry, black and white art, contemporary essays.

A semi-annual literary arts journal focusing on poetry, short fiction and art work from/about the Appalachians from Alabama to Quebec. This is a primary, but not exclusive focus.

Judy Longley, Nzadi Keita, Robert Chute, Patt Carr, Peter Mandel, Jack Coulehan.

Unsolicited Manuscripts Received/Published per Year: 1,600/200+.
Reading Period: year–round.
Payment: in copies.
Reporting Time: 8 weeks.
Copyright held by publisher, reverts to author upon publication.
1989; 2/yr; 800
$11/yr; $6/ea; 40%
104 pp; 5½ x 8½
ISSN: 1041-9926

POTPOURRI

Polly W. Swafford, Senior Editor; Pat Anthony, Poetry Editor
P.O. Box 8278
Prairie Village, KS 66208
(913) 642-1503

Fiction, nonfiction, poetry.

POTPOURRI is a not-for-profit, monthly literary magazine which is published in tabloid form. **POTPOURRI** publishes a broad genre of short stories, poetry, adventure, travel, essays by both professional and novice writers.

David Ray, Layle Silbert, Robert Cooperman, Stuart Friebert.
Unsolicited Manuscripts Received/ Published per Year: 2,700/1,250.
Reading Period: year–round.
Payment: in copies (up to 20).
Reporting Time: 8–12 weeks.
Copyright: yes.
1989; 12/yr; 6,000
$15/yr; $1/sample copy
32 pp; tabloid 11½ x 14
Ad Rates: $10/per column inch = open rate. Contact publisher for different rates/sizes.

POULTRY, A Magazine of Voice

Jack Flavin, Brendan Galvin, George Garrett
P.O. Box 4413
Springfield, MA 01101
(413) 732-0435
Parodies, satire, put-ons, put-downs of contemporary poetry, lit & litbiz.
David R. Slavitt, Douglas A. Powell, Joyce Lamers, Jay Blumenthal, Lyn Lifshin, R. S. Gwynn, Rachel Loden.
Unsolicited Manuscripts Received/ Published per Year: 500/80.
Payment: 10 free copies.
Reporting Time: 2–3 months.
Copyright: first publishing rights.
1979; 2–3/yr; 1,400
$5/yr; $2/ea

PRAIRIE FIRE

Andris Taskans, Managing Editor
423-100 Arthur St.
Winnipeg, Manitoba, R3B 1H3 CANADA
(204) 943-9066
Fiction, poetry, essays, book reviews.
A Canadian magazine with a western perspective, featuring new writing and special issues on topics such as ethnic writing, women's writing, genre writing and more.
Sandra Birdsell, Rudy Wiebe.
Unsolicited Manuscripts Received/ Published per Year: 800/80
Reporting Time: 3–4 months.
Copyright reverts to author upon publication.
1978; 4/yr; 1,000
$24/yr; $7.95/ea; 30%
100 pp; 6 x 9
ISSN: 0821-1124
Canadian Magazine Publishers Association

PRAIRIE JOURNAL/of Canadian Literature

Prairie Journal Trust
P.O. Box 61203, Brentwood P.O.
Calgary, Alberta, T2L 2K6 CANADA
Short fiction, poetry, review, essays, drama.
Literary small press publication.

No US stamps (submissions will not be read or returned without sufficient Canadian postage for return.)

Fred Cogswell, Lorna Crozier, Mick Burrs, Robin Mathews, Bruce Hunter, John V. Hicks, Shaunt Basmajian, George Amabile, Gary Hyland, Glen Sorestad, Peter Baltensperger, Dennis Cooley.

Unsolicited Manuscripts Received/ Published per Year: 200/20.

Payment: Honouraria.

Reporting Time: 3–6 weeks.

Copyright for author.

1983; 2/yr; 500

$6/yr; $3/ea; 40%

60 pp; 7½ x 8

Ad Rates: negotiable

ISSN: 0827-2921

PRAIRIE SCHOONER

Hilda Raz
201 Andrews Hall
University of Nebraska
Lincoln, NE 68588-0334
(402) 472-3191

Poetry, fiction, essays, reviews, translation.

PRAIRIE SCHOONER, a literary quarterly, publishes the best writing available from beginning and established writers: short stories, poems, interviews, imaginative essays of general interest, and reviews of current books of poetry and fiction. Scholarly articles requiring footnote references are generally not published by **PRAIRIE SCHOONER**.

John Keeble, Ursula Hegi, Linda Hasselstrom, Brendan Galvin, Kyoko Mori, Stephen Peters.

Unsolicited Manuscripts Received/ Published per Year: 4,800/120.

Payment: 12 annual writing prizes and grant funds, when available; copies also.

Reporting Time: 3 months.

Copyright held by magazine; reverts to author upon request.

1927; 4/yr; 3,100

$20/yr ind, $22/yr inst; $6.45/ea; 40%

176 pp; 6 x 9

Ad Rates: $150/page (4¾ x 7½)

ISSN: 0032-6682

Ingram, Total

PRIMAVERA

Editorial Board
Box #37-7547
Chicago, IL 60637
(312) 324-5920

Poetry, fiction, photographs, graphics/artwork.

PRIMAVERA focuses on the experiences of women; publishes both established and unknown writers. Literary quality is the most important consideration.

S. L. Marin, Maxine Clair, Janet McCann, Anna Czekanowicz.

Unsolicited Manuscripts Received/ Published per Year: 1,000/25–30.

Payment: in copies.

Reporting Time: 2 weeks–3 months.

Copyright held by magazine; reverts to author upon publication.

1975; 1/yr; 1,000

$9/yr; $9/ea

5½ x 8½

No ads

ISSN: 0364-7609

THE PROSPECT REVIEW

Peter A. Koufos
557 10th St.
Brooklyn, NY 11215
(718) 788-5709

Poetry, fiction.

TPR is a literary journal committed to daring; bridging a gap between the unacknowledged poet and writer with those in academia for cultural unity.

E. Ethelbert Miller, Richard Burgin, Jana Harris, Gina Bergamino.

Unsolicited Manuscripts Received/ Published per Year: many/20.

Payment: copies.

Reporting Time: on or near issue release date.

Copyright reverts to authors upon publication.

1990; 2/yr

$12/yr; $6/ea

86 pp; 6 x 8

Ad Rates: Available on request

ISSN: 1049-0426

DeBoer

PROVINCETOWN ARTS

Christopher Busa
650 Commercial Street
Provincetown, MA 02657
(508) 487-3167

Poetry, fiction, reviews, essays, translation, interviews, photographs, graphics/artwork.

The documentary voice of the artists and writers who visit Cape Cod, **PROVINCETOWN ARTS** focuses on the phenonmenon of the art colony, not as geographical locus, but as a point of view. A large proportion of this annual book-length magazine emphasizes visual art, exploring the relation of visual art to language.

Alan Dugan, Stanley Kunitz, Susan Mitchell, Mark Doty, Cyrus Cassells, Henri Cole.

Unsolicited Manuscripts Received/ Published per Year: 650/5.

Reading Period: Aug.—Feb.

Payment: $25–$125 per poem;

$125–300 per story (fiction & nonfiction).
Reporting Time: 2–4 months.
Copyright: Provincetown Arts, Inc.
1985; 1/yr; 9,500
$10/yr; $6.50/sample; 40%
184 pp; 9 x 12
Ad Rates: $950/page; $550/½ page; $400/⅓ page
Ingram, IPD, New England Circulation Assoc.

PUCK: THE UNOFFICIAL JOURNAL OF THE IRREPRESSIBLE

Brian Clark, Kurt Putnam, Violet Riverrun
900 Tennessee, #15
San Francisco, CA 94107-3014
(415) 648-2175; Internet = bcclark@igc.apc.org
Fiction, essays, reviews, graphics, poetry.
A radical reinterpretation of consensus reality. Color covers, 80 pages, 8½ x 11, printed offset, appearing thrice a year.
Stan Henry, Hugh Fox, Abdel Ishara, etc.
Unsolicited Manuscripts Received/Published per Year: 1,000's/dozens.
Payment: copies and honararium
Reporting Time: 2 weeks–2 months.
Copyright: yes.
1984; 3/yr; 5,000
$17/yr; $6.50/ea; 40%–55%
80 pp; 8½ x 11
Ad Rates: Write, call, or e-mail for rates
ISSN: 1071-7633
Fine Print, Desert Moon, Ubiquity, Bookpeople, Inland

PUCKERBRUSH REVIEW

Constance Hunting
76 Main St.
Orono, ME 04473
(207) 581-3832
Fiction, poetry, reviews, criticism, interviews, essays, graphics/artwork, photographs.
The special focus is on Maine literature and literary figures such as Elizabeth Hardwick, Mary McCarthy, Amy Clampitt, Phillip Booth. The intent is to publish fiction, poetry and reviews by contemporary Maine writers. The purpose is both to reveal and to encourage the literary energy in this isolated state. "Puckerbrush" = new growth.
Deborah Pease, James Laughlin, Sonya Dorman, Farnham Blair, Sanford Phippen.
Unsolicited Manuscripts Received/Published per Year: 200/35.
Payment: in copies.
Copyright held by magazine; reverts to author upon publication.

1978; 2/yr; 450
$8/yr; $4/ea; 40%
75 pp; 8½ x 11
Ad Rates: inquire

250 pp; 6 x 9
Ad Rates: $150/page; $90/½ page; $60/¼ page
ISSN: 0738-517X

PUERTO DEL SOL
Kevin McIlvoy and Antonya Nelson
New Mexico State University
Box 3E
Las Cruces, NM 88003
(505) 646-3931
Poetry, fiction, novel sections, criticism, essays, reviews, translation, interviews, photographs, graphics/artwork.
Though our emphasis is on the Southwest, forty percent of each issue is the poetry, short fiction, artwork, etc. of artists from all over the United States.
Naomi Shihab Nye, Richard Russo, William Stafford, Susan Thornton, Dagoberto Gilb.
Unsolicited Manuscripts Received/Published per Year: 1,000/25 fiction, 35-45 poetry, 5-10 essay.
Reading Period: Sept.—Apr. 1.
Payment: copies.
Reporting Time: 8–12 weeks.
Copyright held by magazine; reverts to author upon publication.
1960; 2/yr; 1,400
$12/yr ind, $10/yr inst; $7/ea; 40%

Q

QUARRY WEST
Kenneth Weisner
c/o Porter College
University of California
Santa Cruz, CA 95064
(408) 459-2155; (408) 459-2951 (messages)
Poetry, fiction, essays, graphics/artwork.
QUARRY WEST combines quality design, graphics, production with about 95 pages of poetry and fiction, plus essays and reviews. We value intensity of voice and variety in form, content, intent. "A controversy of poets." We do symposiums, also: #22, Rexroth; #25, Neruda; #29/30, Dissident Song: Contemporary Asian American Anthology.
Marilyn Chin, Francisco X. Alarcón, Bill Knott, Lucille Clifton, Bruce Weigl.
Unsolicited Manuscripts Received/Published per Year: 800/20.

Payment: 2 contributor's copies.
Copyright held by magazine; reverts to author upon request.
1971; 2/yr; 1,000
$15/yr; $10/ea; $3.50/back issue; 40%
110 pp; 6¾ x 8¼
Ad Rates: inquire
ISSN: 0736-4628

THE QUARTERLY

Gordon Lish
650 Madison Ave.
New York, NY 10021
(212) 888-4769

Poetry, fiction, essay, humor.
A wide-open venue with particular hospitality for the unaffiliated. Fastest, fairest readings.
Unsolicited Manuscripts Received/Published per Year: 25,000/200.
Reading Period: year–round.
Payment: varies.
Copyright held by magazine; reverts to author upon publication.
1987; 4/yr; 15,000
Subscription information available upon request.

QUARTERLY REVIEW OF LITERATURE

Contemporary Poetry Series
Theodore and Renee Weiss
26 Haslet Ave.
Princeton, NJ 08540

Poetry.
QRL, a new concept in poetry, publishes 4 to 6 prize-winning collections of poetry in each volume, chosen through international competition. Called "the most significant event in years" and "the best bargain in poetry" and applauded as "brilliant." Each issue includes: poetry, long poems, poetic plays, poetry translation, plus introductory essays, photographs, and biographies of each author.
Wislava Szymborska, David Schubert, Nancy Esposito, Larry Kramer, Julia Mishkin.
Reading Period: May and Nov.
Payment: $1,000 plus 100 copies per winning manuscript. Please write for more information, with SASE.
Reporting Time: 2 months or less.
Copyright held by magazine.
1943; 1/yr; 3–5,000
$20/2 volumes ind paper, $20/cloth volume inst; $10/ea; 10%
350 pp; 5½ x 8½
Ad Rates: $300/page; $175/½ page
ISSN: 0033-5819

QUARTERLY WEST

M. L. Williams
317 Olpin Union
University of Utah

Salt Lake City, UT 84112
(801) 581-3938

Fiction, poetry, reviews, translation.

We try to publish the best in poetry and fiction, both mainstream and experimental. We conduct a biennial novella competition and also publish reviews and translations. We're not a western genre magazine. Biennial Novella Competition; send S.A.S.E. for details. We accept multiple submissions (just tell us, please).

Andre Dubus, Francine Prose, Ron Carlson, Marvin Bell, Stephen Dobyns, William Stafford, Philip Levine, C.E. Poverman, Antonya Nelson.

Unsolicited Manuscripts Received/ Published per Year: 1,000+/40.

Reading Period: year–round.

Payment: fiction $25–$50; poems and reviews $15–$50 each + 2 copies and 1 yr sub.

Reporting Time: 4–12 weeks.

Copyright held by magazine; reverts to author upon request.

1976; 2/yr; 1,000

$11/yr; $6.50/ea; 25%–40%

200 pp; 6 x 9

Ad Rates: $150/page (4⅜ x 7⅞); $85/½ page (4⅜ x 4)

ISSN: 0194-4231

QUILT

Ishmael Reed, Al Young
660 13th St., #203
Oakland, CA 94612-1241

Poetry, fiction, criticism, essays, interviews, graphics/artwork.

QUILT is a book-length literary journal which represents the quality and diversity of contemporary writing. **QUILT** is multicultural in focus (featuring Asian, Afro, Hispanic, European and Native American authors) and gives voice to new as well as established talent.

Cecil Brown, Frank Chin, Adrienne Kennedy, Harryette Mullen, Cyn Zarco.

Payment: none.

Copyright reverts to author.

1981; 1/yr; 1,000

$7.95/yr; $7.95/ea; 40%

200 pp; 5½ x 8½

No ads

ISSN: 0277-593X

QUIXOTE

Morris Edelson, Melissa Bondy
1812 Marshall
Houston, TX 77098
(713) 529-7944

Poetry, fiction, criticism, essays, translation, interviews.

Social criticism/satire/mucking around.

D. A. Levy, Pablo Neruda, Tuli

Kupferberg, Steve Kowitt, Curt Johnson.
Payment: in copies.
Reporting Time: 6 months.
Copyright held by author.
1965; 12/yr; 300
$15/yr; $2/ea
40–100 pp; 4 x 5–11 x 17

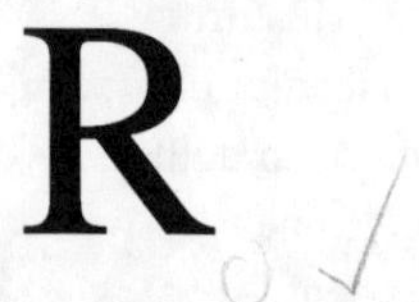

RACCOON

David Spicer
P.O. Box 111327
Memphis, TN 38111-1327
Poetry, fiction, criticism, essays, reviews, translation, interviews, photographs.
A journal of contemporary literature, with poetry, fiction, essay.
Maurya Simon, Pattiann Rogers, David Romtvedt, Jay Meek, Frank Russell.
Payment: poetry–1 year subscription; prose–$50 and 1 copy.
Reporting Time: 6 weeks–3 months.
Copyright reverts to author upon publication.
1977; 3/yr; 500
$12.50/yr; $5/ea; 40%
ISSN: 0148-0162
SPD, Ebsco, Faxon

RAG MAG/Black Hat Press

Beverly Voldseth, Editor and Publisher
Box 12
Goodhue, MN 55027
(612) 923-4590
Poetry, fiction, essays, reviews, plays, photographs, graphics/artwork.
Small ecletic lit mag.
James Lineberger, JoAnne Makela, Egon Ludowese, Susan Thurston Hamerski.
Unsolicited Manuscripts Received/Published per Year: 400/80.
Reading Period: Jan.—Mar.
Payment: in copies.
Reporting Time: 1 week–2 months.
Copyright held by magazine; reverts to author upon publication.
1982; 2/yr; 250
$10/yr. $6/ea
112 pp; 6 x 9
Ad Rates: $35/page (4 x 7⅜); $20/½ page (4 x 3½); $10/¼ page (4 x 1¾); will exchange ads
ISSN: 0742-2768

RAMBUNCTIOUS REVIEW

M. Dellutri, N. Lennon, R. Goldman, E. Hausler
1221 West Pratt Boulevard
Chicago, IL 60626

Poetry, fiction, photographs, graphics/artwork.

We are an annual literary arts magazine devoted to the publication of new and established writers and artists. We sponsor annual poetry and fiction contests and theme issues. Our next issue is focused on "Life."

Elizabeth Eddy, Richard Calisch, Hugh Fox, Richard Kostelanetz.

Unsolicited Manuscripts Received/ Published per Year: 1,000/15.

Reading Period: Sept. 1—May 31.

Payment: 2 issues.

Copyright held by magazine; reverts to author upon publication.

1986; 1/yr; 450

$10/3 issues; $4/sample

48 pp; 7 x 10

No ads

Ingram

RANT

Alfred Vitale
P.O. Box 6872
Yorkville Station
New York, NY 10128
(212) 722-4834

Short fiction, poetry, prose, artwork.

RANT is a hybrid of Zine and Literary Journal . . . unconventional . . . jarring and outspoken writing without pretense . . . features voices that challenge any and all established institutions.

Hal Sirowitz, Gina Grega, Charles Bukowski, Ron Kolm, Arthur Nersesian, Cheryl Townsend, C. F. Roberts.

Unsolicited Manuscripts Received/ Published per Year: 5,000/150.

Payment: copies.

Reporting Time: 1–3 months, but generally within 1 month.

Copyright: yes.

1993; 4/yr; 1,000

$20/yr; $4.95/ea

90 pp; 8½ x 5½

Ad Rates: $100/page; $60/½ page (4 x 5); $40/all other

ISSN: 1068-9419

Ubiquity, Desert Moon

RARITAN

R. Poirier, Editor; Suzanne K. Hyman, Managing Editor
31 Mine St.
New Brunswick, NJ 08903
(908) 932-7887 or 7852

Criticism, essays, reviews, poetry, fiction. A comprehensive critique of contemporary culture.

Stanley Cavell, Clifford Geertz, Vicki Hearne, Edward W. Said.

Unsolicited Manuscripts Received/ Published per Year: 250/7.

Payment: $100/article.

Reporting Time: 2 months.

Copyright reverts to author in 6 months.
1981; 4/yr; 3,500
$16/yr, $26/2 yrs ind, $20/yr, $30/2 yrs inst; $5/ea; $6/back issues; 40%–50%
160 pp; 6 x 9
Ad Rates: $275/page (4½ x 7½)
ISSN: 0275-1607
DeBoer, Ingram

Copyright held by magazine; reverts to author upon publication.
1981; 2/yr; 3,000
$20/3 issues; $35 inst & overseas; $7.50–$10 ea; 40%
150 pp; 8½ x 11
Ad Rates: $300/page; $175/½ page; $75/⅓ page (4 x 5¼)
ISSN: 0883-0126
Ubiquity, Fine Print, Last Gasp, Armadillo, DeBoer, Desert Moon, Central Books (UK)

RED BASS

Jay Murphy
105 W. 28th St.
New York, NY 10001
(212) 239-7470

Poetry, essays, graphics/artwork, criticism, reviews, translation, interviews, fiction, plays, photographs.

RED BASS illuminates the interface between art and politics in a series of thematic book/magazines, usually of a cross-cultural, interdisciplinary nature.

Robert C. Morgan, Luisa Valenzuela, James Purdy, Carolee Schneemann, Etel Adnan.

Unsolicited Manuscripts Received/Published per Year: We are not accepting unsolicited manuscripts.

Payment: in copies, sometimes in cash as funds allow.

Reporting Time: 3 months.

THE RED CEDAR REVIEW

Zachary Chartoff, Laura Klynstra
Department of English
Morrill Hall
Michigan State University
East Lansing, MI 48824
(517) 355-9656

Poetry, fiction, graphics/artwork photography.

Take risks; hit the off-beat, exploit the system: oddities, erotica, humor, sex, drugs and rock and roll. Avoid the mainstream: tree poems, vampire love songs, don't you make my brown eyes blue? ie, love, pornography, and death, as always. SASE required.

Lyn Lifshin, Carol Cavallaro, Hannah Stein, Craig Cotter.

Unsolicited Manuscripts Received/Published per Year: 300/25.

Reading Period: year–round.

$10/yr; $5/ea; $2/sample, 40%
Faxon, Ebsco

RE*MAP MAGAZINE

Todd Baron
8270 Willoughby Ave.
Los Angeles, CA 90046

RENEGADE

Michael Nowicki, Miriam Jones, Larry Snell
P.O. Box 314
Bloomfield Hills, MI 48303
Poems, essays, short stories, plays.
Open literary magazine.
Unsolicited Manuscripts Received/ Published per Year: 500/10–20.
Payment: contributor's copy.
Reporting Time: 2 weeks–6 months.
1989; 2/yr; 100
$5.90/yr; $3/ea
24 pp; 11 x 8½
Ad Rates: free

REPRESENTATIONS

Stephen Greenblatt, Carla Hesse, Co-Chairs; Editorial Board
English Department
University of California
Berkeley, CA 94720
(415) 642-9044
Criticism, essays, translations.
REPRESENTATIONS publishes critical essays on interdisciplinary topics; disciplines included are literature, political theory, art history, and anthropology, and roughly 50 percent of the work published is literary criticism. Of the balance, literary methodology is a substantial influence in essays in other fields such as history, political theory, anthropology, etc.
Unsolicited Manuscripts Received/ Published per Year; 400/28
Payment: none.
Reporting Time: 6–8 weeks.
Copyright held by University of California Press.
1983; 4/yr; 2,200
$22/yr ind; $44/yr inst
152 pp; 7 x 9¾
Ad Rates: $150/page
ISSN: 0734-6018
DeBoer

RESONANCE

Evan and Patty Pritchard
P.O. Box 215
Beacon, NY 12508
(914) 838-1217
Essays, graphics/artwork, poetry, review, photographs, fiction, interviews, music and humor.
RESONANCE is a journal of all forms of creative expression inspired by personal spiritual experience. It strives to create a

popular forum for communication between artists, scientists and the spiritual community, however it does not promote or denigrate any other organizations, spiritual, educational or otherwise. It is a forum for individual spiritual insight.

Heather Hughes-Calero, Susan Hanniford Crowley. Interviews with Chris Williamson, Madeleine L'Engle, Arun Gandhi, Pete Seeger, David Lanz, Joan Houston, others.

Unsolicited Manuscripts Received/Published per Year: 700/10.

Payment: 1 copy.

Reporting Time: 8 weeks.

Copyright held by Evan and Patty Pritchard—compilation only; reverts to author upon publication.

1987; 3/yr; 2,000

$10/yr; $3/ea; 40%

52 pp; 8½ x 11

$100/½ page; $50/¼ page; $25/⅛ page

Ubiquity, Homing Pigeon, Armadillo, L-S Distributors, Book Tech, New Leaf

RESPONSE: A Contemporary Jewish Review

Adam Margolis, Bennett Lovett-Graff

27 W. 20 St. 9th fl.

New York, NY 10011

(212) 675-1168; Fax: (212) 929-3459

Unsolicited Manuscripts Received/Published per Year: 200-300/15.

REVERSE

Jan McLaughlin and Bruce Weber

19 W. 73rd St. #3A

New York, NY 10023

(212) 787-4056

Essays, poetry.

Devoted almost exclusively to essays by poets focusing on issues relevant to poetry. Themes of revent issues: censorship of literature; state of poetry in Florida; forgotten poets. Planning an issue on problems in translation. Includes avantegarde and academic points of view. Often deals with controversial subjects. A poetry journal that thinks.

Carolyn Forché, Barbara Holley, Yvonne Sapia, Jan McLaughlin, Bruce Weber, Lenny Della-Roca.

Payment: $20 upon publication.

Reporting Time: 3–4 months.

Copyright held by author.

1988; 2/yr; 300

$6/yr; $3.50/ea; 40%

16 pp; 8½ x 11

Ad Rates: $50/¼ page; $25/⅛ page

REVIEW

Alfred J. Mac Adam, Daniel Shapiro, Editors
Americas Society
680 Park Ave.
New York, NY 10021
(212) 249-8950

Fiction, poetry, criticism, essays, reviews, translations, interviews, articles on visual arts and music.

REVIEW presents the best of Latin American literature in English translation. It contains a review section as well as major articles on the Latin American visual and performing arts.

Unsolicited Manuscripts Received/Published per Year: 75–100/5.

Payment: $100 and up.

Copyright held by the Americas Society (present); Center for Inter-American Relations (back issues).

1967; 2/yr; 5,000

$16/yr ind, $25/yr inst; $9/ea

100 pp; 8½ x 11

Ad Rates: $700/page (7¾ x 9¾); $400/½ page (5 x 7)

Total, Ingram, Inland

THE REVIEW OF CONTEMPORARY FICTION

John O'Brien, Steven Moore
4241 Illinois State University
Normal, IL 61790-4241

Criticism, essays, reviews, translation, interviews.

Each issue is devoted to criticism on one or two contemporary novelists.

Upcoming issues are devoted to Angela Carter, Raymond Queneau, Edmund White.

Gilbert Sorrentino, Robert Creeley, Paul Metcalf, Carlos Fuentes, Toby Olson.

All manuscripts are by invitation only.

Reporting Time: 2 weeks.

Copyright held by magazine; reverts to author upon publication.

1981; 3/yr; 2,800

$17/yr ind, $24/yr inst; $8/ea; 10%–40%

200 pp; 6 x 9

Ad Rates: $150/page (5 x 7½)

ISSN: 0276-0045

DeBoer, Inland, SPD

RFD

Short Mountain Collective
P.O. Box 68
Liberty, TN 37095
(615) 536-5176

Poetry, fiction, essays, reviews, interviews, photographs, graphics/artwork.

RFD focuses on rural gay men in related areas of human growth and consciousness and is an open forum for new ideas, radical views and controversial issues. The scope includes articles on alternative lifestyles, homesteading skills, collectives, gardening, cooking, contact letters, poetry, fiction, prisoner section, book reviews and graphics.

Harry Hay, Bru Dye, Louise Hay, Robin Walden, Jan Nathen Long.

Unsolicited Manuscripts Received/Published per Year: 50/20.

Payment: 1 copy of issue published in.

Reporting Time: 1–6 months.

Copyright held by author.

1974; 4/yr; 3,300

$25/yr ind 1st class, $18/yr ind 2nd class; $20/yr inst; $5/ea; 40%

72 pp; 8½ x 11

Ad Rates: $350/page (8½ x 11); $185/½ page (4¼ x 11 or 8½ x 5½); $98/¼ page (4¼ x 5$\frac{1}{12}$)

ISSN: 0149-709X

RHINO

8403 W. Normal Ave.
Niles, IL 60714
or
1808 N Larrabee St.
Chicago, IL 60614

Send 3–5 poems to **RHINO** at either address. Please no sentimental verse. Strong free verse with fresh images!

Unsolicited Manuscripts Received/Published per Year: 500+/70.

Reading Period: year–round.

Payment: 1 copy.

Copyright held by author.

1976; 1/yr; 500

$6 + $1.05 postage/ea; back issues are $3/ea plus postage; 40%

90+ pp; 5½ x 8⅜

No ads

RIVER CITY (formerly **MEMPHIS STATE REVIEW**)

Sharon Bryan
English Department
Memphis State University
Memphis, TN 38152
(901) 678-4509

Poetry, fiction, essays, interviews. No novel excerpts.

The magazine sponsors the River City Writing Awards in fiction: 1st prize $2,000; 2nd prize $500; 3rd prize $300. Send SASE for details.

Fred Busch, Marvin Bell, Mona Van Duyn, Pattiann Rogers, Luisa Valenzuela, John Updike.

Unsolicited Manuscripts Received/Published per Year: 1,000/40.

Reading Period: Sept.—May.

Payment: varies.

Reporting Time: 1 month.

Copyright reverts to author.

1980; 2/yr; 1,000

$9/yr; $5/ea

100 pp; 6 x 9
Ad Rates: $40/page

RIVER STYX

Jennifer Tabin, Quincy Troupe and Michael Castro, Editors
14 S. Euclid
St. Louis, MO 63108
(314) 361-0043

Poetry, fiction, interviews, photographs, graphics/artwork.

RIVER STYX is a multicultural journal of poetry, prose and graphic arts publishing works by both established and up and coming writers and artists, significant for their originality, quality, and craftsmanship.

Sharon Olds, Grace Paley, Derek Walcott, Marilyn Hacker, Howard Nemerov.

Unsolicited Manuscripts Received/ Published per Year: 1,500+/50-60.

Reading Period: Sept. and Oct.

Payment: $8/page for literature: $10/page for photographs or drawings.

Copyright held by Big River Association; reverts to author upon publication.

1975; 3/yr; 1,000
$20/yr ind, $28/yr inst; $7/ea; 33%
112 pp; 5½ x 8½
Exchange ads
ISSN: 0149-8851
Ingram

RIVERWIND

C. A. Dubielak, Audrey Naffziger
Hocking College
Nelsonville, OH 45768
(614) 753-3591 ext 2375

Poetry, fiction, nonfiction.

RIVERWIND is more interested in publishing the new poet, the good poet, the challenging, the true as opposed to the well-established and/or predictable. Quality, please. Beginning with our 1993 edition, the focus of Riverwind will be on Appalachian Writers (Ohio, W. Virginia, Kentucky, etc.), themes, characters and concerns.

Simon Percik, James Riley.

Unsolicited Manuscripts Received/ Published per Year: 200/30-50.

Payment: copies.

Reporting Time: 4 weeks–3 months. No summer submissions.

Copyright held by author.

1982; 1/yr; 400
$2.50/yr; $2.50/ea; 60%
80 pp; 6 x 9

ROHWEDDER: International Journal of Literature and Art

H.J. Schacht, Nancy Antell, Robert Dassanowsky-Harris, Angela Baldonado
P.O. Box 29490
Los Angeles, CA 90029

(213) 256-5083

Poetry, fiction, reviews, translation, interviews, photographs, graphics/artwork.

A journal of international literature and art, featuring poetry and prose in original language and English translation, black and white photography and graphics, reviews and essays on pictoral and theater arts and events in the Los Angeles area and globally. We are also interested in language oriented work, experimental forms, theoretical writings on postmodernism, open text work and new lyric poetry. 1993 theme issue: Contemporary Media.

Terry Wolverton, Wanda Coleman, Luis Alfaro, and Robert Peters.

Unsolicited Manuscripts Received/Published per Year: 600/50.

Payment: in copies.

Reporting Time: 3 month.

Copyright held by magazine; reverts to author upon publication.

1986; 1-2/yr; 800–1,000

$5/ea

50 pp; 8½ x 11

Ad Rates: $300/page (8½ x 11); $170/½ page (5½ x 8½); $90/¼ page (4¼ x 5½); $50 (2¾ x 4¼); $30 (1¾ x 4¼)

ISSN: 0892-6956

S

SAGUARO

Charles Tatum
315 Douglass Bldg
The University of Arizona
Tucson, AZ 85721
(602) 621-7551

Fiction, poetry, essays, autobiography and biography, no reviews.

Bilingual (Eng/Span) magazine dedicated to writing by and about Chicano/Latinos. **SAGUARO** seeks works by both established and unknown writers.

Bernice Zamora, Sandra Cisneros, Joel Huerta, Carmen Tafolla, Maria Herrera-Sobek, Max Aguilera-Hellweg.

Unsolicited Manuscripts Received/Published per Year: 200/20.

Payment: in copies.

Reporting Time: variable.

Copyright held by Mexican American Studies & Research Center; reverts to author upon publication.

1984; 1/yr; 500

$10/2 issues; $6/ea; 20–40%

100 pp; 6 x 9

No ads

ISSN: 0885-5013

SALMAGUNDI

Robert and Peggy Boyers, Editors; Thomas S.W. Lewis, Associate Editor, Marc Woodworth, Assistant Editor
Skidmore College
Saratoga Springs, NY 12866
(518) 584-5000, ext 2302

Poetry, fiction, criticism, essays, reviews, translation, interviews.

SALMAGUNDI is an international quarterly of the humanities and social sciences publishing essays and book reviews on literature, contemporary politics, film, dance, and current ideas. General issues also feature original fiction, poetry, photographs and interviews.

George Steiner, Conor Cruise O'Brien, Nadine Gordimer, Christopher Lasch, Susan Sontag, Seamus Heaney.

Unsolicited Manuscripts Received/Published per Year: 2,000/15-20.

Payment: none.

Reporting Time: 1–5 months.

Copyright held by Skidmore; reverts to author upon publication.

1965; 4/yr; 5,600

$15/yr ind, $22/yr inst; $5/ea

160–230 pp; 8½ x 5½

Ad Rates: $150/page (4 x 7); $85/½ page (4 x 3½)

DeBoer

SALTHOUSE
A Geopoetics Journal

DeWitt Clinton
800 W. Main
Department of English
University of Wisconsin
Whitewater, WI 53190
(414) 472-1036

Poetry, fiction, reviews.

Interest is in poetry, fiction and reviews/criticism which is influenced by a sense of anthropology, geography or history.

No immediate plans for publishing future issues. Back issues are available. Ask for a catalog.

ISSN: 0737-5506

SANDHILLS REVIEW
(formerly St. Andrews Review)

Stephen E. Smith, Editor
Sandhills Community College
2200 Airport Rd.
Pinehurst, NC 28374

Publishes fiction, poetry and essays of highest quality from both established writers and promising new authors from all over the U.S. and abroad.

Fred Chappell, Hiroaki Sato, Soichi Furuta, Yukio Mishima, Desmond Egan.

Unsolicited Manuscripts Received/Published per Year: 800/50.

Payment: 1 copy.

Copyright held by magazine; reverts to author upon publication.
1972; 2/yr; 500
$8/ea; 30%
100 pp; 6 x 9
Ad Rates: $200/page (5 x 7); $100/½ page (2½ x 3½); $50/¼ page (1¼ x 1¾)
ISSN: 1061-3579

SAN DIEGO WRITERS' MONTHLY

Charles Harrington Elster, Michael T. McCarthy
3910 Chaman St., Suite D
San Diego, CA 92110
(619) 226-0896; Fax (619) 223-0226
Quincy Troupe, William Murray, Elizabeth George, Joseph Wambaugh, Raymond Feist.
As San Diego's only monthly literary magazine, our goal is to inform, represent, and entertain while promoting writing from all San Diegans, established and aspiring. Our publication crosses all genres and includes a variety of columns, interviews, essays, features, reviews, fiction and poetry written chiefly by county residents.
Payment: $5/poem, $10–25 for fiction/nonfiction.
Reporting Time: 4–5 weeks.
Copyright held by author, although magazine asks for one time North American Serial Rights.
1991; 12/yr; 700
$23/yr ind and inst; $3/ea
36 pp; 8½ x 11
Ad Rates: $375/page (7 x 9½); $300/½ page (3¼ x 9½ or 7 x 4); $200/¼ page (3¼ x 4½)
ISSN: 1054-6774

SAN FERNANDO POETRY JOURNAL

Richard Cloke, Editor; Shirley Rodecker, Managing Editor; Lori C. Smith, Pub. Editor
Kent Publications, Inc.
18301 Halstead St.
Northridge, CA 91325
(818) 349-2080
Poetry.
Seeks to fuse diverse elements of contemporaneity, ranging from evocation of scientific and technical advances–cosmology, subatomic inner space–cyber-punk S.F.–with a pronounced interest in poetry of social protest which illuminates the ills of our time, with special emphasis on ecology.
Stan Proper, Stratton F. Caldwell, Leigh Hunt, Jack Bernier, Phyllis Gershator.
Unsolicited Manuscripts Received/Published per Year: 7-800/2-500.

Payment: in copies, discounts on subs.
Reporting Time: 2–3 weeks.
Copyright reverts to author.
1978; 4/yr; 500
$10/yr; $3/ea; 20%–30%
100 pp; 5½ x 8½
Ad Rates: $50/page (4½ x 7); $25/½ page (4½ x 3½)
ISSN: 0196-2884

SAN FRANCISCO REVIEW OF BOOKS

Donald Paul
2909 McClure St.
Oakland, CA 94609
(510) 286-2020; Fax (510) 286-0220
Reviews, interviews, and profiles of literary works and persons.
Commentary, debates, and essays on everything from baseball to Buddhism, thrillers to post-modernism.
Unsolicited Manuscripts Received/Published per Year: 100/15%
Payment: negotiable.
Copyright held by magazine.
1975; 6/yr; 8,000
$16/yr; $3/ea; 35-50%
48 pp; 8½ x 11
Ad Rates: Full page b/w $995
ISSN: 0194-0724
Eastern News

SANTA FE LITERARY REVIEW

Colleen Rae
P.O. Box 8018
Santa Fe, NM 87504-8018
(505) 989-7641
Fiction, poetry, art/graphics, essays.
The goal of the **SANTA FE LITERARY REVIEW** is to explore art as it can be rather than as it "should" be, which requires a firm knowledge of what has been.
Richard Goldstein, Steven Counsell, Nedra Westwater, Patricia Hinnebusch, Lisa Greenleaf.
Payment: 5 copies and a 1 year subscription
Reporting Time: 6 weeks.
Copyright held by Colleen Rae/Haven Hill Press; reverts to author upon publication.
1991; 4/yr; 1,000
$18/yr; $5/ea; 40%
96 pp; 6 x 9
Ad Rates: $100/page (4 x 7)
ISSN: 1055-8446

THE SANTA MONICA REVIEW

Jim Krusoe
1900 Pico Blvd.
Santa Monica, CA 90405
Fiction, poetry, essays.
Guy Davenport, Charles Baxter,

Barry Hannah, Peter Handke, Amy Gerstler, Alicia Ostriker.
Unsolicited Manuscripts Received/ Published per Year: 2,000/4-6.
Reading Period: year–round.
Payment: copies.
Reporting Time: 1–3 months.
Copyright: first serial rights only.
1988; 2/yr; 1,200
$12/yr; $7/ea
128+ pp; 8 x 5
Ad Rates: vary
ISSN: 0899-9848
Armadillo, DeBoer, Fine Print, Ubiquity

SCARLET

Douglas Oliver / Alice Notley
all mss.—61 rue Lepic
75018, Paris, FRANCE
Inquiries only—Notley/Oliver
848 Union St.
Brooklyn, NY 11215
(718) 789-2846
mss. will not be forwarded.
Poetry, prose, drawings.
SCARLET is a poetry magazine which emphasizes political and spiritual content and is dedicated to the idea that poetry shouldn't be boring.
Amiri Baraka, Denise Riley, Leslie Scalapino.
Unsolicited Manuscripts Received/ Published per Year: about 100/about 10.
Payment: 3 copies.
Reporting Time: varies.
Copyright reverts to author.
1990; 4/yr; 500
$14/yr; $2/sample
24 pp; 8½ x 11

SCREENS AND TASTED PARALLELS

Terrel D. Hale
12714 Barbara St.
Silver Spring, MD 20906
(301) 949-6825
Poetry, some reviews.
Dedicated to providing a forum for a variety of alternative poetries and poetics, some prose, mostly poetry.
Arkadii Dragomoschenko, Guido Zlatkes, Johanna Drucker, Maggie O'Sullivan, Saul Yurkievich.
Unsolicited Manuscripts Received/ Published per Year: 50/10.
Payment: none.
Reporting Time: 3-5 months.
Copyright reverts back to poets.
1989; 1/yr; 800+
$10/yr; $6/sample
239 pp; 8½ x 11
ISSN: 1042-9786
SPD, Spectacular Diseases (UK)

SE LA VIE WRITER'S JOURNAL

Rosalie Avara
P.O. Box 371371

El Paso, TX 79937
(915) 592-4658

Contest winning poems, essays, short stories, cartoons, book reviews, articles about poetry, writing.

A quarterly dedicated to encouraging novice writers, poets and artists by giving them a chance to get published and receive cash prizes.

Philip Eisenberg, Marian Ford Park, Winnie E. Fitzpatrick.

Unsolicited Manuscripts Received/ Published per Year: 150/50.

Payment: 1 copy of issue in which work appears.

Reporting Time: Contest entries—90 days.

Copyright held by Rosalie Avara, Editor/Publisher of Rio Grand Press.

1987; 4/yr; 300+

$16/yr; $4/ea

68+ pp; 8½ x 5

Ad Rates: $25/page; $15/½ page; $10/¼ page; $5/⅛ page

THE SEATTLE REVIEW

Donna Gerstenberger
Padelford Hall, GN-30
University of Washington
Seattle, WA 98195
(206) 543-9865, 543-2690

Poetry, fiction, essays, interviews with writers.

THE SEATTLE REVIEW is a journal of poetry and prose published twice yearly. We try to achieve a balance in our pages between the work of nationally-known writers and that of younger writers of promise.

Rita Dove, W.P. Kinsella, Ursula Le Guin, William Stafford, Frances McCue, Jane McCafferty.

Unsolicited Manuscripts Received/ Published per Year: 2,000-2,500/8-12 fiction, 80 poems, 2 essays, 1-2 interviews.

Reading Period: Sept.—May.

Payment: varies.

Reporting Time: 3–6 months.

Copyright held by magazine; reverts to author upon publication.

$8/yr, $16/2 yrs; $5/ea

100 pp; 6 x 9

Ad Rates: $100/page (5 x 7); $75/½ page (5 x 4½)

ISSN: 0147-6629

SEEMS

Karl Elder
Lakeland College
Box 359
Sheboygan, WI 53082-0359
(414) 565-3871

Poetry, fiction, essays.

Jeffrey Baker, John Birchler, M.J. Echelberger, Chris Halla, Robert Nagler.

Unsolicited Manuscripts Received/Published per Year: 1,000/25.
Payment: 1 copy.
Reporting Time: 1–3 months.
Copyright held by Karl Elder; reverts to author upon publication.
1971; irreg; 350
$16/4 issues; $4/ea
40 pp; 8½ x 7
ISSN: 0095-1730

SEMIOTEXT(E)/AUTONOMEDIA

Sylvere Lotringer, Jim Fleming
P.O. Box 568
Brooklyn, NY 11211
(718) 387-6471
Fiction, criticism, essays, translation, interview, photographs.
Contemporary radical cultural politics, "movement" literatures. Also sponsors "Foreign Agents," and "Native Agents" small book series promoting contemporary radical politics and culture, philosophy and human sciences, and literature.
Michel Foucault, Roland Barthes, Felix Guattari, Jean Baudrillard, Gilles Deleuze, Kathy Acker, William Burroughs.
Unsolicited Manuscripts Received/Published per Year: 150/10-15.
Payment: none.
Reporting Time: 3 months.
Copyright reverts to author upon publication.
1974; irreg; 8,000
$18/3 issues ind, $36/3 issues inst; $10/ea; 40%
320 pp; 7 x 9
ISSN: 0093-5779

SENECA REVIEW

Deborah Tall
Hobart and William Smith Colleges
Geneva, NY 14456
(315) 781-3364
Poetry, criticism, translation, interviews.
Twice a year the **SENECA REVIEW** publishes poetry and prose about poetry, with a special interest in translation.
Seamus Heaney, Rita Dove, Denise Levertov, Hayden Carruth, Cornelius Eady.
Unsolicited Manuscripts Received/Published per Year: 5,000 poems/70 poems.
Reading Period: Sept.—May 1.
Payment: 2 copies.
Reporting Time: 6–10 weeks.
Copyright held by Hobart and William Smith Colleges; reverts to author upon publication.
1970; 2/yr; 1,000
$8/yr, $15/2 yrs; $5/ea; 40%
90 pp; 5½ x 8½
Ad Rates: $75/page (5 x 8)

ISSN: 0037-2145
Small Press Traffic

SENSATIONS MAGAZINE

David Messineo
2 Radio Ave. A5
Secaucus, NJ 07094

Poetry, fiction, photographs, graphics/artwork.
Unsolicited Manuscripts Received/ Published per Year: 200/30.
Reading Period: Aug. and Jan.
Payment: none.
Reporting Time: 2 months after deadline.
Copyright held by author.
1987; 1/yr; 150
$8/sample
50-70 pp; 8½ x 11
Ad Rates: $100/page; $50/½ page; $25/¼ page

SEQUOIA

Carlos Rodriguez
Storke Publications Building
Stanford, CA 94305
(415) 362-3420

Poetry, fiction, photographs, art.
We have no set guidelines, nor do we accept simultaneous submissions.
Rita Dove, Seamus Heaney, Susan Howe, Janet Lewis, James Merrill.
Unsolicited Manuscripts Received/ Published per Year: 2,000/80.
Reading Period: Oct.—May.
Payment: in copies.
Reporting Time: 2 months.
Author retains rights.
1892; 2/yr; 500
$10/yr; $5/ea
80–105 pp; 5½ x 8
Ad Rates: $100/page; $60/½ page
L–S Distributors

THE SEWANEE REVIEW

George Core
University of the South
Sewanee, TN 37375
(615) 598-1245

Poetry, fiction, criticism, essays, reviews.
America's oldest literary quarterly publishes original fiction, poetry, essays on literary and related subjects, book reviews and book notices for well-educated readers who appreciate good American and English literature.
Hayden Carruth, Louis D. Rubin, Jr., George Garrett, Donald Davie, Malcolm Cowley, L.C. Knights.
Payment: $10–$12/printed page; 60¢/line for poetry.
Reporting Time: 4 weeks.
Copyright held by author.
1892; 4/yr; 3,500
$15/yr ind, $20/yr inst; $6/ea
192 pp; 6 x 9
Ad Rates: $175/page (4¼ x 7);

$110/½ page (4¼ x 3⅜);
$80/¼ page

ISSN: 0037-3052

SHENANDOAH

Dabney Stuart, Editor; Lynn Williams, Managing Editor
P.O. Box 722
Lexington, VA 24450
(703) 463-8765

Poetry, fiction, essays, translations, photographs.

Consider work from both new and established writers. Annual prizes in fiction, poetry and the essay.

Seamus Heaney, Northrop Frye, Robert Wrigley, Lisa Sandlin, Shelby Hearon.

Unsolicited Manuscripts Received/ Published per Year: 3,640/less than 1%.

Reading Period: Sept.—May.

Payment: $2.50/line poetry, $25/page fiction.

Reporting Time: 2–4 weeks.

Copyright held by magazine; reverts to author upon publication.

1950; 4/yr; 2,100

$11/yr; $3.50/ea; 50%

120 pp; 6 x 9

Ad Rates: $200/page (4½ x 7); $100/½ page (4½ x 3½)

ISSN: 0037-3583

Armadillo, Fine Print, Ubiquity

SHOOTING STAR REVIEW

Sandra Gould Ford
7123 Race St.
Pittsburgh, PA 15208
(412) 731-7464

Poetry, fiction, essays, reviews, photographs, graphics/artwork.

SHOOTING STAR REVIEW is an award-winning illustrated quarterly that uses the arts to explore the Black experience. Guidelines available with SASE. Sample copy ($3) is sent with next bulk mailing unless 9 x 12 envelope w/$1.21 postage included.

Kristin Hunter, Dennis Brutus, Reginald McKnight, Jerry Ward, Toi Derricote, Doris Jean Austin, Marita Golden.

Unsolicited Manuscripts Received/ Published per Year: 600/60.

Payment: $20/fiction; $10 and up/essays; $4/poems.

Copyright held by magazine; reverts to author upon publication.

1987; 4/yr; 1,500

$12/yr ind, $15/yr inst; $3/ea; 20% consignment, 50% outright purchase

32 pp; 8½ x 11

Ad Rates: $300/page; $150/½ page; $75/¼ page

ISSN: 0892-1407

SHORT FICTION BY WOMEN

Rachel Whalen
Box 1276 Stuyvesant Station
New York, NY 10009

All fiction: short stories, short novels, novel excerpts; 100% original.

Our goals are to encourage woman writers and to give readers an enjoyable, superbly written magazine.

Joan Frank, Edwidge Danticat, Meredith Sue Willis.

Unsolicited Manuscripts Received/Published per Year: 2,500/25. SASE for guidelines.

Payment: depends on length and budget.

Reporting Time: 6 weeks.

Copyright: first serial rights only.

1991; 3/yr; 2,500

$18/yr; $6/ea

128 pp; 5½ x 8½

THE SHORT STORY REVIEW

Dwight Gabbard, Stephen Woodhams, Beth Overson, Catherine Jacob, Melinda Dart, George Knuepfel
450 Irving St. #4
San Francisco, CA 94122

Fiction.

Founded in 1983, **THE SHORT STORY REVIEW** publishes works of fiction.

Molly Giles, Amy Tan, Richard Cortez Day, William Heinesen, Sara Vogan.

Payment: none.

Reporting Time: 8–12 weeks.

Copyright held by author.

1983; 4/yr; 1,500

$10/yr; $2.50/ea; 40%

20 pp; 10 x 13

Ad Rates: $432/page (10 x 13½); $254/½ page (10 x 6⅝); $149/¼ page (4 11/16 x 6⅝)

ISSN: 0741-0786

L-S Distributors, Armadillo

SIBYL-CHILD

Nancy Arbuthnot, Saundra Maley
709 Dahlia St. NW
Washington, DC 20012
(202) 723-5468

Established in 1974, **SIBYL-CHILD** is out of print. Back issues of chapbooks—fiction, poetry, translations—available at $2/ea.

Doris Mozer, David Hall, Ann Slayton, Peter Van Egmond, William Griffiths, Nan Fry.

5½ x 8

ISSN: 0161-715X

SIDEWALKS

Tom Heie
Box 321
Champlin, MN 55316
(612) 421-3512

Poetry, short prose (fiction, memoir, essay), graphics.

A magazine for emerging and established writers of poetry and prose.

Michael Dennis Browne, Mark Vinz, Thom Tammaro, Robert Cooperman, Kenneth Pabo, Phillip Dacey.

Unsolicited Manuscripts Received/Published per Year: 1,000/100.

Payment: copies.

Reporting Time: 1-3 months.

Copyright: Tom Heie.

1991: 2/yr; 500

$8/yr; $5/ea; 40%

60-75 pp; 8 x 5½

ISSN: 1059-2210

THE SIGNAL

Joan Silva, David Chorlton
P.O. Box 67
Emmett, ID 83617
(208) 365-5812

Poetry, fiction, criticism, essays, reviews, translation, interviews, photographs, graphics/artwork.

We would like to create a forum for inter-disciplinary work, bridging between literature, art, music; and ecological, socio/political concerns. We encourage submissions in the socio/scientific area; examples would be archeologic, rare travel experiences/philosophic essays on almost anything, but quality of thought and expression should be rigorous and must have literary merit.

Hans Raimund, Natalya Gorbanevskaga, Michele Zackheim, Maurice Kenny, Lloyd Van Brunt, Olga Cabral, Clarissa Pinkda Estes.

Unsolicited Manuscripts Received/Published per Year: 300+/60+.

Payment: in copies.

Copyright held by magazine; reverts to author upon publication.

1987; 2/yr; 500

$10/yr; $6/ea; 40%

50+ pp; 8½ x 11

Ad Rates: $100/page (8½ x 11); $65/½ page (8½ x 5½); $35/¼ page (4¼ x 2¾)

SILVERFISH REVIEW

Rodger Moody
P.O. Box 3541
Eugene, OR 97403
(503) 344-5060

Poetry, short short stories, reviews, essays, translations, interviews, photographs, annual poetry chapbook contest.

The only criterion for selection of material is quality. In future issues **SILVERFISH REVIEW** wants to showcase essays on creative process and short short stories. **SILVERFISH RE-**

VIEW also sponsors an annual poetry chapbook contest.
Kevin Bowen, Lauren Mesa, Floyd Skloot, Judith Skillman, Robert Ward.
Unsolicited Manuscripts Received/ Published per Year: 800/10-15.
Reading Period: year–round.
Payment: 2 copies plus a year subscription, and $5 per page (when funding permits).
Reporting Time: 2–12 weeks.
Copyright held by author.
1979; 2/yr; 750
$12/3 issues ind, $15/3 issues inst; $50 life subscription (individuals only); $4/ea plus $1.50 postage; 40%
48 pp; 5½ x 8½
Ad Rates: $100/page (4¼ x 7½); $50/½ page (4¼ x 4)
ISSN: 0164-1085
Spring Church Book Company (chapbooks only), Faxon, Ebsco, Boley, Small Changes

SING HEAVENLY MUSE!

P.O. Box 13320
Minneapolis, MN 55414
Fiction, creative prose, poetry.
A magazine to foster women's writing and the writing of men showing an awareness of women's consciousness, in fiction, creative nonfiction and poetry.
Marihl Le Sugur, Chocolate Waters, Ann Ortit de Montellino, etc.
Unsolicited Manuscripts Received/ Published per Year: 1,000/40.
Payment: an honorarium, depending on funding, plus contributor's copies.
Reporting Time: 2 months first reading, 6–9 months if it goes to second reading.
Copyright by magazine, rights revert to authors.
1977; 1/yr; 400
$19/3 issues; $9/ea
approx. 100 pp; 6 x 10
Olson, Ubiquity, Small Changes

SINISTER WISDOM

Elana Dykewomon
P.O. Box 3252
Berkeley, CA 94703
Poetry, fiction, criticism, essays, reviews, interviews, plays, photographs, graphics/artwork by lesbians.
A lesbian/feminist journal of art, literature and politics founded in 1976 by Harriet Desmoines and Catherine Nicholson, passed on in 1981 to Michelle Cliff and Adrienne Rich, in 1983 to Melanie Kaye/Kantrowitz and in 1986 to the current editor. The primary commitment of the magazine is to publish creative work by lesbians from a broad

range of racial, ethnic, cultural and class perspectives.

Sapphire, Gloria Anzaldva, Marilyn Frye, Adrienne Rich, Chrystos, Winn Gilmore, Judith Katz.

Unsolicited Manuscripts Received/ Published per Year: 300-500/60-90.

Payment: 2 copies.

Reporting Time: 6–9 months.

Copyright held by author.

1976; 3–4/yr; 3,000

$17/yr ind, $30/yr inst; $6/ea; 40%

144 pp; 5½ x 8½

Ad Rates: $200/page (5⅛ x 8¼); $100/½ page (5⅛ x 4); $75/⅓ page (5⅛ x 2⅝); $50/¼ page (2½ x 4); $35/2 x 2 or 2⅜ x 2⅜

ISSN: 0196-1853

Inland, Bookpeople

SIPAPU

Noel Peattie
23311 County Rd. 88
Winters, CA 95694
(916) 662-3364

Reviews, interviews, conference news.

Newsletter for librarians, editors, and collectors interested in dissent (feminist, Third World, pacifist, etc.) literature, together with small press poetry. Emphasis on peace and environmental concerns; all must have a print emphasis.

Karl Kempton, Loss P. Glazier, Mary Zeppa, John Daniel, Harry Polkinhorn.

Unsolicited Manuscripts Received/ Published per Year: 2/0.

Payment: 5¢/word.

Reporting Time: 5 months.

Copyright held by editor; reverts to author upon publication.

1970; 450

$8/yr; $4/ea

36 pp; 8½ x 11

No ads

ISSN: 0037-5837

Ebsco, Faxon, Popular Subscription Service, Turner

SISTERSONG: Women Across Cultures

Valerie Staats
P.O. Box 7405
Pittsburgh, PA 15213

Essays, letters, fiction, poetry, book reviews, b&w artwork and photography.

A theme journal dedicated to exploring the conditions of contemporary women's lives through letters and art. New authors and works in translation encouraged. Recent and upcoming themes: work; body; memory; handwork; friendship.

Lynne Hugo deCourcy, Gisela Notz, Ana María Rodas.
Unsolicited Manuscripts Received/Published per Year: 250/60.
Payment: none.
Reporting Time: about 3 months.
Copyright: revert to author on publication.
1992; 3/yr; 1,000
$16/yr ind, $28/yr inst; $24/yr overseas; $6/ea
80 pp; 6 x 9
ISSN: 1063-214X

SLIPSTREAM

Dan Sicoli, Robert Borgatti, Livio Farallo
Box 2071
Niagara Falls, NY 14301
(716) 282-2616 after 5 p.m. E.S.T.
Poetry, short fiction, graphics.
We publish vital writings (poems & fiction) by many excellent writers whose work is often ignored or overlooked by mainstream or academic publishers.
Charles Bukowski, Daryl Rogers, Fred Voss.
Unsolicited Manuscripts Received/Published per Year: 2,000+/100–125.
Reading Period: year–round.
Payment: in copies.
Reporting Time: 2 weeks–2 months.
Copyright reverts to author upon publication.
1981; 1–2/yr; 300
$8.50/2 issues; $5/ea
128 pp; 7 x 8½
No ads
ISSN: 0749-0771

THE SMALL POND MAGAZINE, Inc.

Napoleon St. Cyr
P.O. Box 664
Stratford, CT 06497
(203) 378-4066
Poetry, fiction, essays, reviews, graphics/artwork.
Features contemporary poetry by new and established writers, but also uses short prose pieces of many genres, plus some art work—black and white only.
Marvin Solomon, Fritz Hamilton, Sid Harriet, Rika Lesser, Jane Somerville, H.R. Coursen.
Unsolicited Manuscripts Received/Published per Year: 5,000/75.
Reading Period: year–round.
Payment: 2 copies.
Reporting Time: 10–30 days, longer in summer.
Copyright held by N. St. Cyr. Original mss. which are published become the property of the Beinecke Rare Books & Mss. Lib. at Yale.
1964; 3/yr; 300

$8/yr; $3/ea; random back issue/$2.50; inquire
40 pp; 5½ x 8½
Ad Rates: $40/page (4½ x 7½); $25/½ page (4½ x 3½); $15/¼ page (4½ x 2¼)
ISSN: 0037-721X

SMALL PRESS MAGAZINE

Evie Righter
Kymbolde Way
Wakefield, RI 02879
(401) 789-0074; Fax (401) 789-3793

Articles about independent publishing, book reviews, excerpts.

SMALL PRESS exists to serve small, independent publishers by printing articles for and about small presses, including reviews and excerpts of small press books and magazines.

Unsolicited Manuscripts Received/Published per Year: 50/2.
Reading Period: year–round.
Payment: $50-200
Reporting Time: 1-2 months.
Copyright held by magazine.
1983; 4/yr; 7,500
$29/yr; $7.50/ea
100+pp; 8¼ x 11
Ad Rates: upon request
ISSN: 0000-0485
Eastern News

THE SNAIL'S PACE REVIEW

Darby Penney and Ken Denberg
RR#2 Box 363 Brownell Rd.
Cambridge, NY 12816

Poetry and poetry in translation.

THE SNAIL'S PACE REVIEW publishes contemporary poetry and poetry in translation. The editors especially welcome submissions from women, people of color, and members of ethnic and cultural minorities.

Maurice Kenny, Martha Collins, Ai.
Unsolicited Manuscripts Received/Published per Year: 3,000/60.
Payment: 2 copies.
Reporting Time: 2-3 months.
Copyright reverts to author upon publication.
1991; 2/yr; 300
$7/yr; $4/ea; 40%
32–36 pp; 5½ x 8½
ISSN: 1054-1632

SNAKE NATION REVIEW

Roberta George, Janice Daugharty, Nancy Phillips
110 #2 W. Force St.
Valdosta, GA 31601
(912) 249-8334

Poetry, fiction, essays, photographs, graphics/artwork.

SNAKE NATION REVIEW is a regional quarterly, founded in the fall of 1989. We encourage writing that addresses all areas of life. We look for good writing that encounters change and character; all subjects are acceptable if it meets our one requirement–well written.

Van K. Brock, D. Victor Miller, Judith Otiz Cofer.

Unsolicited Manuscripts Received/ Published per Year: 1,000/45.

Payment: Prize money (editors' choice); 2 copies/contribution.

Reporting Time: 6 months.

Copyright: Snake Nation Press.

1989; 2/yr; 1,000

$15/ yr ind, $20/yr inst; $6/ea; 40%

100 pp; 6 x 9

Ad Rates: $100/page; $50/½ page; $25/¼ page

ISSN: 1046-5006

SONORA REVIEW

Department of English
University of Arizona
Tucson, AZ 85721
(602) 621-1836 or (602) 626-8383

Poetry, fiction, reviews, translation, interviews, criticism, essays.

We're looking for the liveliest new writing we can get our hands on, including experimental and non-conformist work. Most issues are general in nature, though recent special features have profiled "Crossing Borders: Writing from Alternative Traditions" and "Voices from the Southwestern Landscape." We welcome simultaneous submissions.

Jane Miller, David Foster Wallace, Rick Bass, Frances Sherwood, Antonya Nelson.

Unsolicited Manuscripts Received/ Published per Year: 2,000/24.

Payment: copies, annual prizes. $150 and $50 each in fiction, poetry, & creative nonfiction.

Reporting Time: 2–3 months, longer during summer.

Copyright reverts to author.

1980; 2/yr

$10/yr; $20/2 yrs; $5/ea; 40%

120 pp; 6 x 9

SOUNDINGS EAST

Rod Kessler, Claire Keyes
English Dept.
Salem State College
Salem, MA 01970
741- 6270

Original poetry, fiction, artwork.

SOUNDINGS EAST is a collection of original poetry, short fiction, and art work, published biannually by the students of Salem Statem College.

Debra Allbery, Robert Cooperman, Antonya Welson.

Unsolicited Manuscripts Received/ Published per Year: 400/60.

Reading Period: Sept.—Nov., Jan.—April.
Payment: 2 copies.
Reporting Time: 2 to 4 months.
Copyright reverts to author.
1978; 2/yr; 2,000
$6/yr; $3/ea
65 pp; 5½ x 8½

Reading Period: Jan.—May, Sept.—Nov.
Payment: in issues.
Reporting Time: 6–9 months.
Copyright held by magazine.
1968; 2/yr; 600
$7/yr ind; $5/ea; 33⅓%
200 pp; 9 x 6
Ad Rates: negotiable
ISSN: 0038-3163

SOUTH CAROLINA REVIEW

Richard J. Calhoun
English Department
Clemson University
Clemson, SC 29634-1503
(803) 656-3229

Poetry, fiction, criticism, essays, reviews, translation, interviews.

Listed as one of the twenty most outstanding literary magazines in the United States by the *The New York Quarterly*, **THE SOUTH CAROLINA REVIEW** is now in its third decade of publication. Our primary goal is to continue to publish fiction, poetry, and criticism of the quality that has earned us several Pushcart nominations, as well as election to *The Best American Short Stories 1982* and *Prize Stories 1982: The O. Henry Awards.*

Stephen Dixon, Rosanne Coggeshall, Joyce Carol Oates, Cleanth Brooks, Leslie Fiedler.

SOUTH COAST POETRY JOURNAL

John J. Brugaletta
English Department
California State University Fullerton
Fullerton, CA 92634
(714) 773-3163

Poetry, graphics/artwork.

SOUTH COAST POETRY JOURNAL avoids theorizing so as to remain open to every kind of excellence in poetry, no matter what the style or school. Our standards for excellence, however, are high.

Richard Eberhart, Rita Dove, Marge Piercy, William Stafford, John Hollander, Denise Levertov, Mark Strand.

Unsolicited Manuscripts Received/Published per Year: 4,000 poems/80.

Reading Period: Sept.—May.
Payment: in single copies.
Copyright held by magazine; reverts to author upon publication.
1986; 2/yr; 450
$10/yr ind, $12/yr inst; $6/ea; 40%
60 pp; 5½ x 8½
Ads accepted
ISSN: 0887-2074

SOUTH DAKOTA REVIEW

John R. Milton
University of South Dakota
Vermillion, SD 57069
(605) 677-5229

Poetry, fiction, criticism, essays, occasional translation and interviews.

When the material warrants, an emphasis on the American West; writers from the West; Western places or subjects; frequent issues with no geographical emphasis. Periodic special issues on one theme, or one place, or one writer, e.g., Ross MacDonald (Spring 1986), Wallace Stegner (Winter 1985).

Edward Loomis, Max Evans, Frederick Manfred, Lloyd Van Brunt.

Unsolicited Manuscripts Received/Published per Year: 1,000/up to 100.

Reading Period: year–round.

Payment: in copies.

Reporting Time: 2 weeks–2 months, slowest in summer.

1963; 4/yr; 600
$15/yr, $25/2 yrs; $5/ea; 40%
150–190 pp; 6 x 9
ISSN: 0038-3368

THE SOUTHERN CALIFORNIA ANTHOLOGY

James Ragan, Sarah Pearson
Master of Professional Writing Program
University of Southern California
WPH 404
Los Angeles, CA 90089-4034
(213) 740-3252

Poetry, fiction, interviews, graphics/artwork (on cover).

Published through the Master of Professional Writing Program at the University of Southern California, **THE SOUTHERN CALIFORNIA ANTHOLOGY** is a literary journal of fiction, poetry, and interviews. Seventy percent of the pieces are solicited. Volume X (published Dec. 1992) includes works by: Amiri Baraka, Robert Bly, Vance Bourjaily, Donald Hall, John Hollander, David Madden, James Merrill, John Frederick Nims, Joyce Carol Oates, James Ragan, Hubert Selby, Jr., Mark Strand,

Henry Taylor, John Updike, Peter Vierck, Richard Yates.
Unsolicited Manuscripts Received/Published per Year: 1,000/10.
Reading Period: Sept. 1—Jan 1.
Payment: 3 copies.
Copyright held by the University of Southern California, Master of Professional Writing Program; reverts to author upon publication.
1983; 1/yr; 1,000
$9.95/yr; 40%
144 pp; 5½ x 8½
ISBN: 0-9615108-5-4
Blackwell North America, Ballen Booksellers, SPD

SOUTHERN EXPOSURE
Eric Bates
P.O. Box 531
Durham, NC 27702
(919) 419-8311
Essays, reviews, interviews, photographs, graphics/artwork.
SOUTHERN EXPOSURE is a winner of the National Magazine Award and is widely respected as the voice of the progressive South. Investigative journalism and oral history are emphasized. Very little fiction and no poetry; mostly nonfiction articles on social issues.
Unsolicited Manuscripts Received/Published per Year: 1,000/1-2.
Payment: up to $200.
Reporting Time: 6–8 weeks.
Copyright held by magazine.
1973; 4/yr; 4,000
$24/yr; $5/ea; 40%
Ad Rates: $400/page; $270/½ page
64 pp; 8½ x 11
ISSN: 0146-809X
Ingram

SOUTHERN HUMANITIES REVIEW
Dan R. Latimer, R.T. Smith, co-editors
9088 Haley Center
Auburn University
Auburn, AL 36849
(205) 844-9088
Poetry, fiction, essays, reviews.
THE SOUTHERN HUMANITIES REVIEW publishes fiction, poetry and critical essays on the arts, literature, philosophy, religion, and history. Essays, articles, or stories should, in general, range between 3,500 and 5,000 words. Poems should not exceed two pages in length. No multiple submissions.
Margaret Holley, Robert Morgan, Donald Hall, Peter Green, Yannis Ritsos, Reynolds Price.
Unsolicited Manuscripts Received/Published per Year: 1,500-2,000/40-55.
Payment: copies.

Reporting Time: 1–3 months.
Copyright held by Auburn University.
1967; 4/yr; 700
$15/yr; $5/ea
100 pp; 4½ x 7½
Ad Rates: $100/page (4½ x 7½); only with adequate notice.
ISSN: 0038-4186

SOUTHERN POETRY REVIEW

Ken McLaurin
Department of English
University of North Carolina
Charlotte, NC 28223
(704) 547-4309

Poetry, reviews.

Poetry submissions accepted from established and previously unpublished poets. **SPR** is a natural outlet for poets writing in the South, but has no regional bias. Variety in style and content encouraged.

Susan Ludvigson, Linda Pastan, David Keller, Dave Smith, Marge Piercy.
Reading Period: Sept.—May.
Payment: in copies.
Copyright held by magazine; reverts to author upon request.
1958; 2/yr; 1,100
$8/yr; $4.50/ea; 40%
80 pp; 6 x 9
No ads
ISSN: 0038-447X

THE SOUTHERN QUARTERLY: A Journal of the Arts in the South

Stephen Flinn Young
University of Southern Mississippi
Southern Station Box 5078
Hattiesburg, MS 39406-5078
(601) 266-4370

Criticism, essays, reviews, interviews, photographs.

A non-profit scholarly journal, **THE SOUTHERN QUARTERLY** includes essays, articles, interviews and reviews on the arts and society—defined broadly—in the southern U.S. General and special issues include research on music, theatre, dance, literature, film, art, architecture, popular and folk arts.

Unsolicited Manuscripts Received/Published per Year: 30/10.
Payment: 1 year subscription.
Reporting Time: 2–3 months.
Copyright held by University of Southern Mississippi; reverts to author upon publication.
1962; 4/yr; 750
$10/yr ind, $18/2 yrs ind, $25/yr inst; $5/ea; 15%
150 pp; 6 x 9

Ad Rates: $100/page (4½ x 6¾); $75/½ page (4½ x 3⅜)
ISSN: 0038-4496

SOUTHERN READER

Randall J. Bedwell
P.O. Box 1827
Oxford, MS 48655
(601) 234-2596

Cultural commentary, satire, fiction, poetry, essays, reviews.

SOUTHERN READER is a bimonthly publication exploring the South through progressive cultural commentary. **SR** reviews books, music and fiction.

Max Childers, Vernon Chadwick, Greil Marcus, Cynthia Shearer.

Unsolicited Manuscripts Received/Published per Year: 200/6.

Payment: copies unless notified.

Reporting Time: varies.

Copyright: Southern Reader Corp.

1989; 6/yr; 15,000

$12.95/yr; $2.50/ea

24-32 pp; 8½ x 11

Ad Rates: please inquire

ISSN: 1042-6604

Ingram

THE SOUTHERN REVIEW

James Olney, Dave Smith
43 Allen Hall
Louisiana State University
Baton Rouge, LA 70803-5005
(504) 388-5108

Fiction, poetry, criticism, reviews, interviews.

THE SOUTHERN REVIEW publishes poetry, fiction, criticism, essays, reviews and excerpts from novels in progress, with emphasis on contemporary literature in the United States and abroad, and with special interest in Southern history and culture.

Ernest J. Gaines, Reynolds Price, Lee Smith, W. D. Snodgrass, Jill McCorkle, Albert Gelpi.

Unsolicited Manuscripts Received/Published per Year: 10,000/100.

Reading Period: Sept.—May.

Payment: $12/printed page for prose; $20/printed page for poetry; 2 complimentary copies.

Reporting Time: 2 months.

Copyright held by LSU; reverts to author upon publication.

1935 (original series), 1965 (new series); 4/yr; 3,100

$18/yr, $32/2yr, $45/3yr, ind; $35/yr; $55/2yr; $80/3yr; inst, Foreign subscribers: add $3/yr for postage

250 pp; 6¾ x 10

Ad Rates: $250/page (4½ x 7½); $150/½ page (4½ x 3⅝); $100/¼ page (4½ x 1⅔)

ISSN: 0038-4534

DeBoer, Fine Print

SOUTHWEST

Janine Kelley
3490 South Walkup Dr.
Flagstaff, AZ 86001
(602) 774-6159

Fiction, essays, interviews, poetry, film/book reviews.

SOUTHWEST is an international literary magazine celebrating the cultural and artistic diversity of the region publishing writers with a range of light.

Simon Ortiz, James Cervantes, Mary Sojourner, Ruth L. Schwartz, Ann Walka, Ernesto Carriazo-Osorio.

Unsolicited Manuscripts Received/ Published per Year: 500/17.

Reading Period: Mar. 1—June 1.

Payment: copies.

Reporting Time: 2–5 weeks.

Copyright reverts to the author upon publication.

1993; 1/yr; 300–500

$5/yr; $5/ea

72 pp; 6 x 9

Ad Rates: $75/4 x 6

ISSN: 1065-0156

McGaugh's Newsstand

THE SOUTHWEST REVIEW

Willard Spiegelman, Editor-in-Chief; Elizabeth Mills, Senior Editor
307 Fondren Library West
Box 4374
Southern Methodist University
Dallas, TX 75275
(214) 768-1037

Poetry, fiction, essays, interviews.

THE SOUTHWEST REVIEW is a quarterly that serves the interests of its region but is not bound by them. **SWR** has always striven to present the work of writers and scholars from the surrounding states and to offer analyses of problems and themes that are distinctly southwestern and, at the same time, publishes the works of good writers regardless of their locales.

Alice Adams, John Ashbery, Millicent Dillon, Rosellen Brown, Padgett Powell, Reynolds Price, Adrienne Rich, Harvey Sachs.

Unsolicited Manuscripts Received/ Published per Year: 3,600±/60.

Reading Period: Sept.—May 31.

Payment: varies.

Reporting Time: 1 month.

Copyright held by SMU; reverts to author upon publication.

1915; 4/yr; 1,500

$20/yr ind, $25/yr inst; $5/ea; 40%

160 pp; 6 x 9

Ad Rates: $250/page (25 x 42½ picas); $150/½ page (25 x 21 picas)

ISSN: 0038-4712

Fine Print, Total

SOU'WESTER

Fred W. Robbins
School of Humanities,
Southern Illinois University
Edwardsville, IL 62026-1438
(618) 692-3190

Poetry, fiction.

Published three times a year, usually Fall, Winter, Spring; **SOU'WESTER** is somewhat selective and prefers to publish new writers.

Robert Wexelblatt, Jared Carter, Kathleen Thompson, Jeanne Bryner.

Unsolicited Manuscripts Received/Published per Year: 1,000/45.

Reading Period: year–round.

Payment: 2 free copies, 1 yr subscription.

Reporting Time: 3–4 months.

Copyright: first serial rights; released upon request, with acknowledgement.

1960; 3/yr; 300

$10/yr; $5/ea; 40%

84 pp; 6 x 9

Ad Rates: $80/page; $60/½ page; $30/¼ page

ISSN 0098-499X

Literati & Co.

THE SOW'S EAR POETRY REVIEW

Larry Richman, Managing Editor; Mary Calhoun, Graphics Editor
19535 Pleasant View Dr.
Abingdon, VA 24210-6827
(703) 628-2651

Poetry, reviews, interviews, graphics, photography.

Contemporary poetry exported from and imported into Southern Appalachia. No nostalgia. We publish both established and new poets, with no restrictions on subject matter or style. We use B & W art to complement poetry.

Single poem competition, Sept. and Oct., with $500 prize and publication; chapbook competition March and April, $500 prize and publication. SASE for guidelines.

Marge Piercy, Fred Chapell, Lee Smith, David Huddle, Josephine Jacobsen, Jim Wayne Miller.

Unsolicited Manuscripts Received/Published per Year: 3,000/150.

Payment: in copies.

Reporting Time: 3–6 months.

Copyright reverts to author.

1988; 4/yr; 500

$10/4 issues; $3.50/ea; 40%

32 pp; 8½ x 11

SPARROW POVERTY PAMPHLETS

Felix and Selma Stefanile
103 Waldron St.
West Lafayette, IN 47906

(317) 743-1991

Poetry.

The one-poet-an-issue magazine, providing a forum for mature poets. We are in the modernist tradition, with its emphasis on craft, shaped language, unity of voice and vision.

Christopher Bursk, Geraldine C. Little, Roger Finch, Gail White, Gray Burr, Ger Killeen.

Payment: $30, plus royalties of 20%.

Sparrow is in reorganization for 1991. For the time, no new manuscripts are being sought. Query with SASE late in 1991.

Copyright reverts to author on request.

1954; 3/yr; 900

$9/yr; $2/ea for back copies; 35%

28–32 pp; 5½ x 8½

ISSN: 0038-6588

Spring Church (for our chapbooks), SPD

SPEAR SHAKER REVIEW

Stephanie Caruana

P.O. Box 308

Napanoch, NY 12458

(914) 647-3608

Essays, articles, reviews, some poetry.

Explores the authorship of the Shakespeare plays from the point of view that the most likely candidate is Edward de Vere, Earl of Oxford. Within this framework we are open to any relevant material or format.

Dr. Paul Nelson, Gary Goldstein, the Honorable John Paul Stevens.

Unsolicited Manuscripts Received/Published per Year: 50/16.

Payment: 5 copies.

Reporting Time: 2 weeks.

Copyright reverts to author.

1987; 4/yr; 700

$24/yr; $6/ea; 40%

28 pp; 8½ x 11

Ad Rates: $100/page; $60/½ page

ISSN: 0894-8852

SPECTRUM

Robert H. Goepfert

Anna Maria College

Paxton, MA 01612-1198

(508) 849-3450

Non-fiction, fiction, poetry, art, photography.

An interdisciplinary national publication geared to the scholarly non-specialist.

Unsolicited Manuscripts Received/Published per Year: 600/10.

Reading Period: year–round.

Payment: $20 honorarium and 2 free copies.

Reporting Time: 6 weeks.

Copyright First North American serial rights.

1985; 2/yr; 1,000
$7/yr; $4/ea
64 pp; 6 x 9
ISSN: 0895-8270

SPOON RIVER POETRY REVIEW

Lucia Getsi, Jerry Pratt
English Department
Illinois State University 4240
Normal-Bloomington, IL 61790
(309) 438-7906

Poetry, translation, interviews, photographs, reviews.

SRPR wants poetry that is interesting and compelling. Our standards are high—the acceptance rate is about 2%. We publish emerging and established poets, and occasionally feature groups of poets working at the edges and margins of language and American poetics.

Tim Seibles, Diane Glancy, Roger Mitchell, Richard Jackson, Katherine Soniat, Frankie Paino, William Trowbridge.

Unsolicited Manuscripts Received/ Published per Year: 6-7,000/120.

Reading Period: Sept.—May 1.

Payment: one year subscription.

Reporting Time: 8 weeks.

Copyright reverts to author upon publication.

1976; 2/yr; 600

$12/yr ind, $16/yr inst; $6/ea; 40%

128 pp; 5½ x 8½

Ad Rates: $150/page (5 x 8); $75/½ page

ISSN: 0738-8993

Ebsco, Ingram, Faxon, Ubiquity, Fine Print

SPRING: The Journal of the E.E. Cummings Society

Norman Friedman, David V. Forrest
33–54 164 St.
Flushing, NY 11358-1442
(718) 353-3631

Essays, poems, photographs, drawings, bibliographies, etc.

We publish material relating to and about E. E. Cummings. Approaching the centennial of his birth, we feel the time is ripe for re-evaluating and honoring him.

Milton A. Cohen, Richard S. Kennedy, Linda Wagner-Martin.

Unsolicited Manuscripts Received/ Published per Year: 20/10–12.

Reading Period: Oct.—Mar.

Payment: none.

Reporting Time: we publish once a year so far, so there's no hurry.

Copyright held The E. E. Cummings Society.

1992; 1/yr; 2–300

$15/yr; $15/ea
144 pp; 5½ x 8½

STAND MAGAZINE

Jon Silkin, Lorna Tracy, Rodney Pybus
179 Wingrove Road
Newcastle upon Tyne NE4 9DA, UK
(091) 273-3280

STAND MAGAZINE is an independent quarterly of non writing, politically left of center, **STAND** has shown a strong awareness of social injustices and emphasizes the need for commitment between the writer and their community.

Bette Pesetsky, Joyce Carol Oaks, Paul Celar, Rodney Pybus.

Unsolicited Manuscripts Received/Published per Year: 520–624 stories, 1,000–1,300 poems/10–12 stories, 30–40 poems depending on length.

Payment: £30.00 per poem/per thousand words.

Reporting Time: 4–6 weeks.

Copyright reverts to authors, but magazine reserves right of first publication.

1952; 4/yr; 4,500
84 pp; A5 landscape
Ad Rates: £220.00/page; £110.00/½ page; £55.00/¼page
UK ISSN: 0038-9366

STET MAGAZINE

Cassandra L. Oxley
P.O. Box 75, Cambridge MA 02238
(508) 264-4938 (phone and fax)

Poetry, short fiction, nonfiction, art.

We are a small literarry magazine with a national following—we are presently seeking more essays & fiction though we love to present poetry. We hope to publish more regularly in '94.

Max Money, William J. Vernon, Estelle Gilson.

Unsolicited Manuscripts Received/Published per Year: 300–500/60–80.

Reading Period: year–round.

Payment: 2 copies.

Reporting Time: 6 weeks—3 months.

Copyright; 1st rights.

1990 4/yr; 100+
$12/yr; $3.50/ea
44+ pp; 7 x 8½ or 8½ x 11
ISSN 1060-8028

STILETTO

Michael Annis
P.O. Box 27276
Denver, Colorado 80227-0276

Poetry, short stories, essays, excerpts from fiction, plays, "illustrated," experimental, (but accessible etc.); politics & so-

cial works given priority. Bold, uncompromising, often radical.
All genres, street poets to academia. Strong content. Large enough sections to clearly demonstrate the author's ability and vision. If you have a statement to make for posterity, make it here. Guidelines may be found in previous issues. No free samples—these are Cadillacs.
Antler, Wm. Burroughs, Andrei Codrescu, Diane DiPrima, William Heyen, David Ray, Nathaniel Tarn, Diane Wakoski, Anne Waldman, Jimmy Santiago Baca, Charles Bukowski.
Unsolicited Manuscripts Received/Published per Year: many/12.
Reading Period: year–round.
Payment: 20 contributor copies, 1st Ed.
Mss. not selected for **STILETTO** may be considered for inclusion in a companion volume titled *The BEAST*.
Copyright reverts to author/artist.
1989; no schedule latest issue 1992
$31.50 1st Ed. collectors hardbound; $21.50 Commercial Ed. softcover; prices include postage. 30%
250+ pp; 5 x 11¼
ISSN 1043-9501
Howling Dog Press

STORY

Lois Rosenthal
1507 Dana Ave.
Cincinnati, OH 45207
(513) 531-2222
Short fiction.
STORY is devoted to publishing fine short stories.
Bobbie Ann Mason, Joyce Carol Oates, Robert Ward, Madison Smartt Bell, Alice Adams, Tobias Wolff, Rick De Marinis, William Kotzwinkle.
Unsolicited Manuscripts Received/Published per Year: 15,000/50.
Reading Period: year–round.
Payment: $400.
Reporting Time: 1 month.
Copyright: First North American serial rights.
1989; 4/yr; 35,000
$19/yr; $5.95/ea
128 pp; 6½ x 9¼
ISSN: 1045-0831
Ingram, Eastern News

STORY QUARTERLY

Anne Brashler, Diane Williams
P.O. Box 1416
Northbrook, IL 60065
(708) 564-8891
Fiction and interviews.
STORY QUARTERLY is looking for great fiction.
Unsolicited Manuscripts Received/Published per Year: 2,500/20.

Reporting Time: 2 months.
Copyright held by magazine; reverts to author upon publication.
1974; 2/yr; 1,500
$12/4 issues; $5/ea; 40%
110 pp; 6 x 9
ISSN: 0361-0144
DeBoer, Ingram

SUB-TERRAIN MAGAZINE

Brian Kaufman, Dennis Bolen, Paul Pitre, Hilary Green, Bryan Wade, Dirk Beck, Isabella Mori, Ken Gilchrist
P.O. Box 1575, Station A
Vancouver, B.C. V6G 2P7
CANADA
(604) 876-8710; Fax (604) 879-2667

Fiction, poetry, excerpts of novels, essays, art, photography.
SUB-TERRAIN has garnered substantial kudos for its unusual material, daring art, and contentious commentary. We continue to publish a new front line of writers and artists who might otherwise never get the exposure we strive to offer.
Mark Salerno, Tom Osborne, Libby Hart, Pat McKinnon, Simon Perchik.
Unsolicited Manuscripts Received/Published per Year: 7–1,000/75–100.
Reading Period: Sept.—June.
Payment: in copies; payment for solicited material.
Reporting Time: 2–4 months.
Copyright: 1 time only, reverts to author.
1988; 4/yr; 2,000
$10/yr ind, $15/yr inst; $2.95/ea; 40%
32 pp; 7 x 10
Ad Rates: $300/back cover; $210/page; $120/½ page; $65/¼ page
ISSN: 0840-7533
Canada Magazine Publishers Assoc., Fine Print (US)

SULFUR

Clayton Eshleman
210 Washtenaw Ave.
Ypsilanti, MI 48197
(313) 483-9787

Poetry, fiction, criticism, essays, reviews, translation, photographs, graphics/artwork.
Contemporary American poetry, translations, archival materials, book reviews, reproduction of art and photography.
Jerome Rothenberg, John Ashbery, Michael Palmer, William Carlos Williams, Aimé Césaire.
Unsolicited Manuscripts Received/Published per Year: 1,800/10.
Reading Period: year–round.
Payment: $40/contribution.
Reporting Time: 1–2 weeks.

Copyright held by magazine; reverts to author upon publication.
1981; 2/yr; 2,000
$14/yr ind, $20/yr inst; $9/ea; 40%
250 pp; 6 x 9
Ad Rates: $150/page (6 x 9); $85/½ page (6 x 3⅞)
ISSN: 0730-305X
Inland, SPD, DeBoer, Bookpeople, Armadillo, Small Change

SUN DOG: The Southeast Review
Michael Trammell, Ron Wiginton
406 Williams Building
Florida State University
Tallahassee, FL 32306
(904) 644-4230

Poetry, fiction, graphic art.
SUN DOG: The Southeast Review reads both fiction and poetry year-round. We are looking for striking images, incidents, and characters rather than particular styles or genres. We also publish the winner and runners-up of the World's Best Short Short Story Contest, as well as the winner and runners-up of the Richard Eberhart Prize in Poetry.
Janet Burroway, David Bottoms, Jesse Lee Kercheval, Leon Stokesbury, Rick Lott, Helen Norris, David Kirby.
Unsolicited Manuscripts Received/Published per Year: 300-400/12-fiction; 20-poems.
Reading Period: year–round.
Payment: 2 copies.
Copyright held by magazine; reverts to author upon publication.
1979; 2/yr; 1,250
$4/ea; 40%
90 pp; 6 x 9

THE SUN MAGAZINE
Sy Safransky
107 N. Roberson St.
Chapel Hill, NC 27516
(919) 942-5282; Fax (919) 932-3101

Essays, poetry, fiction, interviews, photography.
A monthly magazine in its 20th year of publication, **THE SUN MAGAZINE** celebrates good writing—and the warmth of shared intimacies—in essays, fiction, interviews, and poetry. People write in the magazine of their struggle to understand their lives, often bearing themselves with remarkable candor.
David Budbill, Sharon Claybough, Lou Lipsitz.
Payment: $200/interviews; $100/essays, fiction; $25/poetry.
Reporting Time: 3–6 months.
Copyright held by magazine.
1974; 12/yr; 20,000

40 pp; 8½ x 11
ISSN: 0744-9666
Armadillo, Bear Family, Daybreak, Desert Moon, Olson, Doormouse, Fine Print, Ingram, New Leaf, Small Changes, Ubiquity

SWAMP ROOT

Al Masarik, Editor; Jill Andrea, Managing Editor
Route 2, Box 1098
Hiwassee One
Jacksboro, TN 37757
(615) 562-7082

Poetry, essays, review, interviews, letters, photographs, graphics, artwork.
Contemporary poetry biased toward clarity, brevity, strong imagery; works that speak strongly of the poet's place; works that show a need to be written.
Naomi Shihab Nye, Ted Kooser, Maurya Simon, Linda M. Hasselstrom, William Klorfkorn, Diane Glancy.
Payment: 3 copies, 1 year sub.
Reporting Time: 1 week–1 month.
Copyright reverts to author.
1987; 3/yr; 1,000
$12/yr ind, $15/yr libararies; $5/ea; usual discount
86 pp; 6 x 9
ISSN: 1045-7682

SWIFT KICK

Robin Kay Willoughby
1711 Amherst St.
Buffalo, NY 14214
(716) 837-7778

Poetry, fiction, plays, translation, photographs, graphics/artwork.
We specialize in unusual formats, genres and styles.
Jerry McGuire, Dennis Maloney, Simon Perchik, Penny Kemp, Maurice Kenny.
Payment: in copies.
Reporting Time: varies.
Copyright held by magazine; reverts to author upon publication.
1980; 4/yr; 200
$20/yr ind, $40/yr inst; $6 + postage/sample (checks payable to editor); 40%
ISSN: 0277-447X

SYCAMORE REVIEW

Michael Manley
Department of English
Purdue University
West Lafayette, IN 47907
(317) 494-3783

Fiction, poetry, essays, interviews, translations.
SYCAMORE REVIEW publishes new writers of American contemporary fiction and poetry alongside well-known, experienced writers.
Patricia Henley, H. E. Francis,

Louis Simpson, Lee Upton, Brigit Kelly, Elaine Terranova, Elizabeth Dodd, Julie Schumacher.

Unsolicited Manuscripts Received/Published per Year: 1,000–1,200/40-45.

Reading Period: Sept.—May.

Payments: 2 copies.

Reporting Time: 3 months or less—SASE must be included for response.

Copyright: first serial rights.

1989; 2/yr; 800–1,000

$9/yr; $5/ea

128 pp; 6 x 9

Ad swaps w/other magazines only

ISSN: 1043-1497

T

TALISMAN: A Journal of Contemporary Poetry and Poetics

Edward Foster
Box 1117
Hoboken, NJ 07030
(201) 798-9093

Poetry, essays on poetry and poetics, interviews.

Each issue centers on the poetry and poetics of a major contemporary poet and includes a selection of new work by other important contemporary writers.

Susan Howe, Charles Bernstein, John Yau, Clark Coolidge, Robert Creeley, Rosmarie Waldrop, Ron Padgett, Alice Notley, Leslie Scalapino.

Unsolicited Manuscripts Received/Published per Year: hundreds/20-25.

Reading Period: year—round.

Payments: copies.

Reporting Time: 1 month.

Copyright reverts to author upon publication.

1988; 2/yr; 950

$9/yr ind, $13/yr inst; $5/ea; 40%

224 pp; 5½ x 8½

Ad Rates: $100/page; $50/½ page

ISSN: 0898-8684

DeBoer, Anton J. Mikofsky, SPD, Spectacular Diseases (UK)

TAMPA REVIEW

Richard B. Mathews, Ed., Andy Solomon, Fiction Ed., Kathryn Van Spanckeren & Don Morrill, Poetry Editors.
Box 19F
The University of Tampa
Tampa, FL 33606-1490
(813) 253-3333 ex. #6266

Poetry, fiction, essays, interviews, photographs, graphics/artwork.

The **TAMPA REVIEW** is the faculty-edited literary journal of the University of Tampa. It publishes new works of poetry, fiction, nonfiction and art. Each issue includes works from other countries in order to reflect the international flavor of the city of Tampa and its ties to the international cultural community.

Tom Disch, David Ignatow, Elizabeth Jolley, Denise Levertov, Stephen Dunn.

Unsolicited Manuscripts Received/ Published per Year: 700-1,200/50.

Reading Period: Sept.—Dec.

Payment: $10/page.

Reporting Time: up to 12 weeks after Dec. 31.

Copyright: first serial North American copyrights held by Magazine then reverts to author.

2/yr

$10/yr; $5.95/ea

64-72 pp; 7½ x 10½

ISSN: 0896-064X

TAPROOT: A Journal of Older Writers

Philip W. Quigg, Enid Graf
Fine Arts Center 4290
University at Stony Brook,
Stony Brook, NY 11794-5425
(516) 632-6635

Poetry, fiction, graphics/artwork, reviews.

Publish the works of older writers; interested in "capturing the stories, poems and recountings of events related to and growing from tradition," as well as the realities of our elders' participation in community life. Publication open to members of Taproot Workshops only.

Unsolicited Manuscripts Received/ Published per Year: 15/0.

Payment: 1 copy.

Copyright held by magazine; reverts to author upon publication.

1974; 1/yr; 1,000

$6/ea; 40%

100 pp; 8½ x 11

Ad Rates: $500/page; $300/½ page; $175/¼ page

ISSN: 0887-9257

TAR RIVER POETRY

Peter Makuck
English Department
East Carolina University
Greenville, NC 27834
(919) 757-6041

Poetry, reviews, interviews, essays.

We are looking for poetry that shows skillful use of figurative language. Narrative poems, short image poems, poems in closed and open form are welcome. We are not interested in sentimental, flat statement verse. Though we often publish the work of established poets, we are open to the work of newcomers as well.

A.R. Ammons, Brendan Galvin, Sharon Bryan, Betty Adcock, Susan Ludwigson, Michael Mott, Patricia Goedicke, Leslie Norris, Mark Jarman.

Unsolicited Manuscripts Received/ Published per Year: 4,500/125.

Reading Period: Sept.—April.

Payment: none.

Reporting Time: 5–7 weeks.

Copyright reverts to author.

1965; 2/yr; 1,000

$10/1 yr, $18/2 yr; $5.50/sample; 40%

62 pp; 6 x 9

THE TEXAS REVIEW

Paul Ruffin
English Department
Sam Houston State University
Huntsville, TX 77341
(409) 294-1429

Poetry, fiction, criticism, essays, reviews.

We are interested in the very best fiction and poetry available; our nonfiction may be literary, historical, or "familiar." We are interested principally in reviews of contemporary poetry and fiction.

Fred Chappell, Richard Eberhart, George Garrett, Donald Justice, William Stafford, Richard Wilbur.

Unsolicited Manuscripts Reveived/ Published per Year: 3,000/150.

Reading Period: Sept.—Apr.

Payment: in contributor's copies plus 1 year subscription to magazine.

Copyright held by magazine; reverts to author upon publication.

1979; 2/yr; 750–1,000

$10/yr (ind and inst); $5/ea; 40%

144 pp; 6 x 9

ISSN: 0885-2685

THEMA

Virginia Howard
Thema Literary Society
Box 74109
Metairie, LA 70033-4109
(504) 887-1263

Fiction, poetry.

Stories and poems must relate to premise specified for each issue. Themes for 1994: Mirror Image; The Waiting Room; Is It a Fossil, Higgens? Coming in 1995: Three by a Tremor Tossed; Laughter on the Steps, and more to be announced.

Edith Pearlman, Caitland Burke, Nora Ruth Roberts, Sue Walker.

Unsolicited Manuscripts Received/ Published per Year: 800/75.

Payment: $25 for short story, $10 for poems, $10 for short-shorts and illustrations.

Reporting Time: dependent on deadlines.
Copyright reverts to author.
1988; 3/yr; 300
$16/yr; $8/ea; 40%
200 pp; 5½ x 8½
ISSN: 1041-4851

THIRTEEN

Ken Stone
Box 392
Portlandville, NY 13834
(607) 547-4301

Poetry, fiction, reviews, translations, graphics/artwork.

THIRTEEN is a poetry magazine which specializes in 13-line poetry. We have no special themes or other requirements other than the poem be 13 lines, not including title. All poems should be titled.

Rochelle Holt, Judson Crews, ave jeanne, R. H. Yodice, Sue Saniel Elkind.

Unsolicited Manuscripts Received/ Published per Year: 500/100.
Payment: 1 copy.
Reporting Time: 2 weeks.
Copyright held by author.
1982; 4/yr; 350
$5/yr; $2.50/ea; 40%
40 pp; 8½ x 11½
No ads
ISSN: 0747-9727

13th MOON

Judith E. Johnson
English Department
SUNY
Albany, NY 12222

Poetry, fiction, criticism, essays, reviews, translation, interviews, photographs, graphics/artwork, by women.

13th MOON is a feminist literary magazine, placing primary emphasis on the quality of writing. It is specifically interested in work from feminist, lesbian, third-world, and working-class perspectives.

Joanna Russ, Cheryl Clarke, Nelida Pinon, Marie Ponsot.

Unsolicited Manuscripts Received/ Published per Year: 1,000/30.
Reading Period: Sept.—May.
Payment: in copies.
Reporting Time: varies.
Copyright held by 13th Moon, Inc.; reverts to author upon publication.
1973; 1/yr; 2,500
$10/ind, $20/inst; $10/ea; 40%
200 pp; 6 x 9
Ad Rates: inquire

THE THREEPENNY REVIEW

Wendy Lesser
P.O. Box 9131
Berkeley, CA 94709
(510) 849-4545

Poetry, fiction, criticism, essays, reviews, memoirs, graphics/artwork.

THE THREEPENNY REVIEW is a quarterly journal publishing essays on literature, theater, film, television, dance, music, and the visual arts, as well as new poetry, original fiction, and socio-political articles. While based in California, it is aimed at a nationwide audience.

John Berger, Seamus Heaney, Elizabeth Hardwick, Thom Gunn, Amy Tan.

Unsolicited Manuscripts Received/Published per Year: 5,200/20.

Payment: $100–$200.

Reporting Time: 3 weeks–2 months.

Copyright held by magazine; reverts to author upon publication.

1980; 4/yr; 10,000

$16/yr; $6/ea; 30%–50%

40 pp; 11 x 17

Ad Rates: $900/page (10 x 14); $500/½ page (10 x 7½); $300/¼ page (4½ x 7¼)

ISSN: 0275-1410

Ingram, Ubiquity

THUNDER & HONEY

Akbar Imhotep
P.O. Box 11386
Atlanta, GA 30310
(404) 688-3376

Poetry, fiction, interviews, photographs, graphics/artwork.

THUNDER & HONEY is primarily devoted to poetry and fiction. Future issues will have arts-related articles and some interviews.

Charlie Braxton, Nome Poem, R.F. Smith, Askia Toure, Jeanne Towns.

Payment: 15 copies.

Copyright held by magazine; reverts to author upon publication.

1984; 4/yr; 1,500

$2.50/yr; 75¢/ea

4 pp; 8½ x 11

Ad Rates: $210/page (10 x 16); $120/½ page (10 x 8); $60/¼ page (5 x 4)

TIGHTROPE

Ed Rayher
323 Pelham Rd.
Amherst, MA 01002

Poetry, fiction, translation, graphics/artwork. Not reading short fiction until 1994.

We stress excellence and accessibility to unpublished or little published authors. Our format is erratic, but we always emphasize form as well as content.

Steven Ruhl, Linda Burggraf, Gillian Conoley, Lance Liskus.

Unsolicited Manuscripts Received/Published per Year: 500/25.

Payment: inquire.
Copyright held by magazine; reverts to author upon publication.
1977; 2/yr; 350
$10/yr; $6/ea; 40%
40 pp; size varies; Letterpress

TO: A Journal of Poetry, Prose and the Visual Arts

Seth Frechie, Andrew Mossin
Box 121
Narberth, PA 19072
Biannual.
Contemporary fiction, poetry, and poetics featuring new translation, archival material, essay and review. Each issue features work, in the visual arts with a special emphasis placed on work by contemporary american photographiers.
John Ashbery, Charles Bernstein, Leslie Scalapino, Jack Stuizgers.
Payment: in copies.
Reporting Time: 6 weeks.
Copyright reverts to author.
1992; 2/yr; 1,000
$15/yr ind, $30/yr inst; $8/ea; 40%
approx. 140 pp; 7 x 10 page
Ad Rates: $100/page; $50/½ page
SPD, DeBoer

TOOK MODERN POETRY IN ENGLISH SERIES

Edward Mycue
P.O. Box 640543
San Francisco, CA 94164-0543
Poetry, drama, prose, history, criticism, music, food, art, psychology, self-help, philosophy, film, vinyl/recordings, travel.
Laura Kennelly, Owen Hill, Lawrence Fixel, Martha King, Jules Mann, Betsy Ford, Judy Stedman, Elizabeth Hurst, Agnes McGaha, Helen Sventitsky, Jim Gove, Dan Bellm, William Talcott, Ann Erickson.
Payment: in copies.
Reporting Time: 1 month.
Copyright reverts to the contributors.
1988; occasional; 150
$5/ea
8 to 40 pp; 5½ x 4½
Ad Rates: $50/¼ page

TOP STORIES

Anne Turyn
228 Seventh Ave.
New York, NY 10011
Fiction, graphics/artwork.
TOP STORIES is a prose periodical; a chapbook series which (usually) features the work of one author/artist per issue.
Constance DeJong, Lynne Tillman,

Susan Daitch, Tama Janowitz, Richard Prince.
Payment: varies.
Reporting Time: 1 year.
Copyright held by author.
1979; 3/yr; 1,500
$13.50/yr ind, $14.50/yr inst; $3/ea single issue; $6/ea double issue; 40%
5¼ x 8¼
No ads

TOUCHSTONE: Literary Journal
William Laufer
P.O. Box 8308
Spring, TX 77387-8308
Poetry, criticism, essays, reviews, translation, interviews, graphics/artwork, fiction.
We publish fiction, nonfiction, poetry and graphics. We do not care for "Creative Writing Program" fiction. We welcome minority viewpoints, and look for imaginative, experimental trends. We also publish (poetry and fiction) chapbooks, no theme, no reading fee. Send SASE for submission guidelines.
Lyn Lifshin, Rebecca Gonzales, Ramona Weeks, Vassar Miller, Arthur Smith, Sheila Murphy, Walter McDonald, Annette Sanford.
Reading Period: Jan.—Oct.
Payment: 2 copies (magazine), or 10 copies (chapbooks).
Reporting Time: 6 weeks.
Copyright reverts to author .
1976; 1/yr; 1,000
$5/ea
52–60 pp; 5½ x 8, perfect bound
ISSN: 1715-1697
No ads

TRAFIKA INTERNATIONAL LITERARY REVIEW
Michael Lee, Alfredo Sanchez, Jeffrey Young
Janovskélto 14, 170 00 Prague 7 CZECH REPUBLIC
Short fiction, essays, poetry.
TRAFIKA is a new international literary review for the contemporary poetry, fiction, and essays of established and emerging writers from throughout the world.
Don DeLillo, Arnošt Lustig, Miroslar Holub.
Unsolicited Manuscripts Received/Published per Year: 15,000/100
Payment: contributor's copies.
Reporting Time: 3 months.
Copyright reverts to author upon publication.
1993; 4/yr; 3,000
$35/yr; $10/yr; 25%
224 pp; 6 x 9
Ad Rates: $400(US)/page (5½ x 8¼)
SPD

TRANSLATION

Frank MacShane, Lori Carlson, Timothy Sultan
Room 412 Dodge Hall
Columbia University
New York, NY 10027
(212) 854-2305

Poetry, fiction, translation.

TRANSLATION publishes new English translations of significant contemporary works of prose and poetry. Prose excerpts should not exceed 30 pages. Each volume features solely the literature of a particular language or region.

Payment: varies.

Reporting Time: maximum of 6 months.

Copyright reverts to translator/author upon publication.

1972; 2/yr; 1,500

$18/yr; $9/ea

220 pp; 6 x 9

Ad Rates: $300/page

ISSN: 0093-9307

TRANSLATION REVIEW

Rainer Schulte
Box 830688
University of Texas at Dallas
Richardson, TX 75083-0688

TRANSLATION REVIEW publishes articles on the art and craft of translation, interviews with well known translators, criticisms of revent translations, profiles of publishers.

Payment: yes.

Reporting Time: 3 months.

Copyright held by magazine.

1978; 3/yr; 1,200

$30/yr ind, $125/yr inst; $35/yr Colleges and Univ. Prices in Canada, Mexico and abroad are more.

50 pp; 8½ x 11

Ads Rates: $200/page (7½ x 9) $125/½ page (7½ x 4½ or 3½ x 9); $75/¼ page (2¼ x 3½)

ISSN: 0737-4836

TRIQUARTERLY

Reginald Gibbons
Susan Hahn
Northwestern University
2020 Ridge
Evanston, IL 60208

Fiction, poetry, essays, reviews, translation, interviews, photographs, graphics/artwork.

TRIQUARTERLY is especially dedicated to short fiction, although substantial amounts of poetry are also published regularly in every issue, including long poems. Brief book reviews and occasional essays round out the contents.

Stanley Elkin, Alice Fulton, Linda

McCarriston, Sandra McPherson, Jim Powell, Alan Shapiro, Bruce Weigl.
Unsolicited Manuscripts Received/Published per Year: 8,000/100
Reading Period: Oct.—Mar. 31
Payment: $20/printed page, prose; $1.50/line, poetry.
Reporting Time: 2–3 months.
Copyright reverts to author upon request.
1964; 3/yr; 4,000
$20/yr ind; $26/yr inst; $5/sample; varies
250 pp; 6 x 9¼
Ad Rates: $250/page (6 x 9¼); $150/½ page (6 x 4⅝)
ISSN: 0041-3097
Ingram, DeBoer, Bookpeople, Ubiquity, Inland

TRIVIA: A Journal of Ideas

Erin Rice, Kay Parkhurst
P.O. Box 606
North Amherst, MA 01059
(413) 367-0168

TRIVIA publishes the finest, most "lively and vicious" writing from radical, visionary women. Essays, reviews, translations, interviews, original art and experimental forms that combine rigorous thinking with uncompromising feminist vision. Articles on language and memory, aging, lesbian ethics, feminism's seduction by New Age philosophy.
Nicole Brossard, Michèle Causse, Christina Thürmer-Rohr, Barbara Mor, C. C. Sundance, Lee Maracle, Lou Robinson.
Unsolicited Manuscripts Received/Published per Year: 50–60+/10+.
Reporting Time: 4–6 months.
Copyright reverts to author.
1982; 2/yr; 2,000
$16/3 issues ind; $20/3 issues inst; $5/ea
120 pp; 5½ x 8½
Ad Rates: inquire
ISSN: 0736-928X
Inland, Bookpeople, Small Changes, Fine Print, Spectacular Diseases (UK)

TUCUMCARI LITERARY REVIEW

Troxey Kemper
3108 W. Bellevue Ave.
Los Angeles, CA 90026
(213) 413-0789

Poetry, fiction, essays, nostalgia, memories, vignettes, humor.
TUCUMCARI LITERARY REVIEW is old fashioned and the preference is for types of writing in vogue in the 1930s to 1950s. Most of the poetry is rhyming, in "standard" forms,

not disjointed phrases and odd-shaped lines of prose arranged like poetry. The emphasis is on writing that "says something."

Alice Mackenzie Swaim, Marian Ford Park, Kenneth Johnson, Fontaine Falkoff, Ken MacDonnell, Daniel Kaderli.

Unsolicited Manuscripts Received/Published per Year: 2,000/450.

Payment: in copies upon publication.

Copyright held by author.

1988; 6/yr; 170

$12/yr ind & inst; $2/ea by mail; 40%

40 pp; 5½ x 8½

Ad Rates: free for readers

TURNSTILE

George Witte, Lindsey Crittenden
175 Fifth Avenue, Suite 2348
New York, NY 10010

Fiction, poetry, essays, interviews, photographs, artwork/graphics.

TURNSTILE publishes high-quality fiction, poetry, essays, interviews and artistic works. A passageway for variety and difference, **TURNSTILE** encourage new and emerging writers and artists.

Unsolicited Manuscripts Received/Published per Year: 1,000+/20.

Payment: in copies.

Reporting Time: 6–8 weeks.

Copyright reverts to author upon publication.

1988; 2/yr; 1,200

$22/4 issues; $6.50/ea; 40–50%

128 pp; 6 x 9

$150/page; $100/½ page

ISSN: 0896-5951

Deboer, Inland, Ingram

U

THE UNDERGROUND FOREST—La Selva Subterranea

Joseph Richey, Ann Becker
1701 Bluebell Ave.
Boulder, CO 80302

Nonfiction, poetry, investigative articles, politics.

A bilingual (Spanish-English), hemispheric publication devoted to the dissemination of informed opinions and good writing.

Margaret Randall, Agnes Bushell, Gioconda Belli, Victor Hernandez Cruz.

Payment: 2 copies.

Reporting Time: as soon as we can.

Copyright reverts to author.

1986; 2/yr; 2,000

$12/yr; $3/sample; 40%

96 pp; 17 x 5¼

Ad Rates: Write for information

ISSN: 1045-3660
Maine Writers and Publishers Association, Ubiquity

UNMUZZLED OX

Michael Andre
105 Hudson St.
New York, NY 10013
(212) 226-7170
Poetry, political.
Library Journal called **OX** "Outrageous and outstanding" perhaps because I published Robert Mapplethorpe; given the current climate I'd settle for "lively." We do publish the dead—a forthcoming issue features baroque librettists; plus W. H. Auden, the late Andy Warhol.
John Cage, Robert Creeley, Dan Berrigan, Allen Ginsberg.
Unsolicited Manuscripts Received/Published per Year: 500/4.
Payment: confidential.
Reporting Time: varies.
Copyright held by Michael Andre.
1971; varies; 15,000
$20/yr; $3/ea; varies
150 pp; 5½ x 8½
Ad Rates: inquire.
ISSN: 0049-5557

UNIVERSITY OF WINDSOR REVIEW

Joseph A. Quinn
Department of English
University of Windsor
Windsor, Ontario, M9B 3P4
CANADA
(519) 253-4232 ext. 2303
Poetry, short stories.
Publishes poetry and short fiction. We subscribe to no particular school or "ism."
Kenneth Radu, Budge Wilson, Patrick Roscoe.
Unsolicited Manuscripts Received/Published per Year: 400/50.
Payment: $50/story; $10/poem.
Reporting Time: 6–8 weeks.
Copyright reverts to author.
1965; 2/yr; 450
$12/yr; $6/ea
100 pp; 6 x 9
ISSN: 0042-0352

VERSE

Henry Hart
English Department
William and Mary, P.O. Box 8795
Williamsburg, VA 231817-8795
(804) 253-4758
Poetry, criticism, reviews, translation, interviews.
VERSE is a literary journal, begun in Oxford, England (1984), which publishes poetry in En-

glish and in translation. The focus is on the international scene, and its main purpose is to improve the understanding of the poetries from different countries, especially Britain and the United States.

Seamus Heaney, James Merrill, James Dickey, A.R. Ammons, Galway Kinnell.

Unsolicited Manuscripts Received/Published per Year: 5,000/120.

Payment: none.

Copyright held by author.

1984; 3/yr; 800

$15/yr, $5/ea ind; $21/yr, $7/ea inst

80 pp; 8¼ x 5¾

Ad Rates: $150/page (6 x 4); $75/½ page (3 x 4); $40/¼ page (3 x 2)

ISSN: 0268-3830

THE VINCENT BROTHERS REVIEW

Kimberly A. Willardson, Roger Willardson, Michelle Whitley-Turner

4566 Northern Circle

Mad River Township

Dayton, OH 45424-5789

Fiction, nonfiction, poetry, reviews, essays, artwork, photos.

TVBR's purpose is to encourage, support and support the work of artists, poets, and prose writers through the publication of 3 magazines per year.

Janice Levy, B.Z. Niditch, Constance García-Barria.

Unsolicited Manuscripts Received/Published per Year: 2,600/90.

Payment: $10 minimum for short stories and articles plus 2 copies of issue; 2 copies of issue to all other contributors.

Reporting Time: 4—8 months.

Copyright: all rights revert to artists/authors upon publication.

1988; 3/yr; 400

$12/yr,; $4.50/ea

64–80 pp; 5½ x 8

Ad Rates: $75/page (7 x 4); $45/½ page (3¼ x 4); $25/business card (2 x 3½)

ISSN: 1044-615X

THE VINYL ELEPHANT

Matthew Duncan

P.O. Box 704

Bowling Green, OH 43402

Poetry, Fiction, B/W Art/Photography.

Literary Journal of Experimental work often edged out due to "extravagances" in subtext matter, "contrivances" in voice or diction, and "inconveniences" of structure or layout.

Lyn Lifshin, Thomas Zimmerman, William John Watkins, Edward Myche.

Unsolicited Manuscripts Received/Published per Year: 1,500/100.
Payment: 1 copy.
Reporting Time: 4—6 weeks.
Copyright reverts to author.
1992; 4/yr; 125
$10/6 issues; $3/ea
48 pp; 8½ x 5½, digest
Ad Rates: $25/page; $15/½ page; $10/¼ page: trade for equal

THE VIRGINIA QUARTERLY REVIEW

Staige D. Blackford
One West Range
Charlottesville, VA 22903
(804) 924-3124

Poetry, fiction, essays, reviews.
One of the oldest and most distinguished literary journals in the country; contains articles and essays covering economics, art, the sciences, politics, and literature. Publishes high-quality fiction and poetry by established and newer authors. 75–100 brief, tightly-written book reviews per issue.
George Garrett, Jay Parini, Joyce Carol Oates, Mary Lee Settle, Ann Beattie.
Unsolicited Manuscripts Received/Published per Year: 2,000+/12-16.
Reader Period: year–round.
Payment: $10/page essays & fiction; $1/line for poetry; $50/essay reviews.
Copyright held by magazine/The University of Virginia; reverts to author upon publication.
1925; 4/yr; 4,200
$15/yr ind, $22/yr inst; $5/ea; 50%
188 pp; 5½ x 8
Ad Rates: $150/page (5½ x 8); $75/½ page (5½ x 4 or 2⅜ x 8)
ISSN: 0042-675X

VISIONS–International, The World Journal of Illustrated Poetry

Bradley R. Strahan, Poetry Editor; Shirley Sullivan, Associate Editor
1110 Seaton Lane
Falls Church, VA 22046
(703) 521-0142

Poetry, reviews, translations, graphics/artwork.
We're international in scope and content. We emphasize the interplay between artwork, poem and appearance of the magazine. We look for strong, well-crafted work that has emotional content (without sentimentality). **VISIONS** also publishes issues on special themes (usually once a year). Many of these, including our specials on Scandinavian/ Nordic and Australia/New Zealand poetry,

are still in print. We oppose the trend to publish facile word play instead of meaningful poetry. We are always interested in translations, especially from work that has not previously appeared in English and from less translated languages such as: Frisian, Basque, Telegu, Malayan, Gaelic, Macedonian, etc.

Allen Ginsberg, Ted Hughes, Marilyn Hacker, Louis Simpson, Lawrence Ferlingletti.

Unsolicited Manuscripts Received/Published per Year: 5,000+/250.

Reading Period: year–round.

Payment: in copies or $5–$10 when we get a grant.

Read a sample copy ($3.50) before submitting work

Reporting Time: 1–3 weeks.

Copyright held by VIAS; reverts to author upon publication.

1979; 3/yr; 750

$14/yr; $4.50/ea; 30%–40%

56 pp; 5½ x 8½

ISSN: 0194-1690

VIVO

Carolyn Miller
1195 Green St.
San Francisco, CA 94109
(415) 885-5695

Art, photographs, cartoons, essays, fiction, poetry, humorous, and serious work.

VIVO is a lively little magazine of art, fiction, essays, and poetry that mixes humorous and serious work.

Carol Snow, Terry Ehret, Jeanne Lohmann, Gerald Fleming.

Unsolicited Manuscripts Received/Published per Year: 250/8.

Payment: 2 copies of magazine.

Reporting Time: 6 weeks.

Copyright reverts to author on request.

1991; 1/yr; 700

$8/2 issues; $4/ea (postpaid); 40% bookstores, 50% newsstands

16 pp; tabloid 11 x 17

Ad Rates: $120/¼ page (4½ x 7½); $15/2 column inch.

ISSN 1056-3474

Fine Print, Inland, Armadillo

VOICES INTERNATIONAL

Clovita Rice
1115 Gillette Dr.
Little Rock, AR 72207
(501) 225-0166

Poetry, essays, photographs, graphics/artwork.

VOICES INTERNATIONAL focuses on high literary quality poetry, accepting for publication poetry with strong visual imagery and haunting impact. We encourage the beginner and have no preference in subject matter (as long as in good taste)

if it presents a fresh approach and special awareness.
Sarah Singer, Eunice de Chazeau, Frederick Zydek.
Unsolicited Manuscripts Received/ Published per Year: 160–180
Reading Period: year–round.
Payment: in copies.
Reporting Time: averages 6 weeks.
Copyright held by magazine.
1966; 4/yr; 325
$10/yr; $2.50/ea
32 pp; 6 x 9

VREMYA I MY (TIME AND WE)
Victor Perelman
409 Highwood Ave.
Leonia, NJ 07605
(201) 592-6155
Russian language literature and commentary. Fiction, essays, poetry, criticism, translation, graphics/artwork, interviews, photographs.
$59/yr ind, $86/yr inst; $19/ea; 40%

WASHINGTON REVIEW
Clarissa Wittenberg, Editor; Mary Swift, Managing Editor; Pat Kolmer, Jeff Richards, Joe Ross, Ross Taylor, Anne Pierce, Editorial Board
P.O. Box 50132
Washington, DC 20091
(202) 638-0515
Poetry, fiction, essays, reviews, plays, interviews, photographs, graphics/artwork.
Bi-monthly tabloid-size journal of arts and literature including poetry, fiction, book and art reviews, essays on the arts, original art work. Emphasis on arts of Washington, D.C. One special issue on single topic each year.
Terence Winch, Doug Lang, Lee Fleming.
Unsolicited Manuscripts Received/ Published per Year: 150 fiction, 150 poetry/5-6 fiction, 15-20 poetry.
Payment: $15–20/review, $50–100/article if available.
Reporting Time: 2 months.
Copyright held by magazine; reverts to author upon publication.
1975; 6/yr; 1,500
$12/yr ind, $20/2 yrs, $8.50/yr inst; $2/ea; 40%
Ad Rates: $250/page (16 x 11¼); $175/½ page (8 x 11¼); $135/⅓ page (7⅜ x 8)
ISSN: 0163-903X

WATERWAYS

Barbara Fisher, Richard Alan Spiegel
393 St. Pauls Ave.
Staten Island, NY 10304-2127
(718) 442-7429

Poetry, graphics.

We publish poets of all ages and types provided we like their work and it pertains to our monthly themes. Our page size is small to encourage portability and accessibility.

Joanne Seltzer, Kit Knight, Arthur Winfield Knight, Albert Huffstickler, Ida Fasel.

Unsolicited Manuscripts Received/ Published per Year: 200/20.

Reading Period: year–round.

Payment: 1 copy.

Reporting Time: 1 month.

Copyright held by Ten Penny Players; reverts to author upon publication.

1977; 11/yr; 100–200

$20/yr; $2/ea; 40%–60%

48 pp; 7 x 4¼

ISSN: 0197-4777

WEBSTER REVIEW

Nancy Schapiro
Webster University
470 East Lockwood
St. Louis, MO 63119
(314) 432-2657

Poetry, fiction, essays, translation, interviews.

WEBSTER REVIEW emphasizes translations of contemporary fiction, poetry and essays. We look for quality original work in those categories. We are particularly open at this time to non-fiction of a general literary nature.

William Stafford, Jared Carter, Barbara Lefcowitz, Charles Edward Easton, Etelvina Astrada.

Unsolicited Manuscripts Received/ Published per Year: 1,200/50.

Payment: in copies.

Copyright held by magazine; reverts to author upon publication.

1974; 1/yr; 1,100

$5/yr; $2.50/ea; 40%

128 pp; 5½ x 8½

ISSN: 0363-1230

WEST BRANCH

Karl Patten, Robert Taylor
Bucknell Hall
Bucknell University
Lewisburg, PA 17837
(717) 524-1853

Poetry, fiction, reviews.

A twice-yearly magazine of poetry, fiction, and reviews.

Denise Duhamel, Robert Freedman, Julia Kasdorf, Sandra Kohler, Sharon Sheehe Stark.

Unsolicited Manuscripts Received/ Published per Year: 800+/90.
Reading Period: year–round.
Payment: 2 copies and 1 year subscription.
Reporting Time: 6–8 weeks.
Copyright held by magazine; reverts to author upon publication.
1977; 2/yr; 500
$7/yr, $11/2 yrs; $4/ea
88–106 pp; 5½ x 8½
No ads
ISSN: 0149-6441

WEST HILLS REVIEW

William Fahey
246 Old Walt Whitman Rd.
Huntington Station, NY 11746
(516) 427-5240
Poetry, essays, photographs, graphics/artwork.
Good lyric poetry. Prose related to Walt Whitman.
John Ciardi, Dave Smith, Gay Wilson Allen, David Ignatow, Edmund Pennant.
Payment: none.
Reporting Time: 3 months.
Copyright held by magazine; reverts to author upon publication.
1979; 1/yr; 500
$5/yr; $5/ea; 50%
125 pp; 5 x 8

WESTERN HUMANITIES REVIEW

David Kranes, Richard Howard, Barry Weller
341 OSH/ University of Utah
Salt Lake City, UT 84112
(801) 581-6070
Poetry, fiction, criticism, essays, reviews, nonfiction.
We print fiction, poetry, articles on the humanities (we prefer 2–3M words). Our standard is excellence; we publish work by established writers as well as new writers.
Mary Oliver, Charles Simic, Francine Prose, Sandra McPherson, Philip Levine, Joseph Brodsky.
Unsolicited Manuscripts Received/ Published per Year: 4,000+/70+.
Reading Period: Sept.—May.
Payment: $50/poem, $150/story-criticism.
Copyright held by magazine.
1947; 4/yr; 1,100
$20/yr ind, $26/yr inst; $5/ea; 40%; 50% to distributors
96 pp; 6 x 9
No ads
ISSN: 0043-3845

WHETSTONE

Barrington Area Arts Council
Sandra Berris, Julie Fleenor, Marsha Portnoy, Jean Tolle
P.O. Box 1266

Barrington, IL 60011
(708) 382-5626

Poetry, short stories, novel excerpts, interviews, creative nonfiction.

Prefer to see 3–7 poems or up to 25 pages of fiction or nonfiction. Include SASE.

Reginald Gibbons, Rebecca Rule, Bill Roorbach, Eleanore Divine, Tom Grimes, Alision Baker, John Jacob, Peyton Houston, Paulette Roeske, Lucia Getsi.

Unsolicited Manuscripts Received/ Published per Year: 1,000+/15-25.

Reading Period: year–round.

Payment: variable. Work accepted is eligible for annual Whetstone Prizes which are cash awards. Total 1993 prizes—$800.

Reporting Time: 3 months.

Copyright reverts to author.

1983; 1/yr; 600

$6.25/ea postpaid; sample copies $3.25 post paid; Trade disc.

100–120 pp; 5⅞ x 9

Will consider ads for 1994 issue.

WHISPERS

Stuart David Schiff
70 Highland Ave.
Binghamton, NY 13905
(607) 729-6020

Fiction, criticism, reviews, graphics/artwork.

WHISPERS is a literary magazine of fantasy and horror. The journal publishes original fiction and art as well as news and reviews.

Stephen King, William Nolan, Ray Bradbury, Harlan Ellison, Ray Russell.

Unsolicited Manuscripts Received/ Published per Year: 300/2.

Payment: varies.

Reporting Time: 1–3 months.

Copyright held by Stuart David Schiff; reverts to author upon publication.

1973; 2/yr; 3,000

No subscriptions; 40%

176 pp; 5½ x 8½

Ad Rates: $90/page (4⅜ x 8); $50/½ page (4¾ x 4½); $30/¼ page (4¾ x 2¼)

WHITE CLOUDS REVUE

Scott Preston
P.O. Box 462
Ketchum, ID 83340

Poetry, one prose piece in 4 issues so far.

WCR is a serially-issued journal specifically interested in delineating and suggesting trends in inter-mountain American West Poetics, divergent from those foisted on hapless readers & writers by the homogenized tyranny of regional MFA syndromes and syndicates.

Charles Potts, Ed Dorn, Rosalie Sorrels, Bruce Embree, Peter Boweb, Brooke Medicine Eagle.

Payment: several copies.

Reporting Time: 2 weeks–2 months.

Copyright reverts to author.

1987; 1½/yr; 200+

$12/4 issues; $3.50/ea; 30%

28–44 pp; 7 x 8½

WHOLE NOTES

Nancy Peters Hastings
P.O. Box 1374
Las Cruces, NM 88004
(505) 382-7446

Poetry.

WHOLE NOTES features work by unknown or beginning writers as well as established poets. It is intentionally kept small so that it is affordable—and highly readable.

William Stafford, Harold Witt, Ted Kooser, and Carole Oles.

Unsolicited Manuscripts Received/Published per Year: 800/40.

Reading Period: year-round.

Payment: in copies.

Reporting Time: 3 weeks.

Copyright held by Nancy Peters Hastings.

1984; 2/yr; 400

$6/yr ind & inst; $3/ea; 40%

28 pp; 5½ x 8½

Ad Rates: Contact CLMP for information.

THE WILLIAM AND MARY REVIEW

Andrew Zawacki, Editor
P.O. Box 8795
The College of William & Mary
Williamsburg, VA 23187-8795
(804) 221-3290

Poetry, fiction, criticism, interviews, photographs, graphics/artwork.

THE WILLIAM AND MARY REVIEW is an internationally-distributed literary magazine published by graduate and undergraduate students of The College of William and Mary, without faculty supervision or censorship. It is the express purpose of **THE WILLIAM AND MARY REVIEW** to publish the work of established writers as well as that of—and with an emphasis on—new, vital voices.

Amy Clampitt, Julie Agoos, Carole Glickfeld, David Ignatow, Dana Gioia, Robert Hershon, Elizabeth Alexander, W. D. Snodgrass, Cornelius Eady.

Unsolicited Manuscripts Received/Published per Year: 300/10.

Reading Period: Sept.—Apr.

Payment: in copies.

Copyright held by College of William and Mary and Editor; reverts to author upon publication.
1962; 1/yr; 3,500
$5.50/yr ind, $8/yr inst; $6/ea; 40%
120 pp; 6 x 9
ISSN: 0043-5600

Reporting Time: 1-2 months.
Copyright reverts to author upon publication.
1969; 1/yr; 1,000
$10/3 years; $4/ea; 40%
82 pp; 6 x 9
Ad Rates: We accept ads up to ½ page.

WILLOW REVIEW

Paulette Roeske
19351 West Washington St.
Grayslake, IL 60030
(708) 223-6601 ext. 555

Poetry, short fiction, creative nonfiction.

WILLOW REVIEW is a flat-spined annual which publishes poetry, short fiction and creative nonfiction (up to 4,000 words). Its orientation is toward high quality, literary work as opposed to genre fiction and light verse.

Lisel Mueller, Bruce Guernsey, John Dickson, Mark Perlberg, Gregory Orr, Gloria Naylor.

Unsolicited Manuscripts Received/Published per Year: 1,500/30-35.

Reading Period: Sept.—May.

Payment: Awards of $100, $50, and $25 in both prose and poetry each year for work deemed best of issue; all contributors receive 2 copies.

WILLOW SPRINGS

Nance Van Winckel, Editor
MS-1
Eastern Washington University
Cheney, WA 99004
(509) 458-6429

Poetry, fiction, essays, reviews, translation, interviews.

WILLOW SPRINGS is committed to the imagination and the power of language fully engaged in the act of telling. We publish high quality poetry, fiction, translation, essays, and art.

Russell Edson, Thomas Lux, Alberto Rios, Madeline DeFrees, Olga Broumas, Jane Miller, Donald Revell, Charlie Smith.

Unsolicited Manuscripts Received/Published per Year: 1,000/50.

Reading Period: Sept. 15—May 15.

Payment: small honorarium plus 2 copies on publication.

Reporting Time: 6 weeks.

Copyright reverts to author.

1977; 2/yr; 1,000

$7/yr; $4/ea; 40%
104 pp; 6 x 9
Ad Rates: $125/page (4¼ x 7); $75/½ page (4¼ x 3½); $50/¼ page (2⅛ x 3½)
ISSN: 0739-1277
Pacific Pipeline, Small Changes

WIND

Steven R. Cope, Charlie G. Hughes
P.O. Box 24548
Lexington, KY 40524
Poetry, fiction, reviews from small presses only.
Focus and emphasis are on the writers who have something special to say: nothing cold and lifeless. **WIND** is highly eclectic; any form, subject matter or approach.
Peter Wild, Larry Rubin, T.M. McNally, Richard E. Brown, Carolyn Osborn.
Unsolicited Manuscripts Received/Published per Year: 4,200/2%
Payment: in copies.
Reporting Time: 2–4 weeks.
Copyright held by author.
1971; 2/yr; 450
$10/yr ind, $12/yr inst, $15/yr foreign; $5.50/ea; $3.50/backissue
82 pp; 5½ x 8¼
ISSN: 0361-2481

WINDFALL

Ron Ellis
Friends of Poetry
c/o Department of English
University of Wisconsin
Whitewater, WI 53190
(414) 472-1036
Poetry.
We are interested in short, intense, highly-crafted poems in any form. Longer poems occasionally considered. No xerox or dot matrix.
William Stafford, Ralph Mills, Francine Sterle, Sheila Murphy, Joanne Hart.
Unsolicited Manuscripts Received/Published per Year: 400/30.
Payment: contributor's copies.
Reporting Time: 8 weeks.
Copyright held by Friends of Poetry; reverts to author upon publication.
1979; 2/yr; 400
$5/yr; $3/ea
40 pp; 5½ x 8½
ISSN: 0893-3375

THE WINDLESS ORCHARD

Robert Novak
English Department
Indiana University
2101 East Coliseum
Fort Wayne, IN 46805
(219) 483-6845

Poetry, criticism, review, photographs, graphics/artwork.

Our muse is interested only in the beautiful, the sacred, and the erotic. Excited, organic forms, with thinking and feeling done in imagery and epigram.

Ruth Moon Kempher, Elliot Richman, Mike Martone, Michael Emery.

Unsolicited Manuscripts Received/Published per Year: 920/44.

Payment: 2 copies.

Reporting Time: 1 week and up.

Copyright reverts to author.

1970; irregular; 320

$10/yr; $4/ea

52 pp; 5½ x 8

No ads

WITHOUT HALOS

Frank Finale, Lora Dunetz, Barbara Finale, H.G. Stacy, W. Swayhoover, Rich Youmans, Judi Beach

P.O. Box 1342

Pt. Pleasant Beach, NJ 08742

Poetry, graphics/artwork.

We consider all types of poetry—mainstream, avant-garde, haiku, light verse, etc. We judge each poem not on a poet's name but on the passion it displays, the honesty of its roots.

Harold Witt, Michael Bugeja, Gale Elen Harvey, Alicia Ostriker, Robert Cooperman, Madeline Tiger.

Unsolicited Manuscripts Received/Published per Year: 2,000/70.

Reading Period: Jan.—June 30.

Payment: 1 copy.

Reporting Time: 3–4 months.

Copyright held by author.

1983; 1/yr; 1,000

$6.25/ea

112 pp; 8½ x 5½

No ads

ISSN: 1052-3162

WITNESS

Peter Stine

Oakland Community College

27055 Orchard Lake Rd.

Farmington Hills, MI 48334

(313) 471-7740

Fiction, essays, poetry, interviews, photographs, graphics/artwork.

WITNESS presents nationally known writers, as well as new talent, and highlights the role of the modern writer as witness. The magazine features a diverse selection of writings—fiction, poetry, essays, journalism, interviews—and regularly devotes every other issue to illuminating a single subject of wide concern.

Gordon Lish, Joyce Carol Oates, Robert Coover, Lynn Sharon Schwartz, Madison Smartt Bell.

Unsolicited Manuscripts Received/ Published per Year: 1,000/20.

Reading Period: year–round.

Payment: $6/page for prose, $10/page for poetry.

Reporting Time: 2–3 months.

Copyright held by magazine; reverts to author upon publication.

1987; 2/yr

192 pp; 6 x 9

Ad Rates: $100/page (5 x 7); $60/½ page (5 x 3½)

ISSN: 0891-1371

DeBoer, Ingram, Fine Print

WOMAN POET

Elaine Dallman

P.O. Box 60550

Reno, NV 89506

(702) 972-1671

Poetry, criticism, photos, interviews.

The West, the East, the Midwest, the South.

Marilyn Hacker, Lisel Mueller, Judith Minty, Rosalie Moore.

Unsolicited Manuscripts Received/ Published per Year: 150/varies.

$12.95/ea paperback; $19.95/ea hardcover. Resale discount varies.

WOMEN & PERFORMANCE: A JOURNAL OF FEMINIST THEORY

Editorial Board; Judy Burns, Jennifer Fink, Judy Rosenthal, Leslie Satin

721 Broadway, 6th Fl.

New York, NY 10003

(212) 998-1625

Essays, criticism, plays, reviews, interviews, translation.

Hélène Cixous, Marianne Goldberg, Sue-Ellen Case, Jill Dolan, Lila Abu Lugnod, E. Ann Kaplan, Peggy Phelan, Lucy Fischer.

Number of Unsolicited Manuscripts Received/Published per Year: 50/1-2

Reading Period: Sept.—June.

$14/yr ind, $25/yr inst; $7/ea; $9/back issue; 40%

THE WOMEN'S REVIEW OF BOOKS

Linda Gardiner

Wellesley College Center for Research on Women

Wellesley, MA 02181

(617) 431-1453

Reviews, poetry.

In-depth reviews of books by and about women, in all areas, both academic and general-interest; feminist in orientation but not committed to any one brand of

feminism or any specific political position.
June Jordan, Diane Wakoski, Gerda Lerner, Michelle Cliff, Jane Marcus.
Unsolicited Manuscripts Received/Published per Year: 60/2.
Payment: varies, $50 minimum.
Reporting Time: 1 month–6 weeks.
Copyright held by magazine; reverts to author upon publication.
1983; 11/yr; 14,000
$17/yr ind, $30/yr inst: $2/ea; 40%
28 pp; 10 x 15
Ad Rates: $1,375 (page/10 x 15); $750/½ page (10 x 7½); $395/¼ page (4¾ x 7½)
ISSN: 0738-1433

WOMEN'S WORDS: A JOURNAL OF CAROLINA WRITING

Lisa Granered, Editor; Elaine Selden, Designer
128 E. Hargett St., Suite 10
Raleigh, NC 27601
(919) 829-3711
Poetry, some fiction and essay, graphics.
WOMEN'S WORDS is a journal seeking to promote women writers in North Carolina.
Jaki Shelton-Green, Tara Allan, Laura Bolger.
Payment: none.
Copyright held by the Women's Center, reverts to author upon publication.
1992; 1/yr; 1,000
$11/yr; $11/ea; 40%
100 pp; 8½ x7
ISSN: 1069-4609

WOMEN'S WORK

Andrea Damm
602 Ave. A
Snohomish, WA 98290
(206) 568-5914
Articles, interviews, biography, fiction & poetry.
Publishes previously unpublished and emerging writers, writers of diverse cultural and economic backgrounds; explores traditional and modern definitions and expressions of "Women's Work."
Carole Bellacera, Sue Pace.
Unsolicited Manuscripts Received/Published per Year: 750/50–60.
Reading Period: year–round.
Payment: currently in copies; may soon pay by word.
Reporting Time: 2–6 months.
Copyright: first serial rights.
1991; 6/yr; 3,000
$12/yr; $2/ea; 40%
32–48 pp; 8½ x 11
Ad Rates: write or call for quote
ISSN: 1058-4870

THE WORCESTER REVIEW

Rodger Martin
6 Chatham St.
Worcester, MA 01609
(508) 797-4770 or (603) 924-7342

Poetry, fiction, criticism, essays, graphics/artwork, photographs.

We look for quality poetry and fiction, and also articles and essays about poetry that have a New England connection.

Stephen Dunn, Walter McDonald, William Stafford, Kathleen Spivack, Stanley Kunitz.

Payment: 2 copies plus honorarium dependant upon grants.

Reporting Time: 4–5 months.

Copyright held by Worcester Review of the Worcester County Poetry Assoc.; reverts to author upon publication.

1973; 1/yr; 1,000

$10/yr; $6/ea; $5 sample; 40%

150 pp; 6 x 9

Ad Rates: $195/page; $100/½ page; $55/¼ page

ISSN: 8756-5277

THE WORLD

Lewis Warsh
c/o St. Mark's Church
10th St. & 2nd Ave.
New York, NY 10003
(212) 674-0910

Poetry, fiction.

A magazine of experimental writing.

Lorenzo Thomas, Chris Tysh, Ron Padgett.

Payment: none.

Reporting Time: 3 weeks.

Copyright held by author.

1966; 3/yr; 500

$20/4 issues; $5/ea

122 pp; 6 x 9

ISSN: 0043-8154

SPD

WORLD LETTER

Jon Cone
2726 E. Court St.
Iowa City, IA 52245
(319) 337-6022

Poetry, short prose, translations.

An international literary review. Do not send unsolicited manuscripts. Query first.

Cesar Vallejo, Charles Bukowski, Edouard Roditi, Cid Corman.

Unsolicited Manuscripts Received/Published per Year: 200/1.

Payment: in copies.

Reporting Time: 1 week or as soon as possible.

Copyright reverts to author upon publication.

1991; 1/yr; 200–300

$6/yr; $6/ea; 40%

48 pp; 6½ x 10

ISSN: 1054-8823

Water Row Books, Longhouse Books, Anton Mikofsky, Alyscamp Press

O

THE WORMWOOD REVIEW

Marvin Malone
P.O. Box 4698
Stockton, CA 95204-0698
(209) 466-8231

Poetry, reviews, translation, graphics/artwork.

Poetry and prose-poems reflecting the temper and depth of the present time. All types and schools from traditional-economic through concrete, dada and extreme avant-garde. Special fondness for prose poems and fables. Each issue has a special section devoted to one poet or topic. One chapbook per year.

Charles Bukowski, Lyn Lifshin, Ronald Koertge, Gerald Locklin, Judson Crews.

Unsolicited Manuscripts Received/Published per Year: 6,000+/350+.

Payment: 3–6 copies of magazine or cash equivalent.

Copyright held by Wormwood Books & Magazines; reverts to author upon request.

1959; 4/yr; 700

$8/yr ind, $10/yr inst; $4/ea;

48 pp; 5½ x 8½

ISSN: 0043-9401

THE WRITERS' BAR-B-Q

Editorial Board: Timothy Osburn, Becky Bradway, Gary Smith, Marcia Womack, and Myra Epping
924 Bryn Mawr Blvd.
Springfield, IL 62703
(217) 525-6987

Fiction, photographs, graphics/artwork.

THE WRITERS' BAR-B-Q publishes stories and novel excerpts. Our preference is for realistic work that has strong characterization and story. We are looking for excellent, spirited, daring writing from all genres. We encourage work by gays and lesbians, people of color, and other writers who may have trouble fitting into the usual venues. Our idea is to publish good stories, and to have fun doing it. **THE WRITERS' BAR-B-Q** is a potluck of styles, subjects and characters. Almost all stories are fully illustrated.

Lowry Pei, Sharon Sloan Fiffer, Michael C. White, Martha M. Vertreace, Shannon Keith Kelley, Nolan Porterfield, Deborah Insel, Paul Lisicky.

Payment: 3 copies, upon publication.

Copyright held by Sangamon

Writers, Inc.; reverts to author upon publication.
1987; 1–2/yr; 1,000.
$10/yr; $5/ea
100 pp; 8½ x 11
Ad Rates: $75/½ page (4½ x 7½); inquire.
DeBoer

WRITERS FORUM

Alex Blackburn, Editor; Craig Lesley, Bret Lott, Fiction Editors; Victoria McCabe, Poetry Editor; robert Dassanovsky–Harris, Managing Editor; Paul Scott Malone, Corresponding Editor
University of Colorado at Colorado Springs
Colorado Springs, CO 80933-7150
(719) 599-4023
Poetry, fiction.
We want the finest in contemporary short story and poetry, with some focus and emphasis on the trans-Mississippi West with its varieties of place and experience.
Gladys Swan, Ron Carlson, Frank Waters, Robert Olen Butler, Simon Ortiz.
Unsolicited Manuscripts Received/Published per Year: 600/35.
Payment: none.
Reporting Time: 3–6 weeks.
Copyright held by UCCS; reverts to author upon publication.
1974; 1/yr; 1,000
Note: Our prices now include cost of postage.
$10/yr ind, $8.20/yr inst; $10/ea
200 pp; 8½ x 5½

WRITER'S JOURNAL

Valerie Hockert
3585 N. Lexington Ave.
Suite 328
Arden Hills, MN 55112
(612) 486-7818
Essays, poetry, reviews, criticism, interviews, commentaries, writing techniques.
Provides writers and poets with practical advice and guidance, motivation and authorative instruction in the craft of writing. Includes book reviews, software reviews, poetry, advice and references.
Anthony Vasquez, Betty Ulrich, Ester M. Leiper, Cheryl Kempf.
Unsolicited Manuscripts Received/Published per Year: 600/36.
Payment: variable.
Reporting Time: 2–6 weeks.
Copyright held by Minnesota Ink, Inc., reverts to author upon publication.
1980; 6/yr; 49,000
$14/yr; $4/ea; 50%
48 pp; 8 x 10½
Ad Rates: $845/page (6¾ x 8½);

$465/½ page (6¾ x 4¼ or 3⅛ x 8 ½)
ISSN: 0891-9759
Ingram, Armadillo, IPD, Fine Print, ADS

XANADU: A Literary Journal
Mildred M. Jeffrey, Barbara Lucas, Weslea Sidon, Mitzie Grossman, Lois V. Walker, Sue-Kain, Editors
Box 773
Huntington, NY 11743
(516) 741-7188
Poetry, essays.
XANADU publishes contemporary poetry and literary criticism.
Karen Swenson, David Ignatow, Edmund Pennant, William Stafford.
Unsolicited Manuscripts Received/Published per Year: 500/30.
Reading Period: year–round.
Payment: 1 copy per contributor.
Reporting Time: 3 months.
Copyright reverts to author upon publication.
1975; 1/yr; 300
$5/ea 20%–40%
64–76 pp; 5½ x 8½
ISSN: 0146-0463

XAVIER REVIEW
Thomas Bonner, Jr., Editor;
Robert E. Skinner, Managing Ediitor
Box 110C, Xavier University
New Orleans, LA 70125
(504) 483-7304 (504) 486-7411
Poetry, fiction, criticism, essays, reviews, translation, interviews.
XAVIER REVIEW is interested in the usual genres of literature and articles in the area of Black literature, Southern literature, religion and literature and Latin American literature (although not exclusively).
Alex Haley, Andrew Salkey, Fred Chappell, John Keller, Gordon Osing, James Baldwin, Andre Dubus, Ernest J. Gaines, Patty Friedmann.
Unsolicited Manuscripts Received/Published per Year: 300/35.
Payment: none.
Reporting Time: 2 months.
Copyright held by magazine.
1980; 2/yr; 500
$10/year ind, $15/year inst; $5/each; 40%
70-75 pp; 6 x 9
ISSN: 0887-6681

xib
Tolek
P.O. Box 262112,
San Diego, Ca 92126
(619) 298-4927

Poems, drawings, photos, Fiction.
Writing and visual. Gritty, tight, slick, lean, tasty. Visual and writing.
Gerald Locklin, Richard Kostelanetz, Oberc.
Unsolicited Manuscripts Received/Published per Year: 2,000/4%.
Reading Period: year–round.
Payment: 1 copy.
Reporting Time: 2½ weeks.
Copyright: Yes—First time author rights.
1990; 2/yr; 500
$10/year; $5/ea; 35%
54 pp; 8½ x 7
Ad Rates: varies, inquire
ISSN: 1058-420x

YARROW

Harry Humes, Editor; Arnold Newman, Associate Editor
English Department
Kutztown University
Kutztown, PA 19530
(215) 683-4353
Poetry, interviews.
A journal of poetry.
William Pitt Root, Gerald Stern, John Engels, Gibbons Ruark, Lola Haskins, Fleda Brown Jackson, Sally Jo Sorenson.
Unsolicited Manuscripts Received/Published per Year: 400–500/50-95.
Reading Period: year–round.
Payment: in copies.
Reporting Time: 1 month.
1981; 2/yr; 350
$5/2 yrs; $1.50/ea
36 pp; 6 x 9

YELLOW SILK: Journal of Erotic Arts

Lily Pond
P.O. Box 6374
Albany, CA 94706
(510) 644-4188
Fiction, poetry, essays, reviews, translations, photography, graphics/artwork, fine arts, science fiction, humor.
YELLOW SILK: Journal of Erotic Arts: Stunning sophisticated stories and poems meet explicit photographs and paintings in what may be the world's only fine literary magazine that is unabashedly erotic.
Marilyn Hacker, Galway Kinnell, Sharon Olds, Mary Oliver, Louise Erdrich.
Payment: 3 copies, 1 year subscription, and varying cash payments.

Reporting Time: approximately 3 months.
Copyright reverts to author after one year following publication; the magazine keeps non-exclusive reprint, electronic, and anthology rights.
1981; 4/yr; 16,000
$30/yr ind, $38/yr inst; $7.50/ea; 40%
60 pp; 8½ x 11
ISSN: 0736-9212
Bookpeople, Inland, Ingram, Ubiquity

YET ANOTHER SMALL MAGAZINE
Candace Catlin Hall
Box 14353
Hartford, CT 06114
(203) 549-6723
Poetry.
YASM publishes short, imagistic poems—special interest in lesser known poets— started broadside inclusion highlighting a single poem.
Lyn Lifshin, Charles Darling, Pat Bridges, Sister Mary Ann Henn, Neil Grill.
Reading Period: Aug. 1—Oct. 31.
Payment: in copies.
Reporting Time: November.
Copyright reverts to author.
1981; 1/yr; 300
$1.98/ea
8–12 pp; 11 x 17
ISSN: 0278-9442

Z

ZEBRA, a journal of literature & opinion
Mario Gortwin
P.O. Box 421584
San Francisco, CA 94142
(415) 753-4600
Poetry, fiction, nonfiction. No romance per se.
Leonard Sanazaro, Phyllis Stowell.
Unsolicited Manuscripts Received/Published per Year: 1,100/200.
Payment: copies.
Reporting Time: 6–8 weeks.
Copyright reverts on publication.
1990; 2/yr; 200
$10/yr; $6/ea; 40%
56–80 pp; 5½ x 8½
Ad Rates: query
ISSN 1052-4967

ZUKUNFT
Prof. Yonia Fain, Joseph Mlotek, Matis Olitzki, Morris Steingart
25 East 21st St.
New York, NY 10010

Poetry, fiction, criticism, essays, reviews.

The **ZUKUNFT** is an independent literary publication. It serves as a vehicle for writers from many countries and is concerned with problems of Jewish life throught the world. In 1992 the **ZUKUNFT**, the oldest continously published Yiddish journal in the world, is celebrating its centennial. It has served to stimulate literary creativity for generations throughout Yiddish speaking communities.

Unsolicited Manuscripts Received/Published per Year: 60/7.

Reading Period (Yiddish mss.): year–round.

Copyright held by Congress for Jewish Culture; reverts to author upon publication.

1892; 6/yr; 2,500

$25/yr ind; $3/ea; 20%

44 pp; 7½ x 10½

Ad Rates: $100/page; $50/½ page; $25/¼ page

ZUZU'S PETALS QUARTERLY

T. Dunn, Editor-in-Chief, D. DuCap, Associate Editor

P.O. Box 4476

Allentown, PA 18105-4476

(215) 821-1324

Literary fiction, essays, poetry, articles, book reviews, chapbook reviews, poetry audio tapes.

Our magazine is a celebration of all aspects of the human experience, and is named after Jimmy Stewart's daughter in the film classic "It's A Wonderful Life".

Max Greenberg, Gayle Elen Harvey, Mark Soifer, Laura Telford.

Unsolicited Manuscripts Received/Published per Year: approx. 2,000/100.

Payment: 1 contributor's copy.

Reporting Time: 2 weeks–2 months

1991; 4/yr; 350

$17/yr; $5/ea; $3/yr discount

46 pp; 8½ x 11

No ads

ISSN 1060-9571

ZYZZYVA

Howard Junker

41 Sutter St., Suite 1400

San Francisco, CA 94104

(415) 255-1282

Fiction, essays, plays, poetry, translations, photographs, prints, drawings.

West Coast writers, artists, and publishers.

Sherman Alexie, Peter Bacho, Alison Baker, Chitra Diva Karuni, Alice Jones, Philip Levine.

Unsolicited Manuscripts Received/Published per Year: 4,000/40.

Payment: \$50–\$250.
Reporting Time: prompt.
Copyright held by magazine; reverts to author upon publication.
1985; 4/yr; 4,000
\$28/yr ind, \$36/yr inst; \$9/ea
144 pp; 6 x 9
Ad Rates: \$500/page (5 x 7¾); \$300/½ page (5 x 3¹³⁄₁₆); \$200/¼ page (2⁷⁄₁₆ x 3¹³⁄₁₆)
ISSN: 8756-5633
Bookpeople, Ingram, Inland, SPD

INDEX BY STATE

COLORADO

CONNECTICUT

DISTRICT OF COLUMBIA

FLORIDA

GEORGIA

HAWAII

INDEX BY STATE

MAINE

MARYLAND

MASSACHUSETTS

MICHIGAN

MINNESOTA

MISSISSIPPI

MISSOURI

NORTH CAROLINA

Sent
Philosophy
Carlos
Melnick
term?

The Quarterly
Long Shot

teaching
Self Discipline